Where the World Ended

Where the World Ended

RE-UNIFICATION AND IDENTITY
IN THE GERMAN BORDERLAND

DAPHNE BERDAHL

UNIVERSITY OF CALIFORNIA PRESS
Berkeley   Los Angeles   London

An earlier version of chapter 7 appeared in *A User's Guide to German Cultural Studies*, edited by Scott Denham, Irene Kacandes, and Jonathan Petropolous. Ann Arbor: University of Michigan Press, 1997.

University of California Press
Berkeley and Los Angeles, California

University of California Press, Ltd.
London, England

Library of Congress Cataloging-in-Publication Data

Berdahl, Daphne.
    Where the world ended : re-unification and identity in the German
borderland / Daphne Berdahl.
        p.   cm.
    Includes bibliographical references and index
    ISBN 0-520-21476-5 (alk. paper). — ISBN 0-520-21477-3 (alk. paper)
        1. Germany (East)—Boundaries—Case studies.   2. Germany—
History—Unification, 1990—Case studies.   3. Ethnology—
Germany—Case studies.   4. Kella (Germany)—Case studies.
5. Kella (Germany)—Social life and customs—20th century.
6. Social change—Germany—Kella.   I. Title.
DD289.5 D47   1999
341.4'2—dc21   98-7099

Printed in the United States of America

08 07 06 05 04 03 02

9 8 7 6 5 4 3

The paper used in this publication meets the minimum requirements of
ANSI/ NISO Z39.48-1992 (R 1997) (*Permanence of Paper*). ∞

For John
and
the people of Kella

Contents

Maps and Figures

Acknowledgments

This book has been made possible through collective effort; it is the product of countless dialogues, intellectual engagements, and human support. I am thus indebted and deeply grateful to the many individuals and institutions that have contributed to all phases of this work. Above all, I thank the people of Kella. Their support, sense of humor, and friendship not only made this project possible but have enriched my life far beyond what I have captured on these pages. Although I have used pseudonyms in the book to protect their privacy, I would like to note my appreciation to several villagers here, using their real names. I especially thank Dorothea and Werner Bierschenk and their children (particularly Verena) for generously supplying us with regular meals, lessons in pig slaughtering, and loving companionship; "Tante Elli" (Elizabeth Henning), whose remarkable talent and passion for storytelling turned out to be my good fortune; Elmar Manegold for his friendship, creativity, and help with numerous requests after I left Kella; Siegfried Manegold, whose insights and willingness to share them have greatly enhanced this study; Evelyn and Werner Marx, and their children Sylvia and Alexandra, for welcoming us so warmly into their home; Inge Montag, for her tolerance, patience, and kindness in the face of my incessant questions; Bernhard Sendler, whose interest and effort contributed to this project in a variety of ways; and Harri Töpfer for his valuable assistance in response to many inquiries. Too many other Kellans or former Kellans were helpful to mention them all by name, but several deserve at least brief recognition: Gisela and Siegfried Bierschenk, Marianne and Erwin Bierschenk, Rosa and Hermann Bierschenk, Holger Braun, Birgit Feiertag, Sylvia Feiertag, Waltraud Günther, Gerlinde and Frank Hacketal, Dr. Werner Henning, Willi and Wigbert Henning, Elvira Hoffmann, Jutta Jost, Gisela Lange, Helga Manegold, Karl Manegold, Ernst Montag, Erika Pappe, Erhard Rudelt, Gisela Schade, Angelika and Uwe Schenk, Bettina and Edgar Schneider, and Sabine Stier. Finally, I thank Jutta Rudelt for her help, compassion, humanity, and, above all, friendship. If she had not been working late one dark December afternoon, I would never have found my way to Kella.

The research on which this study is based was supported by several agencies and institutions, including the Council for European Studies, the University of Chicago Division of Social Sciences, and the Fulbright Commission. A Mellon Fellowship in the Humanities supported several years of graduate study and a year of dissertation writing. A James Bryant Conant Fellowship from the Minda de Gunzburg Center for European Studies at Harvard University during the academic year 1996–1997 provided valuable space and assistance for revisions and follow-up research. The University of Minnesota Graduate School and College of Liberal Arts funded the final preparation of photographs and maps. I thank them all for their support.

Numerous friends, teachers, and colleagues have generously given their time and energy to this project. I am deeply indebted to Edward Bruner, not only for his enduring support and advice over the years but also for introducing me to anthropology and encouraging me to make it my profession. At the University of Chicago, I benefited greatly from the intellectual guidance and nurturing of James Fernandez, Bernard Cohn, Michael Geyer, and Sharon Stephens. In Germany, my thanks go to Carola Lipp, Alf Lüdtke, Helga Lüdtke, Doris Bachmann-Medick, and Hans Medick for their engagement with this work, as well as to the Storre and Ullmann families in Göttingen for their dear friendship. I also thank the members of the Department of Anthropology at Harvard, particularly Mary Steedly, James Watson, and Rubie Watson, for their warm welcome during the year that I taught there. Among my former colleagues at Harvard, I owe a special debt of gratitude to Ken George for his support and encouragement and to Michael Herzfeld, who not only read a version of this manuscript in its entirety and offered valuable suggestions for revision but also provided cherished support, guidance, and friendship.

Other friends and colleagues graciously read and commented on various versions or sections of the manuscript. I am especially indebted to Matti Bunzl for his critical readings and spirited engagement. I also thank Hermine De Soto, Kriszti Fehervary, Jason James, Martha Lampland, Bill Kelleher, Renate Lellep Fernandez, Janet Morford, Kari Robinson, Mary Scoggin, Janelle Taylor, and members of the Anthropology of Europe Workshop at the University of Chicago. Susie Bullington provided valuable assistance in tracking down references. Terry Casey's indexing prowess exceeded all expectations.

At the University of California Press, Stan Holwitz has been a wonderfully supportive, persistent, and patient editor. Many thanks as well to the two anonymous readers for the press for their helpful comments and criticisms and to Sarah Myers for her meticulous copyediting and her interest in this book.

Finally, I thank my family. My parents, Bob and Peg Berdahl, have provided emotional sustenance, loving support, and exemplary partnership; additionally, my father's particular contributions as scholar and teacher have been invaluable. I also thank my sisters, Jennifer and Barbara Berdahl, for their interest, support, and unique sense of humor.

John Baldwin has lived with, and devoted much of himself to, this project. His contributions range from having served as an indispensable partner in fieldwork to the keen insights, advice, support, loyalty, humor, and love he has provided throughout. Our daughter, Audrey, born during the course of this work, has brightened every day with the wonder of her life. To both of them, my deepest thanks and my love.

Introduction

This is a book about borders, boundaries, and the spaces between them. It is about how geographical borders may be invested with cultural meanings far beyond their political intentions and how their dismantling may be so destabilizing as to generate new cultural practices and identities. Arguing that articulations, ambiguities, and contradictions of identity are especially visible in moments of social upheaval, I portray the rapid transformations in everyday life of an East German border village, Kella, after the fall of the Berlin Wall. I ask what happens to people's sense of identity and personhood when a political and economic system collapses overnight, and I explore how people negotiate and manipulate a liminal condition created by the disappearance of a significant frame of reference.

My study derives from a borderland situation, where this state of transition can be observed in particularly bold relief. Kella, the village in which I lived and conducted fieldwork between December 1990 and August 1992, is directly on, and is partially encircled by, the former border between East and West Germany. Under the socialist regime it was situated not only within the *Sperrgebiet*, a restricted zone extending a width of 5 kilometers along the boundary, but also within the more restricted *Schutzstreifen*, or high-security zone, a 500-meter strip edging the border. A single road was the village's lifeline to the rest of East Germany. Its 600 residents needed special passes to reenter Kella, and only close relatives with police clearance were permitted to visit. To deter potential "escapes," all road signs pointing to Kella were removed and, like other Schutzstreifen communities, the village was discreetly omitted from nearly every map produced in the German Democratic Republic (GDR). The crest of the wooded hills surrounding the isolated village lay in the West, where a lookout point ("the window to Kella") with a parking lot large enough to accommodate several tour buses provided a site from which westerners could gaze down on and ponder the Otherness of the East.

Almost overnight, the village was thrust from this extreme margin of the GDR to the geographical center of re-unified Germany.[1] As a participant in and observer of most aspects of daily life—including parties, family gatherings, village festivals, church activities, village council meetings, weddings, funerals, shopping, cleaning, gardening, cooking, even pig slaughtering—I was able to witness and, to a large extent, experience a multitude of changes in Kella during my two-year stay. I observed, for example, the border fence being slowly dismantled, noting that as the political border disappeared, a cultural boundary between East and West was being maintained, indeed invented. I listened to the stories of many people, including former Communist Party (Sozialistsche Einheitspartei Deutschlands [SED], or Socialist Unity Party) members, struggling to come to terms with a devalued past. I witnessed the church, once an alternative institution preaching against the official values of the socialist regime, react to its diminished political function. I talked with women, those most affected by unemployment, about their feelings of superfluousness and isolation, and I watched as many villagers who were fortunate to have found work in the West struggled with feelings of humiliation and anger arising out of encounters with West

German coworkers. As face-to-face interaction in the village drastically declined through the closings of local factories and state-owned facilities, the disappearance of a barter economy, the dissolution of most village clubs and social organizations, the discontinuation of the village public-address system, and the installation in 1992 of telephones in every home, I heard people lament the loss of community—as well as occasionally applaud the loss of social control such interactions had entailed. I witnessed people negotiate their way through an influx of consumer goods as they discovered new ways of using consumption in the construction and expression of identity and difference. I observed how people responded to—and resisted—the opportunity, pressure, and desire to look and function like the West.

One of my principal aims in this project is to explore the way in which extralocal economic, political, and social processes intersect with the individual lives of people in a community, for it is "in the actions of individuals living in time and place" that these forces are embodied, interpreted, contested, and negotiated (Abu-Lughod 1991: 156). In doing so, I consider Kella as a borderland, both literally and metaphorically, a site for the construction and articulation of identities and distinctions through boundary-maintaining practices, as well as an interstitial zone, a place betwixt and between cultures. Kella is, as Gloria Anzaldúa writes of her borderland: "a vague and undetermined place created by the emotional residue of an unnatural boundary. It is in a constant state of transition" (1987: 3).

This study, then, is both an ethnographic account of German reunification and an attempt to understand the paradoxical human condition of a borderland.

BOUNDARIES, BORDERLANDS, AND BORDER ZONES

Boundaries are symbols through which states, nations, and localities define themselves. They define at once territorial limits and sociocultural space. A boundary is, as Georg Simmel has noted, "not a spatial fact with sociological effects, but a sociological fact which forms space" (1908: 623). Boundaries—cultural, geographical, and territorial—identify people; they define who is inside and who is outside. The simple crossing of a border is a "territorial passage" that may alter spatiotemporal experience (Kelleher n.d.; Van Gennep 1960). Indeed, it is an act of definition and a declaration of identity, transforming one, in an instant, from a citizen into a foreigner.

Anthropologists have long emphasized the importance of studying cultural boundaries and processes of boundary maintenance as a means of understanding the dynamics of identity formation and expression. E. E. Evans-Pritchard's classic study of the Nuer (1940) implicitly examined how group identity and boundaries are relational concepts: community, ethnic or social identities, loyalties, and allegiances are constructed largely in relation if not in opposition to other social groups. Acculturation studies of the 1950s introduced the concept of "boundary-maintaining mechanisms" to explain how "closure" was achieved in cultural systems (SSRC 1953: 975). According to this view, cultural boundaries are maintained through "devices" like ritual initiations, secret activities, or legal barriers that function to restrict knowledge to group members and to shield a culture from external influences. In an important and influential argument, Fredrik Barth challenged certain assumptions of earlier acculturation theories and pointed out that "boundaries persist despite a flow of personnel across them" (1969: 9). Arguing that ethnic identity becomes meaningful only at the boundaries of ethnicity, Barth insisted on shifting the focus of investigation to "the ethnic boundary that defines the group, not the cultural stuff that it encloses" (p. 15).

While Barth's emphasis on boundaries is extremely valuable, his theory is less concerned with how they are constructed or sustained, especially when ethnic or other differences are absent. Indeed, it can be argued that it is precisely the "cultural stuff" that impels the very dynamics of boundary construction and maintenance (Mewett 1986: 73). N. D. Fustel de Coulanges recognized this in his study *The Ancient City*, first published in 1864, in which he discussed how certain rituals, beliefs, everyday rites, and memory consecrated the "sacred bounds" of ancient cities and fortified demarcation lines between them (1980). Such practices thus functioned as "boundary-maintaining mechanisms," in that they "expressed and sustained the corporate identity of social groups" (Munn 1973: 582).

During the 1980s, several ethnographic studies of British communities stressed the symbolic construction in practice of community and cultural boundaries (Cohen 1982, 1986). Anthony P. Cohen (1987), for example, shows how practices of everyday life in a Shetland Island community provide its population with a link to the past and thereby enable people to experience and express a sense of boundedness, distinctiveness, and common identity. In this view, boundaries are both spatial delineators and territorial reifications of social processes, as Peter Mewett points out: "The territorial boundary is a secondary thing, however: it provides the physical symbol differentiating one natural unit from another, but its construction occurs in socio-cultural space. In this sense the boundary can exist only for as long as that which it bounds continues to construct it" (1986: 83). As symbolic entities constituted in human action and interaction, boundaries are constructed out of preexisting differences, which they, in their turn, act not only to reinforce but also to create; the sense of difference they mark is as important as the cultural forms and practices they enclose.

Boundaries thus may shape social life by providing a means for social classification and ordering (Heiberg 1989).[2] While the studies of British communities effectively demonstrate this, they often overlook the degree to which identities and boundaries are externally defined by, and articulate with, larger social, political, and economic processes. Further, as Hastings Donnan and Thomas M. Wilson have pointed out in a critique of this work (1994: 4), the focus on boundedness and coherence not only perpetuates "uncritical views of homogeneity" in ethnic or cultural groups that obscures significant diversities and contradictions in social life but also replicates a now widely criticized tendency within anthropology to overemphasize boundedness, coherence, and homogeneity in its study of "culture" (Gupta and Ferguson 1992; Rosaldo 1989).

Until relatively recently, few anthropological studies of boundaries have focused on actual national or territorial boundaries.[3] Peter Sahlins's study of the boundary between France and Spain has been particularly important in recognizing both local and external factors that contributed to the invention of a territorial line and the formation of national identities. Challenging the notion that the nation-state was constructed from the center outward, Sahlins shows that as identity came to be grounded in territory, local interests and disputes were voiced in nationalist terms, thus giving shape to a national territorial boundary and distinct national identities. He notes, significantly, that "boundaries are privileged sites for the articulation of national distinctions" (Sahlins 1989: 271). The focus of his historical study is on the duality of the border, however, with little attention to boundary transgressions or the spaces in between.

A recent surge of interest in boundaries within anthropology, history, and cultural and literary studies has attempted to move away from such binarisms of the border by focusing on the interstitial and hybrid space of the borderland.[4] As Homi Bhabha writes, "this hither and thither of the stairwell, the temporal movement and passage it allows, prevents identities at either end of it from settling into primordial polarities" (1994: 4). Influenced by writings emerging out of or about the U.S.-Mexican borderland, this perspective rejects a static, bounded, and monolithic notion of culture in favor of a more dynamic understanding of the multiplicities, complexities, and contradictions of social life.[5]

The borderlands concept also offers new possibilities for theorizing and conceptualizing social space and identity. Akhil Gupta and James Ferguson, for example, suggest:

> The borderlands are just such a place of incommensurable contradictions. The term does not indicate a fixed topographical site between two other fixed locales (nations, societies, cultures), but an interstitial zone of displacement and deterritorialization that shapes the identity of the hybridized subject. Rather than dismissing them as insignificant, as marginal zones, thin slivers of land between stable places, we want to contend that the notion of borderlands is a more adequate conceptualization of the "normal" locale of the postmodern subject. (Gupta and Ferguson 1992: 18)

In this view, the borderland is as much a metaphor as a physical space, or what Roger Rouse has called "an alternative cartography of social space" (1991: 9).

Renato Rosaldo, who has been at the forefront of anthropology in theorizing the concept of a borderland, retains both a literal and metaphorical notion of a borderland in arguing for studies of people living on cultural and national borders. For Rosaldo, the borderland suggests ways of "redefining the concept of culture": "borderlands should be regarded not as analytically empty transitional zones but as sites of creative cultural production that require investigation. . . . Such cultural border zones are always in motion, not frozen for inspection" (1989: 208, 217). Moreover, the border zones of daily life may form around a variety of social boundaries: "More than we usually care to think, our everyday lives are crisscrossed by border zones, pockets and eruptions of all kinds. Social borders frequently become salient around such lines as sexual orientation, gender, class, race, ethnicity, nationality, age, politics, dress, food, or taste" (pp. 207–8).

In many respects, this view of borderlands and border zones offers a particularly compelling way of conceptualizing identity and social life. Such an approach not only highlights the processual, fluid, and multidimensional aspects of identity but also stresses how identities are contextually defined, constructed, and articulated. Indeed, border zones are often fields of heightened consciousness that demand articulation or identification. People's daily routines move them through a variety of contexts in which different forms of identity and identification are experienced, negotiated, and expressed. Rather than viewing these movements as productive of split, fragmented, or hybrid identities—notions that still imply stasis or coherence—the notion of a border zone, with its emphasis on motion and creative production within a particular arena of social life, suggests a more fluid and contextual notion of identity. Many of the dynamics of social and cultural life, I maintain, are the result of an interplay among these various domains.

As intersecting, overlapping, and, often, mutually constitutive cultural fields, border zones need not be spatially grounded, although they may also have real spatial dimensions and implications. Indeed, they may also form around existing (or, as in the German case, recently vanished) territorial or national borders. Although the theoretical or figurative conception of a borderland is based on literal geopolitical boundaries, much of the recent border theorizing has neglected the contextual specificity and dense materiality of borders in favor of an almost exclusively metaphorical and very general understanding of borders as zones of fluidity, ambiguity, deterritorialization, marginality, liminality, hybridity, resistance, or cultural diversity and difference.[6] Such depictions often overlook the fact that border zones are also places of intense and inflexible lucidity. Borders, like the one I study, generate stories, legends, events, and incidents; they are contested and negotiated in culturally specific ways by individuals and the state; they are resources for both legal and illegal exchanges of goods and services; they are sites of surveillance, control, regulation, and inspection; and they are places of secrecy, fear, danger, and desire.[7]

One of my principal aims in this study is to explore such multiple border zones—both real and imagined—in a place where tangible, indeed concrete, borders have been a powerful presence. None of the theoretical literature on borders and boundaries, in fact, deals with two of the distinguishing features of the territorial border I discuss here: its impermeability (crossing it could have been a fatal act), and then its sudden disappearance. This was a border that once divided East from West, state socialism from western capitalism, and Kella from easy and normal contact with the rest of the world. This study examines the impact of the inter-German border on daily life under socialist rule, arguing that it was not only a means by which state power was inscribed onto space and bodies but also an essential aspect of the *Zwischenraum,* a German term I employ to describe the space between the boundaries of the known in which people negotiated the limits of the possible and, in so doing, helped define them. I explore the changing meaning of the border as a symbolic construction over time, noting the kinds of borderland identities it has (en)gendered as well as recent struggles over the construction, production, and negotiation of memory surrounding the former border fence itself.

Thus I also attempt to unpack the different meanings of a borderland. Moving among different border zones, I seek to illuminate how a figurative borderland, characterized by fluidity, liminality, ambiguity, resistance, negotiation, and creativity, is dynamically heightened, accelerated, and complicated in the literal borderland of Kella, where the specificities of both come into especially sharp relief. While I would concur with the notion of a borderland as a site of "creative cultural production" (Rosaldo 1989: 208), for example, I would caution against any tendency to celebrate the interstitiality and creativity of the borderland without attending to the reality of certain power dynamics in which it may be situated. As Smadar Lavie and Ted Swedenburg have noted, borders are "not just places of imaginative interminglings and happy hybridities" (1996: 15).[8] Like other borderlands, the border I describe is characterized by an uneven and asymmetrical intersection of cultures. It is a site of cultural confrontation, articulation, and, to a large extent, penetration, where struggles over the production of cultural meanings occur in the context of asymmetrical relations between East and West. Although borderland residents may be in-between cultures, both geographically and metaphorically, the hegemony of the West here conveys a sense that they are, or should be, moving in a particular direction. They are not just "halfway beings" of the borderland (Castillo 1995), nor are they passive eastern Germans who have accepted and internalized western projections of them as inferior.[9] Instead, through a dynamic and subtle interplay of imitation and resistance, the inhabitants of this borderland are seeking and asserting new forms of identity.

STATES OF TRANSITION: AN ANTHROPOLOGY OF POSTSOCIALISM

As anthropological studies of socialism have argued and demonstrated, the tools of ethnographic analysis are well suited to the study of socialist societies and postsocialist transitions.[10] With their focus on the fine-grained detail of everyday life, anthropological studies not only have contributed a unique awareness of and perspective on the experiences of the "transition" but also have examined its multiple dimensions and trajectories. In doing so, anthropologists have challenged a certain linear, teleological thinking surrounding the collapse of socialism and pointed to the contradictions, paradoxes, and different trajectories of postsocialist societies.[11] Katherine Verdery, for example, has pointed to the ideological significance and triumphalist connotations of "the main themes"—including "privatization" and the "market economy," "demo-cratization," "nationalism," or "civil society"—of an expanding field that has come to be called "transitology" (1996: 11). At the same time, an-thropologists have also begun to examine these "main themes" from an ethnographically informed perspective. Gail Kligman's focus on the pro-cess of constructing civil society in Romania (1990), for example, cau-tions against reifications of state–society dichotomies, while Susan Gal (1996) points to the concept's gendered dimensions. Studies collected by David Kideckel (1995) examine the impact of decollectivization and pri-vatization on local politics, identities, and social organization in rural eastern European communities; Ladislaw Holy's study of national iden-tity challenges certain "vacuum theories" of nationalism that attribute its ascent after 1989 to a need to fill an ideological vacuum left by the col-lapse of socialism (Holy 1996; see also Verdery 1996).

In contrast to many observers of the transitions in eastern Europe who tend to support a "big bang" theory of socialism's collapse (Verdery 1996), ethnographically grounded studies have emphasized important continuities between socialist and postsocialist societies. David Kideckel (1995) and Gerald Creed (1995) point to parallels between certain struc-tures and experiences of collectivization and decollectivization. In a his-torical ethnography of collectivization in a Hungarian village, Martha Lampland (1995) demonstrates significant similarities between socialist and capitalist political economic practices and illuminates how com-modification under socialism in Hungary helped to pave the way for many of the transitions that have followed. Carole Nagengast (1991), in a study of class and social differentiation in a rural Polish community, similarly argues that the reinstitution of capitalism in Poland does not represent a systemic rupture but reflects important "continuities in ear-lier, class-based *social* relations that masqueraded as *socialist* relations for four and a half decades" (p. 1, emphases in the original). In a discussion of the elaborate social and economic networks formed under socialism's "second society" in Poland, Janine Wedel (1992) also notes how critical these relations will be in shaping Poland's future. More generally, the work of Katherine Verdery (1996) has been devoted to highlighting con-tinuities in many arenas of social, political, and economic life.

Anthropologically informed studies of postsocialist transitions have also pointed to valuable topics outside these "main themes." Important work on the gender regimes of socialism as well as on abortion debates in many postsocialist societies have contributed to theoretical understandings of the relationship between gender and nation (De Soto 1994; Dölling 1991; Gal 1994; Goven 1993; Kligman 1992; Verdery 1996). In a different vein, analyses of ethnic and nationalist conflicts have demonstrated that these are not simply a revival of old tensions suppressed by socialist rule but hostilities that must be re-created anew (Verdery 1996: 95; see also Bringa 1995; Denich 1994; Hayden 1996). Other scholars have examined the pervasiveness of memory and the uses and burdens of the past (Borneman 1997; Hayden 1994; Lass 1994). Another important topic highlighted by anthropological studies of postsocialist transitions is the changing cultural meanings and politics of consumption (Berdahl, Bunzl, and Lampland 1999; Humphrey 1995; Konstantinov 1996; Verdery 1996). Underlying most of these studies, explicitly or implicitly, is the salient question of identity and its rearticulation in altered economic, social, and national contexts (Berdahl, Bunzl, and Lampland 1999; De Soto and Anderson 1993; Kennedy 1994; Kürti and Langman 1997; Slobin 1996). Among other things, this book addresses several of these alternative "transition themes," including national identity, memory, gender, and consumption.

For anthropology, postsocialist transitions offer opportunities to explore some of the central issues of the discipline: the relationship among economic systems, political entities, and culture; the construction of identity, ethnicity, and nationalism; social and cultural change. Similarly, anthropology's long interest in conditions of liminality offers a particularly useful tool for analyzing and conceptualizing these moments of tremendous change (Verdery 1996: 231). Defined by Victor Turner as the ambiguous, interstructural, paradoxical, "betwixt and between" status endured by initiates during a rite of passage, the liminal period is a transition "between states" (Turner 1967: 93). As Turner himself suggests, the term *state* may be interpreted very broadly—even, I would propose, quite literally.

Turner's notion of liminality is drawn from Arnold Van Gennep's writings on *rites de passage*, and it is no accident that one of Van Gennep's images for this concept is a territorial boundary. For it is here at the border, he argues, that a transition between two worlds is most pronounced (1960: 18). In my study of a transition between two German states, I strive to wed the anthropological concept of liminality to more recent theories of borders and borderlands, where—with a few exceptions—it has been surprisingly absent.[12]

In the course of the incorporation of the East into the West, I argue, people like the residents of Kella have invented—and, in some cases, ritualized—certain forms of negotiations and rites of passage that mark a transition. Many of these negotiations and ritualizations have emerged from the interstices of social life: from walks along the former East-West boundary; from spaces between popular faith and institutionalized religion; from consumption practices shaped under a cultural order of socialism in the new context of a market economy; from tensions produced by competing gender ideologies; from the space between the boundaries of remembering and forgetting; and, under socialism, in the Zwischenraum, the space between the boundaries of the known.

The interstitiality of the borderland is thus not confined to the more literal border zone that has formed around the recently vanished territorial boundary, although it may be in this context that its in-betweenness is most visible. In addition to its spatial implications, I also use the borderland here as a temporal, political, and cultural metaphor for a state of and in transition.

PROCESSES AND PARTICULARS

An additional objective of this study, therefore, is to illuminate how people negotiate and manipulate rapid social change in a world of increasingly malleable boundaries, where identities crystallize around borders as well as transcend them. I thus highlight processes of change, contestation, and identity formation that are especially visible in moments of social discord and that take on particular significance at the former border. Throughout the book, I draw on "revelatory incidents" and "ethnographies of the particular" to describe the circumstances and experiences of individuals and a community (Fernandez 1986; Abu-Lughod 1991).[13]

This focus on particulars does not entail a privileging of micropro-
cesses over macroprocesses, however. Instead, it is an attempt to move
away from an emphasis on coherence, boundedness, and homogeneity
that has characterized much of "traditional" anthropology in general
(Gupta and Ferguson 1992; Rosaldo 1989) and European ethnography
in particular. As anthropology returned "part-way home" to study
European cultures, it often carried with it the discipline's traditional
focus on isolated, bounded, and homogeneous communities (Cole 1977).
Viewing change as unilineal and unidirectional, European village studies have traditionally treated localities as bounded social entities and focused on issues of tradition, modernization, adaptation, and continuity
in rural life.[14] An approach emphasizing local identity and culture as
products of large-scale processes, while extremely valuable, may risk
discounting the productive potential and rich detail of human experience, cultural practices, and individual action in social life.[15]

Although its focus is on the village of Kella, this study, like much contemporary ethnography, strives to transcend the "village-study paradigm" as well as other monolithic "culture concepts" by exploring the effects of long-term and extralocal processes as they are manifested and
refracted in a multiplicity of small-scale processes, local practices, and
individual actions (Abu-Lughod 1991: 143). Another aim here, then, is to
tell stories that reflect particular intersections of the large and the small.
Some of these stories focus on individuals, like Werner Schmidt, one of
the few "really reds" in Kella; Emma Hauser, a "religious virtuoso";[16]
"J. R.," nicknamed after the character in the American television series
Dallas; or Ralf Fischer, a traveler of maps. Other stories are about places,
like the Seventh Station, the Kella chapel, or the landscape of the border
fence. And some stories focus on events, like the fall of the Wall on November 9, 1989, or Kella's procession in honor of re-unification on October 3, 1990.

Together, the stories, anecdotes, and vignettes are an attempt to represent ethnographically "a world riven with cultural contradiction"
(Limón 1991: 116). For, as Michael Herzfeld has noted, it is often these
"humbler moments" or "'mere anecdotes'" that reveal what moves
people to action" (1997: 24).[17] I do not claim to explain these events or
experiences "as they really were" to those concerned; experience and

its recollections, reconstructions, and interpretations—including my own—are subjective, situated, and inherently dialogical.[18] Informed by the well-known critiques of anthropology, then, my ethnographic story-telling aims to avoid the distancing, totalizing, and essentializing discourses of generalization; I hope to show that people's experiences of the rapid transformations surrounding the fall of the Wall have been highly differentiated—even in a tiny border village.

ETHNOGRAPHIC RESEARCH AND WRITING

Ethnographic fieldwork, like most research, is often a matter of structured serendipity. Indeed, my choice of a field site and my relationships in the field were the products of a mysterious interplay of luck and systematic research. I cannot claim, for example, that the selection of Kella as a field site was a carefully calculated one. Instead, it was the only village that met my criteria in which I was able to find housing. My interest in borders and boundaries had led me to select the Catholic Eichs-feld region as a research site in order to explore issues of regional identi-ties and boundary maintenance. My second principal criterion was a *Schutzstreifengemeinde,* a village located in the highly restricted 500-meter border zone, which limited me to approximately fifteen villages in the Eichsfeld. Because these villages had been inaccessible under socialism and the construction of new homes restricted, it was difficult to locate housing, for most homes were shared by three or four generations of one family.

As it turned out, however, Kella could not have been better suited to my research aims and interests. It is located directly on the former East-West border, which is also the Protestant-Catholic boundary of the Eichs-feld region, a Catholic enclave in Protestant central Germany with a long tradition of constructing and maintaining a strong sense of regional iden-tity. As I discuss in chapter 1, the former GDR border also corresponds to an earlier boundary between Prussia and Hesse, which now divides Hesse from Thuringia. Furthermore, several unique places and events made Kella a particularly interesting site for my research. I discuss most of these in the chapters that follow, including the chapel between the fences, the Seventh Station, and the procession on October 3 that was broadcast on a regional television station basing its coverage of re-unification events in the village. The videotapes of this coverage and the 1989 border opening in Kella that were sitting on the mayor's desk the day we arranged housing only seemed to confirm that I had landed there by a fortunate twist of fate.

As should be evident by the theoretical issues discussed above, "rep-resentativeness" and "typicality" are not among my major concerns here. The degree to which Kella, with its variety of "exceptional" historical cir-cumstances—borderland location, Catholicism, Eichsfeld regionalism—may represent the practices, behaviors, and experiences of "typical" east-ern Germans before and after the *Wende* (turning point, or the fall of the Berlin Wall and collapse of socialist rule) is, of course, questionable. While I am convinced that many of the experiences, stories, and events portrayed in this study will resonate with those of other eastern Ger-mans—a conviction that derives from having kept careful track of dis-cussions in the regional and national press, from conversations during visits to other areas of Germany, and from observations by friends and colleagues who have spent time in post-Wall Germany—it is not my in-tent here to establish representativeness by sociological measure. In-stead, my aim is to explore issues of identity formation and negotiation that demand and can profit from a local focus in the context of the social, cultural, economic, and political transformations surrounding the fall of the Berlin Wall and German re-unification. In doing so, I hope to gener-ate insights not only into the politics of everyday life in re-unified Ger-many as well as under socialism in the GDR, but also under such condi-tions whenever and wherever they occur.[19]

Research Methodology and Practice

Doing fieldwork in a village that was inaccessible to outsiders for more than thirty years posed its own unique challenges.[20] When I ar-rived with my husband, John, in early December 1990, just days after arranging housing with the local mayor, the entire village had already heard we were coming. Our reception was cool at first, a result of what several villagers later called "suspicious mentalities," which they attributed to the village's isolation under socialism; it was also the product, many later explained, of simple curiosity about Americans ("class enemy number one"). People peered from behind lace window curtains as we walked by, rarely returned a greeting, or simply stopped what they were doing to watch us.

Most anthropologists seem to have their own "fieldwork turning-point narrative"; mine—now often told and retold in a variety of contexts, including among people in Kella—involves music. After failing to elicit even a greeting from anyone but our landlords, we were grateful when the local priest, Father Münster, asked John, a professional violinist, to play in church on Christmas Eve. It was the first time, I later learned, that most villagers had heard a solo violin. After he had filled the packed, candle-lit sanctuary with his music, John was introduced to the congregation by Kella's priest. Much to my surprise, Father Münster explained that I was writing a dissertation about the "Wende in the Eichsfeld," and that although we were not Catholic, my husband and I should be welcomed into the community. His introduction and stamp of approval seemed to work immediately: after church we were greeted and welcomed by several villagers; only days later we were being invited into people's homes. While it is, of course, impossible to determine how much impact the priest or John's memorable performance—or perhaps both—had on the subsequent direction and success of my research, the event did represent a substantial and noticeable change in our reception in the community.

Throughout the course of the next twenty months of field research, I worked to establish and cultivate a network of relations across a diverse range of social, kinship, and age groups in the village. Most of my research thus entailed the total immersion that is typical of ethnographic observation: occasionally joined by John (whose long hours playing in the Staatstheater Kassel orchestra often kept him away from Kella), I attended church, first communions, weddings, funerals, sessions of the village council, and meetings of the local *Heimatverein* (voluntary association dedicated to the cultivation of *Heimat,* or homeland). I participated in social gatherings, dinner parties, religious processions, and local festivals like *Fasching* (the pre-Lent carnival) or *Kirmes* (the annual festival commemorating the dedication of the community church); I shopped with teenagers, entire families, and women friends in Eschwege, Göttingen, and Heiligenstadt; I picked (and ate) cherries with older villagers in their gardens as I caught up on local gossip; I hiked the Silberklippe, the highest of the hills surrounding Kella, with everyone from ten-year-old Sylvia to the village priest; I went dancing with villagers my own age at nearby discos; and I traveled to Tirol with the largely middle-aged Heimatverein. Thanks to the lack of telephones in Kella during my research, which necessitated face-to-face interaction for all communication, I was able to see many people on a regular, often daily, basis. By the end of my stay in Kella, I had come to know most—although not all—villagers, some very well. I have maintained contact with many of them since leaving the field, and I was able to renew relationships during visits in February 1994 and the spring of 1996.

In addition to ethnographic observation and informal interviews, I also selected ten villagers, from a range of age, gender, religious, political, and social groups, with whom I taped "life-history" interviews. These more formal interviews involved an average of three two-hour sessions with each person over a period of several months and were enhanced by daily interaction with the same individuals throughout my stay. In order to establish a basis for understanding village kinship relations and social structure, I also collected oral genealogies of several families. Here I paid particular attention to relatives living in West Germany, social differentiation, and family patterns of party membership. I supplemented these with genealogical records for the entire village, recreated from church records beginning in 1910. Although time consuming, these genealogies turned out to be essential for understanding many aspects of village social relations and organization, particularly in my analysis of social organization and differentiation in chapter 4. Church records also enabled me to compile information on population trends, birthrates, and marriage rates.

Finally, my study involved research in the village archives. Minutes of village council and special committee meetings, Volkspolizei (People's

Police) reports, state mass-organization and party-membership lists, and records of organized village activities and elections provided a wealth of information—inaccessible before the Wende—on everyday life in the GDR. Although I did have access to archival materials from the Nazi period in Kella, I opted not to pursue this line of inquiry for several reasons. First, an in-depth local history of the village during Nazi rule exceeds the scope of my project; archival and oral-history research on this period would have required me to devote significantly less time to ethnographic research, thus limiting my ability to observe and record the tremendous changes in Kella after the fall of the Wall. Because of the rapid pace of transition during the course of my fieldwork, I felt compelled, as it were, to "seize the moment." My second reason was methodological: I was concerned that my positioning as an ethnographer would be affected if I asked probing questions about the village's Nazi past and that this would impede my ability to become integrated into the community. Instead, I have chosen to address this particular period of history as it pertains to other issues explored in this study: continuities between resistive religious practices under the Nazi and SED regimes, for example, or the differences in memory construction of the Nazi past in East and West Germany as a critical element in current negotiations of memory and national identity in the new Germany.

The material on which this study is based is thus drawn from diverse sources. The quotations throughout the book stem from taped interviews, notes taken during informal interviews, or observations recorded in my field notes. Although individuals' names used in the book are pseudonyms, Kella is not. I was initially inclined to use individuals' real names, feeling that this would be a more appropriate and respectful acknowledgment of the people who had so generously shared their lives and experiences with me, but in the end I opted for pseudonyms primarily "to return to them at least a small part of the power to decide whether or not to reveal themselves" (Rogers 1991: xiii). Although most individuals quoted or portrayed here will be well known to people in Kella, I have made every effort to conceal their identity.

The decision to retain the village name, however, is made largely at the Kellans' request. Although people expressed different reasons for this desire—an enduring local pride and sense of Heimat or the misguided anticipation of a burgeoning tourist industry that might be enhanced by my study (despite my repeated attempts to claim otherwise)—underlying their collective request, it seemed to me, was the hope that I might be able to help put Kella back on the map. And in its way, perhaps this study does that.

The Organization of This Study

Boundaries and border zones are the organizing metaphor of the book as well as its object of study. In some respects, the project appears to share certain aspects of the traditional village studies it attempts to transcend with its chapters organized around religion, social organization, or gender. Yet instead of viewing these subjects as separate categories, I treat these and other arenas of social life as multilayered, overlapping, and often interdependent border zones that crisscross people's daily lives. The border zones I describe here are ones whose boundaries "become salient around lines" of social differentiation, religion, nationality, and gender (Rosaldo 1989: 207). They provide contexts for the articulation, negotiation, and construction of different forms of identity and memory, and their dynamics are often closely linked to other kinds of borders and borderlands—geopolitical, regional, metaphorical, or concrete. They are also the areas of social life that have been particularly affected by the collapse of socialism and German re-unification.

This organization of chapters around particular border zones is also intended to reflect a flow of themes in the book—from publicity and secrecy, to religion, consumption, identity, gender, and memory—that draw together related issues of nation building, identity formation, and a micropolitics of everyday life. Negotiations of socialist state power in relation to practices of publicity and secrecy, for example, are essential for understanding comparable negotiations of a consumer market economy after the fall of the Wall; the history of religious presence in the Eichsfeld region continues to be an important factor in the ongoing negotiation of gender, regional, and religious identities as well as in the construction and expression of memory; practices of social distinction and consumption under socialism have informed and structured transformations in the meanings, politics, and en-gendering of consumption in postsocialist eastern Germany. Taken together, these interwoven themes, I suggest, not only illustrate important continuities between socialism and postsocialism but also illuminate the multiple ways in which the nation-state—both the GDR and the new Germany—attempts to implant itself, at different moments more or less successfully, into everyday life. What makes the German state and its borderland a site of ethnographic inquiry is the historically and culturally specific nature of the border—once looming and impenetrable, now dismantled and reinvented—where power and difference are intimately articulated, exercised, contested, and potentially transformed.

Chapter 1 describes Kella as it was when I arrived in December 1990. Intended to provide readers with a general history and outline of the village, the chapter also offers a basis for gauging the tremendous changes I have witnessed there over the past six years. Chapter 2 focuses on the politics of everyday life under socialism. Drawing from archival research as well as oral histories, I examine state institutions and organizations that formed the microfoundations of power in everyday interaction. The state and its actions became something people had to interpret, I argue, and the regime derived power from the way it was interpreted, experienced, and even resisted. This interplay between above and below, between the state and its citizens, was crucial in sustaining the socialist regime.

In Chapter 3 my focus is on religious identities and practices and their relationship to a dynamic interplay among religion, place, and belonging in Kella. As part of the Eichsfeld region, the village remained devoutly Catholic despite the socialist state's attempts to undermine religion in the GDR. I examine how religion could be both an expression of and reason for resistance under socialism, and I explore transformations in the dynamic relationship between popular faith and institutionalized religion since the Wende. These changes, I argue, have resulted in a renegotiation and redefinition of religious identities and practices. Underlying my argument in this chapter is the assumption that religion may be viewed not as a distinct sphere of cultural life but, rather, as something that permeates, and is permeated by, complex negotiations of identity within changing political and economic structures.

Chapter 4 explores the production and reproduction of inequality in village social relations over time. I focus on the kinds of constructions used to classify social differentiation, and I examine the emergence of new strategies of social distinction after the virtual elimination of private property under socialism. I argue that a new group of village elites asserted itself through the social capital of connections and show how these new practices of distinction occurred primarily in the realm of the second economy, in which consumption became productive in new and strategic ways: it both reflected and constituted difference. With the fall of the Wall, consumption has taken on new meanings and roles in the construction of difference as inequalities are reorganized according to the principles of a consumer market economy.

In many respects, chapter 5 forms the core of the book, for it sets up and expands on the borderland argument. I explore the development and experience of the border under socialism, the events surrounding the fall of the Wall, and the dynamic of boundary maintenance and invention on both sides of the former border after the Wende. I examine the emergence of certain "initiation rites" into the new society for eastern Germans, particularly in the realm of consumption, and discuss how certain taxonomies of classification, of identifying who is an *Ossi* and who is a *Wessi,* have become part of everyday life. Over a relatively short period of time, I argue, new forms of identity have been created, invented, and asserted.

Chapter 6 argues that these real and invented distinctions between East and West are often structured in gendered terms. I examine several ideological and practical tensions in social life that have informed the construction and negotiation of gender before and after the Wende in Kella, and I focus in particular on how the influx of western images and ideologies of womanhood have challenged forty years of women's experience as workers and mothers under socialism. I explore how these contrasting gender ideologies are tension-laden, and I argue that this tension and the social transformations of which it is a part are both gendered and gendering. National identity must thus be viewed as a gendered phenomenon.

Chapter 7 explores the construction, production, and negotiation of historical memory since the fall of the Wall. It focuses on several arenas in which this negotiation and contestation take place, including performative ceremonies, shifting discourses of historical memory and their relationship to local practices, and struggles over the commemoration and representation of the GDR past. I return here to the book's central theme of borders and boundaries in a discussion of the politics of memory surrounding the former border fence itself. Arguing that memory is an interactive, infinitely malleable, and highly contested phenomenon, this final chapter examines the role of the past in the present.

1   The Village on the Border

SHIFTING BOUNDARIES

When I first arrived in Kella in 1990, crossing the border from West Germany to East Germany entailed much more than a simple territorial passage. The gradual transition in the roads leading to the village was itself a liminal space, a product of the roads' borderland location as well as of a consciousness of their temporary remoteness that was heightened by the new pavement and construction that surrounded other border crossings. To reach Kella, you had to exit the fast-paced western German highway (B27) near the town of Eschwege, follow wide, well-paved roads through the western village of Grebendorf, and then take a narrow asphalt road winding through the hills to the spot overlooking Kella known to locals as "Braunrode." An "Eschweger Klosterbräu" placard signaled the entry to an abandoned restaurant that used to serve the tourists who would come for a glimpse of the famous Iron Curtain and the people it enclosed.[1] At this point, the end of the western German terrain, the winding road turned to gravel; a sharp two-meter drop on the right forced you to slow down and weave through large potholes, a stark contrast to the smooth pace of traffic in the West just moments, even meters, ago. A wide, rough-edged opening in the three-meter-high border fence that surrounded the village marked the passage into the "East;" seconds later, a colorful wooden crucifix on the left indicated that you had also entered the Catholic Eichsfeld.

The village of Kella, like the Eichsfeld region of which it is a part, has a long history as a borderland (Map 1). In fact, it has been a village on many borders. Over the past two hundred years, the boundary line on which Kella is situated has delineated not only East and West but also Prussia and Hesse, Thuringia and Hesse, Catholic and Protestant, and the Eichsfeld and a variety of states and principalities (Figures 1 and 2). Fluctuations in this multilayered and shifting boundary have influenced many aspects of the community's history, economy, and social landscape. As I discuss at various points in the book, these multiple boundaries—regional, religious, territorial, national—are also an important part of a local identifying narrative.

The first mention of Kella in the public record dates back to 1141. The village name reportedly stems from the old German *Këla*, meaning valley or ravine, and alludes to the community's location at the foothills of the eastern Hessian mountains. The locality's history is closely tied to that of the Eichsfeld, a rural area nestled between the Harz mountains to the north and the Thuringian basin to the south. From the twelfth century until 1803, the Eichsfeld was a principality governed by the archbishop of Mainz; as an ecclesiastical territory, the region remained a Catholic enclave after the territories surrounding it became Protestant during the Reformation.[2] Its territorial borders thus became cultural boundaries as a sense of beleaguered religious isolation shaped a regional identity of the Eichsfelders. This cultural, religious, and, to some extent, economic separation from its neighbors continued after the region came under Prussian control in 1803. In the aftermath of the defeat of Prussia by Napoleon and the Peace of Tilsit in 1807, the Eichsfeld spent a brief

Map 1. The Eichsfeld.
(Cartography by the University of Minnesota Cartography Laboratory)

period under French rule as part of the newly formed Kingdom of Westphalia. It returned to Prussian rule in 1813 until the redrawing of boundaries at the Congress of Vienna in 1815 divided the Eichsfeld between Hanover and Prussia. Kella, in the southwestern corner of the Eichsfeld, bordered Hesse and remained under Prussian control. The Eichsfeld remained divided until Prussia annexed both Hanover and Hesse, along with several other states, after the Austro-Prussian War in 1866. Although partitioned into different administrative districts, the Eichsfeld as a geographical, religious, and cultural region remained united under different German states for the next eighty years.

The bonds between villages in the northern Eichsfeld, forged by centuries of common interest, religious unity, trade, and intermarriage, were

Figures 1 and 2. Old boundary stones of Prussia (left) and the GDR (right) along the same borderline near Kella. (Photographs by the author)

ruptured after 1945, when the boundary between East and West Germany was drawn through the northwestern part of the region. Using the boundaries of prewar administrative districts, the Allied powers divided the country into four zones of occupation. Like the East-West border near Kella that was also the boundary of the Eichsfeld as well as a demarcation between the lands of Thuringia and Hesse before the war, many of these boundaries corresponded to earlier lines of division drawn during the various treaties of the nineteenth century. The division of the Eichsfeld after the war was especially devastating to the area because nearly one-half of the eastern Eichsfeld was located in the Sperrgebiet, thus making it inaccessible to the majority of Eichsfeld residents. As we shall see in the next chapter, villages in this zone, especially those like Kella within the even more restricted 500-meter Schutzstreifen, were subject to particularly strict surveillance and control by the East German regime.

Much of Eichsfeld history, memory, and local identity is thus ordered through a notion of boundaries. There are *the* border (the *Grenze*, or former inter-German border), the Sperrgebiet and Schutzstreifen boundaries, the Protestant-Catholic boundaries of the Eichsfeld enclave, and linguistic boundaries. These linguistic distinctions denote a local Eichsfeld dialect separate from the surrounding region as well as a boundary within the Eichsfeld that differentiates a Low German from a Thuringian dialect.[3] The latter linguistic boundary runs southeast of the former east-west border and historically distinguished the "upper Eichsfeld" from the "lower Eichsfeld," a distinction alluding to geological elevation. The border of 1815 (and later of 1945, which ran along the same line) shifted the boundary between the upper and lower Eichsfeld north, where it is today. This historical distinction corresponds to an enduring economic inequality between the two Eichsfelds resulting from the richer, more fertile soil of the lower Eichsfeld—a gap that was widened by the region's division into the capitalist West and socialist East.

POSTWAR KELLA

As many older villagers are apt to remind the younger generation, Kella fell on the eastern side of the border through an accident of history. The village, along with several other regions of Thuringia, was first occupied by American troops in April 1945. Following an agreement between the Allied powers on June 5, 1945, the United States and Britain traded their occupied parts of Saxony, Thuringia, and Mecklenburg for regions of Berlin. On July 1, the American troops left Kella; five days later, Russian troops arrived, and the village became part of the Soviet occupation zone. "They traded us off for Berlin," villagers say.

Like many large-scale historical processes, these shifts were manifested locally and specifically through their instantiation in particular events and individuals. World War II and National Socialist rule in Kella were experienced, among other things, in the loss of forty-one young men in battle; a few regional Nazi party members who lacked broad support among the local population; struggles with the state over freedom of religious expression; the bombing of Kassel 60 miles away in 1943, which reportedly shook village window panes; the bombing of the Eschwege airstrip in 1944, which claimed the life of a local father of five; the influx of war refugees, which reached its peak at 200 evacuees housed in village homes during the winter of 1944/1945; and the downing of two German fighter planes near Kella on April 2, 1945, the pilots of which are buried in the village cemetery. The end of the war was signaled by the arrival of American troops in Kella, as reflected in the following account written by a thirteen-year-old girl in September 1945. The Americans arrived in Kella on April 8, the Sunday after Easter and the day of Kella's annual first communion celebrations.

> When mass was over and we were on our way home, we saw a white flag up on Braunrode. I said to mother: "Who could that be?" And mother said: "That's certainly nobody from Kella!" And she was right, because we learned that one of the evacuated women from Cologne, along with her father, had gathered the courage to head out carrying a white flag.
>   There was much excitement when we got home, but I thought without really thinking, that it was somehow fitting that the Americans should come the Sunday after Easter. Just as I was going to look in on my sick brother I heard a woman in the street yelling, "The Americans are coming! The Americans are coming!" Mother said: "I'm going to look from upstairs to see if it's true." As she looked out the window, she saw an American standing below. She was frightened as she came

down the stairs and yelled, "Get dressed, they're already standing down below!" Then an American came inside and said [in broken German]: "[Have] no fear. Everything [is being handled] at the mayor's." We started to cry right when we saw the strange soldiers, because we all thought the village would be set on fire and ransacked. We also realized that we had lost the war.[4]

This image of emerging from the church to see American troops standing on the Braunrode hill appears frequently in residents' accounts of the end of the war. During the two months of American occupation, still referred to locally in typical GDR terminology as the period "when the Americans first liberated us," the village housed between 6 and 150 troops.[5]

The transfer of the region from American to Soviet control was also noted initially in the movement of troops. On July 1, 1945, the Americans suddenly left Kella. Two days later, without notice or explanation, access to Eschwege was barricaded. For the next several days, American troops fortified the new border, reportedly shooting at anyone who attempted to cross illegally. The unrest generated by these actions, coupled with the news that the region had been transferred to Soviet control, led to a sudden increase in people attempting to flee eastern Germany. Kella and the surrounding region were inundated with refugees, as the priest's 1946 chronicle describes: "There was much unrest in the village. All at once many strangers appeared. Evacuees wanted to get over the border quickly—mothers to their children and children to their mothers.... One could hear many a groan [of exhaustion] at the foot of the Silberklippe and see many anxious faces scurrying through the bushes." On July 6, five days after the Americans' departure, Soviet troops arrived in Kella. Shortly thereafter, a Soviet commander attempted to allay villagers' fears of Soviet occupation by calling a community meeting. According to the priest's chronicle, the officer announced: "We may be in power here, but we don't intend to oppress and we will leave the church in freedom." Several homes along one village street were emptied to house the fifty newly arrived Soviet soldiers.

Despite the commanding officer's assurances, however, the border quickly became increasingly fortified through stricter Soviet surveillance and curfews, the establishment of official border crossings, and the construction of sentry boxes and underground bunkers at control check-points. Because the densely forested hills surrounding the village made surveillance of the border difficult, the operating borderline was drawn at the base of the woods. As Kella's priest wrote in his 1946 chronicle: "Our Stations of the Cross fell into 'foreign territory.' . . . Kella had become a border village."[6]

ECONOMY

Throughout much of its history, economic development in the Eichsfeld was hindered by the region's distance from its ruling electorate in Mainz, a problem that was compounded by the frequent boundary changes and political affiliations after the end of ecclesiastical control during the nineteenth century. As in the rest of the Eichsfeld, Kella's economy was largely supported until the mid–nineteenth century by small-scale agricultural production and, from the seventeenth through the nineteenth centuries, by cottage industries, particularly spinning and weaving.[7] The unique lime soil surrounding Kella was especially fertile for fruit trees; efficient use of the land as both an orchard and a grazing pasture for sheep enabled many villagers to earn a living close to home. The tradition of partible inheritance, however, which was practiced throughout the Eichsfeld for centuries, had substantially reduced the size of family property holdings; by the early nineteenth century it was difficult for most Eichsfelders to earn a living from the land. Economic circumstances of the local population worsened throughout the nineteenth century after the Industrial Revolution displaced the once prosperous local textile production in the Eichsfeld. Many residents of Kella, together with people from throughout the region, were forced by economic necessity to seek work elsewhere.[8] Many villagers were able to find employment in nearby Hesse, often taking away work from the Hessian population because Eichsfelders were willing to work for lower wages. Others were forced to seek work through seasonal migration. Leaving at Easter and returning in the fall for Kirmes, men from the Eichsfeld, including many from Kella, earned their livings as masons in the Rhineland or as laborers in the brickyards of most German industrial cities; in the winter, many found work in the sugar factories of Saxony. Although less common, women from Kella (usually unmarried) also found work as seasonal agricultural laborers in Magdeburg or as day laborers in Hesse. The opening in 1911 of a small cigar factory in Kella, a typical Eichsfeld industry, enabled many local women to find work close to home. For many villagers, however, the economic need for seasonal work continued into the twentieth century: in 1924, for example, more than 25 percent of the working-age population in Kella earned a living as migrant laborers (Müller and others 1966: 11).

During the period of National Socialist rule and World War II, most women in Kella continued to work in the local cigar factory until production was halted in the final war years. Men who were too old for military service found employment in nearby Eschwege. The jobs generated by Hitler's war machine, including street and Autobahn construction as well as work at the Eschwege airstrip, were a welcome relief not only from the mass unemployment of the Weimar period but also from the many years and generations of migrant labor throughout the Eichsfeld's history.

As part of the socialist state's campaign to industrialize the Eichsfeld and thereby end its plight as the "poor house of Prussia," several industries were established in the region after the advent of socialist rule. Kella's village economy was principally supported by two of these local industries until 1989. The local cigar factory was reopened in 1953 under the direction of the state-owned VEB Gildemann Dingelstädt and provided work for fifty women from Kella. In 1966, the facility was taken over by the VEB Kleinmetalwerk Heiligenstadt for the production of suspender clips. Approximately eighty women, more than half of the working-age women in Kella, assembled clips here until the factory closed in the spring of 1991. A toy factory in the neighboring village of Pfaffschwende (three kilometers from Kella) opened in 1955; the vertical organization of its production line employed more than one-third of working-age adults in Kella as draftspeople, toolmakers, masons, mechanics, bookkeepers, cooks, or assembly line workers. It, too, dismissed nearly all of its employees during the course of my fieldwork. Other villagers worked on the regional collective farm, and a few commuted thirty kilometers to Heiligenstadt, the regional center and seat of the *Kreis* (district).[9] Most of these jobs also disappeared after the collapse of socialist rule.

The rapidly increasing unemployment rate in the former GDR was thus reflected in Kella: during the period of my research, nearly every household had at least one member without work, usually a woman. Despite this relatively high unemployment rate, however, Kella was able to escape the worst of the economic crisis that hit the former GDR after re-unification. Owing to its close proximity to the West, many villagers were able to find employment in western Germany, usually in the nearby town of Eschwege. Within two years of the Wende, more than half of the men and many of the younger women had found work in the West. Aided by their training in masonry and extensive construction projects made possible by the federal government–subsidized efforts to "rebuild" East Germany after re-unification, the vast majority of village men employed in the West worked in construction. Women, who were primarily hired as part-time workers, worked as office assistants, as store clerks, or in housekeeping.

In many respects, these one-sided border crossings from East to West have entailed a resumption of economic ties that existed before the establishment of the border between East and West Germany in 1945, when many locals worked, shopped, or sold their wares in Hesse. Residents of Kella and its neighboring villages go to Eschwege to shop, to visit relatives, and to work once again for lower wages—not as Eichsfelders now but as Ossis.

DECEMBER 1990

In 1990, a border crossing from West to East was most quickly and richly apparent to the senses.[10] The brown coal emissions from every chimney in the village, mixed with the oily blue exhaust of Trabants, the poorly built, slow, small, boxy automobiles owned by most East Germans, produced a very distinctive odor. The brownish haze that hovered over the village, trapped by the surrounding hills, confirmed visually what the olfactory senses had already perceived. As throughout eastern

Germany, this "GDR air" was largely responsible for the dirty, graying stucco that covered many of the buildings in the community, not to mention the reportedly related health problems (bronchitis, asthma, migraines) of the local population.

Kella sounded different, too. Many of these sounds emanated from the patterns of village life: the clucking of chickens, the bleating of sheep, the occasional terrified squeal of a pig headed to slaughter. In December 1990, most households still maintained some form of small-scale agricultural production, a leftover from life under socialism when such production had been necessary to ensure adequate supplies for household consumption as well as to fulfill prescribed amounts of eggs, poultry, or pork set by the latest five-year state plan. "Bio-hens," as local chickens came to be called by villagers who liked to poke fun at West German organic-food terminology, spent their days mingling on the village soccer field; at night they would return to their respective homes. Sheep, whose wool commanded a decent price in the GDR, spent their time in the barn behind the family home or grazing under the cherry or apple trees in a household garden plot.

Other sounds in Kella, and the habitual practices they generated, were more distinctly East German. The noise of spluttering Trabants could be heard from afar, giving most villagers enough time to make it to a window, peer out from behind lace curtains, and ascertain, as well as comment on, its driver and passengers. This practice was largely a product of forty years of life in a Schutzstreifengemeinde, people told me, when knowledge of villagers' comings and goings was not only the work of various agents of state control but also part of the social control that is frequently part of life in a small community; in Kella such social control was intensified by the village's enforced isolation. A local sense of sound was often so well developed that people could not only tell the difference between a Trabi (the nickname for a Trabant), a Wartburg, or a Lada (the range of automobile possibilities in the GDR) but could also make distinctions among them and thus identify individual automobiles. For some, the influx of western automobiles after the Wende was confusing, causing them to abandon this taxonomy of sounds; for others, it was an opportunity to expand their repertoire and thus adapt to a new range of

Figure 3. The loudspeaker that was part of the village public-address system used during socialist rule; behind it is one of the community bulletin boards that replaced the public-address system in 1991. (Photograph by the author)

possibilities and their corresponding social distinctions as the status and value of eastern automobiles plummeted.

On any given weekday, but usually on Friday mornings, echoes of the village public-address system could also be heard on most street corners in Kella (Figure 3). Despite being renovated shortly before the Wende, the sound quality of the system was relatively poor. In order to alert residents of the coming announcements, music too distorted to even identify would typically blast for several minutes out of the cone-shaped speakers mounted on narrow poles. This would be followed by a clearer (although not always audible) voice of one of the women employed in the mayor's office relaying information about garbage pickup, recycling drop-offs, village council meetings, mayoral office hours, or gatherings of local voluntary associations and clubs. Even in chilly weather, the distinctive sounds of this public-address system would bring people out of their homes, providing an occasion to gather, visit, and exchange information. On bitterly cold days, when people would lean out of their windows to hear the announcements, it provided an opportunity for brief, face-to-face contact and exchange of neighborly greetings. An important source of local knowledge, it was through the village public-address system that most residents learned of the dissolution of the Sperrgebiet on November 10, 1989.

In December 1990, the village landscape contained evidence of Kella's past interspersed with glimpses of an anticipated future (Map 2). The peeling brown stucco and faded yellow sign ("Goods for Everyday Needs") on Kella's only store, a branch of the Konsum retail chain in its last days of management by the state trade organization, contrasted sharply with the colorful advertisements and western products in its windows (Figure 4).[11] The bright yellow telephone booth just a block away, which had been installed after the Wende and contained a notice announcing its connection to West German lines—a point of pride as much as information—similarly not only contrasted with the gray and brown houses that surrounded it but also recalled the phoneless households of nearly all village residents. The once inaccessible chapel on the border, elegantly and efficiently restored less than half a year after the fall of the Wall, reflected the hopes and promises of progress to come.

At the end of 1990, the local suspender-clips factory was still in operation. As in other areas of the former GDR, women were working fewer hours and employees over the age of fifty had been ushered into early retirement; but those with work were grateful for employment. The Pfaffschwende toy factory, too, was still in operation when I arrived in 1990, although an aura of uncertainty surrounded its future as well. "Who knows how much longer it will go on," was a frequent utterance in relation to both factories, reflecting a sense of collective anxiety after the loss of the guaranteed employment enjoyed in the GDR. Other

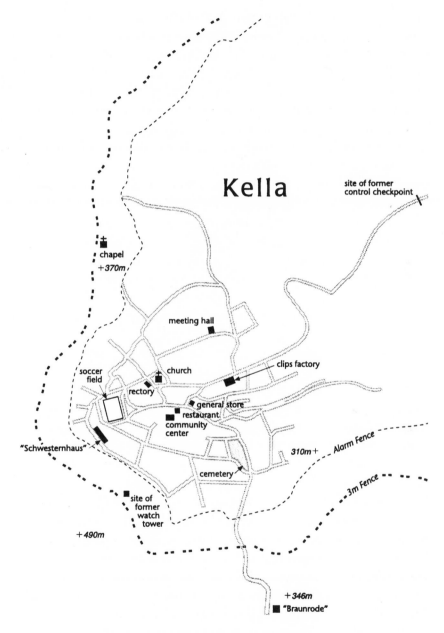

Kella

site of former
control checkpoint

chapel
+370m

meeting hall

soccer
field

church

clips factory

rectory

general store

restaurant

community
center

"Schwesternhaus"

310m+   Alarm Fence

cemetery

3m Fence

site of
former
watch
tower

+490m

+346m
"Braunrode"

Map 2. Kella. (Cartography by the University of
Minnesota Cartography Laboratory)

Figure 4. The village Konsum store,
featuring the faded GDR logo, "Goods
for Everyday Needs," which contrasts
with colorful new emblems of western
consumer goods, 1991. (Photograph
by the author)

villagers were still employed on the regional collective farm, and several continued commuting to Heiligenstadt. A few local women also
worked in the state kindergarten and day-care facilities, housed in the recently completed community building that was also home to a local post
office branch and a hair salon. A few steps from this centrally located
community building was the village pub. Run by a local family and
administered by the same trade organization as the local store, the pub
was patronized almost exclusively by village men, including a group of
regulars.

The local pub, the community building, and the Konsum store were all in the village center, the part of Kella to which people still allude when they say they are going "into the village," even if they live less than a block away. Other landmarks of community life, located in the hills surrounding this village center, included a cultural center, whose large hall has long been the site of most village festivals and celebrations; two soccer fields, neither of which was in use in 1990 because the local soccer team had dissolved immediately following the Wende; and ecclesiastical buildings like the village church built in 1752, the Schwesternhaus (nuns' home), and the chapel between the fences. Two bus stops, one at the eastern entrance to Kella and the other near the main village soccer field, were the spots where many began and concluded their school or work days. In 1990, there was still regular bus service to Heiligenstadt and several villages along the way, including Pfaffschwende, where children from Kella attended school.

Also nestled in these hills are most of the village's 150 houses. Ranging from older, timbered homes to recently completed two-family dwellings, most houses in Kella border directly on the street. During my stay in the village, the private space of the household was most frequently demarcated by a fenced enclosure; to reach the front door of homes, one typically had to enter first through a heavy gate and then cross a courtyard separating living quarters from a barn or shed (Figure 5). In 1990, the intimate spheres of these village homes were usually being shared by several generations. Like many living quarters in socialist eastern Europe, domestic spaces in Kella had what Slavenka Drakulic has described as "the strange ability to divide and multiply" (1991: 82). Although the village population was always in gradual decline throughout the socialist period,[12] there was, as elsewhere in the GDR, always a shortage of living quarters—a problem compounded in Kella by the fact that building permits for new homes were more difficult to obtain in the Schutzstreifen than in other areas in the GDR. People thus creatively manipulated and reshaped space, turning one room into two, an attic into a small apartment, a bathroom into a kitchen.

In December 1990, many of these buildings in Kella appeared unfinished to a western eye, including mine. Like many houses through-

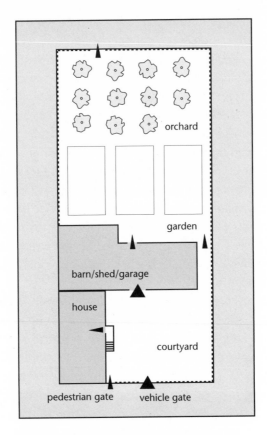

Figure 5. Typical organization of a Kella house,
courtyard, barn, and grounds, 1990.
(Drafting by the University of Minnesota
Cartography Laboratory)

out the former GDR, these homes were lacking stucco, something that
was particularly difficult to obtain during the period of socialist rule. I
soon came to appreciate, however, that the rough, richly textured outside
walls of these homes reflected not only the realities of an economy of
shortage but also the care, effort, and resourcefulness that went into securing and creatively piecing together diverse shapes and sizes of building materials, often over a period of several years (Figure 6). Such creativity, I would come to learn, was not limited to the building of homes

Figure 6. A house in Kella, photographed
in 1991, in which the layering of bricks
reflects scarce building materials patiently
acquired and creatively assembled over
time. (Photograph by the author)

but was reflected in a range of daily practices both during and after the
period of socialist rule.

In December 1990, most of the local institutions that provided the fabric
of daily life in the village were on the brink of dissolution, extinction, or,
at least, transformation. By the time I left Kella two years later, most had
disappeared. Except for a few remaining employees of the toy factory in
Pfaffschwende, nearly all residents had changed or lost their jobs. Both
the state-sponsored day-care center and kindergarten had closed due to
lack of funds and declining enrollments of children whose unemployed
mothers no longer needed child-care services.[13] The local pub had also

Figure 7. In one of many home and village "beautification" projects, photographed in 1992, a local worker finishes the renovation of a house facade with newly available building materials. (Photograph by the author)

closed, replaced shortly thereafter by a family business run by former Communist Party members near the village's western entrance. Survival of the village Konsum store, now under private ownership, was threatened as villagers were lured by the wider selection and lower prices of western discount stores in Eschwege. The still-functioning public-address system had been replaced by community bulletin boards, thus supplanting the simultaneous collective experience of local news with individual responsibility for the latest community announcements (Figure 3). Face-to-face interaction similarly declined through the installation of telephones in every village home; no longer was the single yellow telephone booth the only line of communication to the outside world.

Like many areas of the former GDR, Kella often felt like a giant construction site. Roads were torn up in order to install cables for television and telephones; streets were newly paved; houses were whitened by stucco or paint; facades of community buildings were renovated; and new communal spaces like walking trails, park benches, and green areas were created through make-work projects sponsored by the state or by the newly founded local Heimatverein. By the time I left in 1992, the feel of the village had changed. The experience of abrupt transition from West to East was dramatically reduced after the border crossing near Kella was paved in the fall of 1991. Similarly, the distinctive smell of "GDR air" had dissipated as Trabis became a second automobile for most families (usually relegated to the wife) and as brown-coal ovens were replaced with more prestigious and environmentally sound oil heating. With the widespread availability of quality meats, few families were still slaughtering their own pigs for domestic consumption; the sounds of bleating sheep and squealing pigs faded as barn stalls were renovated to make room for a garage for a western automobile or to create additional living space for an expanding family. On returning for a visit a year after settling in West Germany in 1991, one young woman exclaimed: "I don't even recognize my Heimat!" The consequences of these dramatic changes, as well as what happened in between, is the subject of the remainder of this book.

2 Publicity, Secrecy, and the Politics of Everyday Life

Even more than in other regions of the GDR, the state was a constant and highly visible presence in Kella. Because of its immediate proximity to the border between East and West Germany, sirens, army jeeps, border guards, and watch towers were part of daily life (Figure 8). A "signal fence," armed with an optical and acoustic alarm system as well as multiple rows of barbed wire, ran directly behind many village homes and gardens. Curfew was usually set at 11 P.M., but during periods of especially strict state control people had to be back in the village by sundown. In a culture of surveillance where everyone owned binoculars, border guards watched residents, residents watched border guards, western relatives peered down into the village from the hilltop "window to Kella" in search of the familiar, and villagers looked eagerly, though cautiously, through their lenses to see whether distant visitors were

Figure 8.   The two border fences that surrounded Kella and the no-man's-land between them, 1989. The hills, including this hilltop, known locally as the Silberklippe,
mark the actual former geopolitical boundary between East and West Germany
as well as multiple historical boundaries, including that of the Catholic Eichsfeld.
At the lower tree line is a road made of concrete slabs used for surveillance jeeps.
(Photograph courtesy of Gisela Lange)

people they recognized. The presence of state structures was so internalized by people living here, in fact, that a year after the Wall fell some
people were still taking their feet off their automobile accelerators or
reaching for their identity cards while approaching the site where a barrier and control point for the Schutzstreifen used to be.

Despite the state's high visibility—in which certain rules and the consequences of breaking them were well known—much of the regime remained an enigma. With its actions (and some actors) shrouded in secrecy and with its seemingly arbitrary use of power, the state was able to
sustain a mystique of the unknown. This sense of secrecy not only created a space in which people sought to determine "the boundaries of the
possible" (Geyer n.d.); it also endowed the regime with an almost super-

natural quality. The state and its actions became something people had to interpret, and the regime derived power from the way in which it was interpreted, enacted, even resisted. The interplay between above and below, between the known and the unknown, between the state and its citizens was crucial in sustaining the socialist system in East Germany.

My principal aim in this chapter is to explore how the regime was affirmed and contested in everyday practice by focusing on the experiences of residents of Kella under socialism. Viewing the state not as a thing but as a set "of social processes and relations," in this chapter I attempt to provide what Katherine Verdery has called "an ethnography of the state" (1996: 209).[1] I begin by examining daily routines and practices of the socialist state, including institutions and organizations that formed the microfoundations of power in everyday interaction, and I note the degrees of complicity and conformity such interaction entailed. Of particular relevance is the way in which these institutions, and individual participation in them, contributed to an "affirmation of the regime through controlled dissent" (Geyer n.d.). I suggest the German term Zwischenraum (space between) as a concept to describe the space between the parameters of the known, in which people negotiated the limits of the posible and, in so doing, helped define them. This notion of a Zwischenraum, with its spatial implications and connotations of interstitiality, obviously shares certain affinities with the borderland metaphor employed throughout the book; yet it is also distinct from this metaphor (hence my choice of a different term) because of its relationship to a dynamic of state power.[2] Certain everyday practices, I argue, often emerging from this interstitial space, invested the state with an idealized power and knowledge—an imagined omniscience based on the state's omnipresence.

MICROFOUNDATIONS OF POWER

Kella is a place where people tend to describe themselves as "simple workers," "simple folk," or "good Catholics." Until the Wende, the majority of its residents were factory or construction workers. As part

Figure 9.   Kella's chapel between the fences on a hilltop behind the village, 1985. Separated from Kella by the alarm fence, the chapel fell into the no-man's-land and was inaccessible to villagers for years. (Photograph courtesy of Gisela Lange)

of the Eichsfeld region, Kella remained devoutly Catholic despite the socialist state's attempts to root out religion in the GDR. When church services were prohibited in Kella in 1953 and 1954, for example, villagers walked ten kilometers every Sunday to attend mass in a neighboring village outside the Schutzstreifen. Church services in Kella resumed after that, and except for prominent SED members, who were strongly discouraged by the party from going to church, people were free to attend. Although the state had succumbed to popular demand regarding religious practices, it symbolically conveyed its ultimate authority on the issue: a pilgrimage chapel overlooking the village, completed after the end of World War II, fell into the no-man's-land between the fences and was inaccessible for more than thirty years (Figure 9).

This strong Catholic tradition formed much of the basis for opposition to the regime in Kella. Viewing the Christian and socialist doctrines as incompatible, people refused to join the Communist Party on religious grounds. "The SED was an atheist party," one woman explained, "any-one who joined was considered scum of the earth." Whereas among the general population in East Germany one in every five adults was a party member (Jarausch 1994: 35), fewer than 6 percent of Kella's residents joined the party, and less than half of these were natives of the village. Parents also objected to the state initiation ceremony, *Jugendweihe*, for religious reasons. Intended as a secular equivalent to the Catholic first communion or Protestant confirmation, the Jugendweihe was a socialist rite of passage in which fourteen-year-olds were asked to swear alle-giance to socialist state; around 97 percent of young East Germans par-ticipated (Smith 1985: 72). Despite persistent efforts of party officials in Kella—including special sessions of village council meetings, pressure by teachers on students in school, and home visits to parents—minutes of the village council indicate that Jugendweihe participation rarely ex-ceeded 50 percent.

This is not to suggest that residents of Kella successfully avoided com-pliance with the regime, but rather that the church was a pocket of dis-sent here to which the state was, to some extent, willing to concede. By permitting a certain degree of dissent in this area—and granting it the semblance of resistance—the state was more effectively able to per-meate and control other spheres of daily life. Through a multitude of po-litical organizations and practices (often under the thinly veiled guise of social groups), the regime was able to involve many individuals in its operations.

In addition to the largely obligatory membership in work brigades, the trade union, the German-Soviet Friendship League, and, for young people, the Free German Youth (Freie Deutsche Jugend [FDJ]), residents voluntarily joined mass organizations like the Civil Defense Club, the Democratic Women's Federation (Demokratischer Frauenbund Deutsch-lands [DFD]), the German Red Cross, the People's Solidarity League for senior citizens, and the volunteer fire department. The quarterly meet-ings of these groups were largely social in nature, but never free of ideo-logical content. As in other socialist states, the function of these mass or-ganizations was to convey the party program to target groups; Lenin had once called them "transmission belts between the party and the masses" (in Kornai 1992: 40).[3]

To supplement the mass organizations, more than twenty men from the village were involved in the regional *Kampfgruppe*, or People's Militia, complete with its own arsenal and commanders, which was instituted throughout the GDR after the June 1953 uprising to prevent any future riots. Another thirty residents were members of the village council, and additional membership in subcommittees increased the number of villagers engaged in local politics. All in all, such organizations were successful in involving nearly one-half of the adult population (about one member per household) in state activities and functions. Much of village social life in Kella was, then, inseparable from the state.

The workings of a centralized or "rational redistributive" economy (Konrad and Szelenyi 1979) also penetrated nearly every sphere of daily life. On the one hand were the empty store shelves and the hours spent in food lines, reminders of the constant shortage of consumer goods; on the other hand, the continuing pressure to fulfill production norms.[4] In addition to these production norms, for which posters covered factory walls and work units were rewarded through party-organized production rituals, residents in rural areas like Kella were obligated to fulfill work requirements for the local agricultural collective as well as quotas from private agricultural production; people were required to submit prescribed quantities of vegetables, eggs, poultry, and pork to the state.[5] Similarly, male residents of Kella were regularly enlisted in voluntary weekend work brigades to assist in community construction projects. Such "seizures of time" by the state, represented especially by shortages of goods and the resulting queues, entail what Verdery has aptly called the "etatization of time," a "time tax" that served to both enhance and display state power through the appropriation of citizens' time (1996).

Of utmost importance in the border regions was the *Ordnung und Sicherheit der Grenze* (order and security of the border), and the state was remarkably successful in coopting individuals to maintain it. When the border first became impermeable in 1952, villagers were employed to build a ten-meter-wide patrol strip. All residents were thereafter required to ask "outsiders" appearing in Kella to identify themselves; any person without the proper identification and pass was considered to be in violation of the *Grenzordnung* (order of the border) and was supposed to be reported immediately. A mayor's speech in 1967 boasted that 60 percent of all arrests on the border that year were made by citizens themselves.

Although such figures were most likely embellished for senior state authorities, I was told of several incidents of citizen's arrests. Some of these were inadvertent: a school class, for example, that pointed and giggled at an unfamiliar couple crouching in the bushes was later awarded medals for preventing an escape. Many citizens reported activities out of fear or suspicion that the outsider was a Stasi (state security) agent sent to test villagers' compliance. In one instance I was told that a resident confronted a strange man walking back and forth so close to the border fence that the villager figured he had to be an agent. On asking the man for identification, the villager discovered he was Karl Eduard von Schnitzler, host of the infamous television show *Der schwarze Kanal* (The Black Channel) and for thirty years the GDR's leading antiwestern propagandist. Although this resident had done his duty, he was more concerned about what he had revealed by not recognizing the television host: not only that he did not watch von Schnitzler's show but also that he probably watched only western television and might thus be subject to closer scrutiny.

A variety of agents and institutions were responsible for boundary maintenance. Until a few years before the Wende, a full-time policeman (Abschnittsbevollmächtiger [ABV]) was stationed in Kella. The "local sheriff," as villagers called him, worked closely with the border police and the mayor to ensure the Ordnung und Sicherheit der Grenze. He was also a main source of information about Kella and its residents for Kreis officials, an agent of communication with the mysterious power of the state. Residents were never sure about the nature of his activities and duties. As a state bureaucrat, an ostensibly devoted communist, and an "outsider" (no villager ever served as an ABV), the village policeman was perceived as a known evil. People watched what they said when he was around.

Border police were draftees as well as career officers in the national army (Nationale Volksarmee [NVA]). Housed in army barracks in a neighboring village, border guards (*Grenzer*) were drawn from far outside the region in order to prevent locals from becoming familiar with the structure and operations of the border. Their interaction with residents occurred daily at checkpoints, through binoculars from a guard tower, from an army jeep on its hourly border patrol, and even at the local bar or village festivals. Depending on the time of day and the level of border security (which was heightened whenever a "violation of the order of the border" occurred), between two and eight border guards would be present in the village at all times. Despite their obvious embodiment of state authority, border police were rarely targets of villagers' animosity. As one woman explained:

> During the first years when the army was still voluntary, the relations between people and border guards were bad. . . . Mother always said, "Never go out with a Grenzer." But when the army became mandatory for all men, relations between people and the guards improved. Everyone knew it could be their own son, that they couldn't help it that they had to serve on the border. Mother sometimes brought them drinks or a slice of bread. We even brought the ones at the checkpoint chocolate for Christmas.

Despite friendly relations, however, girls were still cautioned against marrying a border guard. Although residents felt a certain empathy for the guards—as they, too, were being required to acquiesce at some level—a certain distance remained.

Much policing of citizens by other citizens was done by villagers themselves. Referred to as *Grenzhelfer* (border-guard helpers) and *Volkspolizeihelfer* (People's Police helpers), these residents patrolled the strip along the border fence (*streifenlaufen*), assisted at control checkpoints, and were supposed to report any unusual activities or strangers in the area. The twenty-six men who served as such helpers wore special armbands and were thus identifiable, as opposed to the more extreme form of self-policing, Stasi informants, who to this day remain unknown in Kella.[6]

Residents with certain occupations were frequently sought out to fulfill more informal duties of self-policing. Unbeknownst to most residents of Kella, for example, was the fact that the local bus driver, who transported more than half the village population to their workplaces in

Pfaffschwende or Heiligenstadt, was required to give guards at the control checkpoint to Kella a signal when a nonresident was aboard. According to one former party member, this kind of cooperation was essential in maintaining the Grenzordnung and helped keep Kella's statistical average for "escapes" (*Republikflucht*) comparatively low.

The reasons people give today for having joined various state organizations vary. In one unusual case, a man who had been a border guard elsewhere claimed he had enjoyed that duty so much that he continued it as a Grenzhelfer in Kella. Others simply appreciated the supplemental monthly allowance for their work as a Volkspolizeihelfer or Grenzhelfer, while some insist they did it out of good intentions—the "lesser evil defense" (Rosenberg 1995)—to protect villagers from someone who may have exercised power maliciously. Many felt forced into compliance, although the perceived gradations of compulsory versus voluntary participation are wide-ranging. I was frequently told that people became active in one organization, like the Civil Defense Club, in order to avoid being pressured into joining others.

Village activities and organizations thus ranged from officially prescribed, formally sanctioned but voluntary, compensated and uncompensated, to merely tolerated, and proscribed. As individuals struggled to make their peace with the system, they were confronted with choices, disagreed with each other about their decisions, experienced changes in their circumstances and aspirations, and often made conflicting statements about their own view of specific events and issues. In what follows, I focus on a few individuals whose histories illustrate particular degrees and measures of responsibility and complicity; the stories also show the way in which such particulars were a critical aspect of daily life in the GDR.

When I first met Thorsten Müller, a mason in his midtwenties, one of the first things I learned about him was that he had not taken part in the Jugendweihe ceremony. His former school classmate was showing me her photograph album when he joined us, and, on seeing pictures of her Jugendweihe, he joked with her about how he had not been lured into the ceremony by the promise of a trip to Hungary, as she had been. His refusal to participate was due partly to the influence of his Catholic parents, he later admitted, but at the time of our first meeting it was presented as his decision. Using a slight physical disability as an excuse, Thorsten was also able to avoid mandatory military education for males in the ninth and tenth grades. He was not, however, exempted from the compulsory eighteen months of military service. Later, after he had started working in the nearby toy factory, he became active in the FDJ, motivated largely by the hope of winning a much-coveted FDJ-sponsored trip abroad. At about this time, he also became a member of the local Kampfgruppe, but he feels he was pressured into joining. "Sometimes you had little choice about things," he explained. "I was called into the factory office and asked to join the Kampfgruppe. When I said no they said I'd have to join the reserves. I still refused, but a week later I received a notice drafting me into the reserves in Berlin, so I joined the Kampfgruppe in order to stay at home." He remains convinced that this series of events was orchestrated by party officials in the factory, including his own brother-in-law.

Despite his involvement in these state organizations, Thorsten views himself as free of responsibility for having participated in the system in any way. Using categories similar to those described to me by several villagers, he explained that people who had participated were either "red" or "very red." "Red were those who joined the party in order to get ahead in their careers, to study what they wanted, or to practice a hobby," he said, citing as examples the names of several men from Kella who had joined the party in order to be permitted to hunt. "Very red were those who *really* participated: party officials, Stasi, those who went willingly to [state-sponsored] demonstrations—everyone who really believed in the system." One measure of complicity Thorsten frequently referred to, as did many villagers, was church attendance. According to Thorsten, party members who attended church fell into the "red" category and were thus viewed as hypocritical; the "really reds" demonstrated their genuine convictions by refusing to attend. While many villagers disapproved of these individuals leaving the church, ironically these "really red," who after the Wende were willing to "stand by their past," enjoy more respect in the community than do former party members who now disavow themselves from any involvement.

One of the few "really reds" is Werner Schmidt. As the leader of the

Kampfgruppe, head of the trade union and assistant mayor, he was an especially prominent party member in the village. He comes from a family with an unusual history of leftist political leanings: his father, the first mayor in Kella under the communist regime, is remembered for having said as a young man, even before the war, that his "gaze was directed toward Moscow." Werner recalls fondly the excitement he felt in the early years of the GDR: "I must admit there were things that we youths liked back then. Many of us were really excited about building the so-called new Germany." He attended the first national meeting of the FDJ in Berlin, became a party member at the age of nineteen, voluntarily joined the army for three years, and returned to Kella to become active in local politics. Although his wife is a devout church member, Werner rarely attended mass and finally left the church officially in 1984. He personally never saw a contradiction between church and party membership, but he felt forced out of the church by both sides:

> I was born here, was baptized here, went to my first holy communion in April 1945, just like everyone else . . . and I never saw any conflict in attending church on Sundays. But I couldn't, because I was a party member. . . . I often sensed that many faithful churchgoers would say that all SED members—all the "reds," as one says today—those are bad people. You know, I have never counted myself among the bad people!

Now in his fifties, Werner and his family were the first to open a private restaurant in the village—nicknamed affectionately by villagers "the Red Ox," "the Red Star," or "the Kremlin" because of the family's "red" past. As we sat in his restaurant one Sunday afternoon, he explained why he refuses to be ashamed of his past:

> Today some people are embarrassed or afraid to admit they once were in civil defense, or that they were a People's Police helper in the former GDR, so they don't want to mention it. Someone recently said to me here in the restaurant: "Hey, you were red, weren't you?" And I replied, "Yes, of course. Do you really believe I would lie about my thirty-six years of party membership? To say I never really agreed with it? It would seem as though I were ashamed of it." You know, I can stand by my past! After all, it's what I lived through! . . . People say: "You were in the Kampfgruppe." Of course I was in the Kampfgruppe, and for thirty years. Why

should I lie about that? I can say this to anyone openly and to their face. And for each individual resolution passed by the village council or executive committee, my signature still stands today.

Werner maintains that he tried to use his position to improve life in the community. With his assistance and leadership, roads were paved, a sewage system was installed, a new community center was built, and the village cemetery was renovated. In his capacity as assistant mayor and head of the trade union, he strove to assist and support individual villagers. In one case he was able to help a teenager from the village, Martin Schneider, who, in a drunken stupor, had attempted to escape over the fence near Kella in 1983. In his effort to avoid damaging his prized western jeans given to him by a relative who had recently returned from a brief visit to West Germany, the youth had tossed them over the fence. Before he was ready to join his pants, however, he became overcome with fear of the potential deadly consequences of his actions. Martin hurried home, leaving the jeans on the western side of the fence. He was tried for attempted unlawful border crossing, sentenced to a year in prison, and prohibited from entering the Sperrgebiet, including his hometown of Kella, for three years. The language of the state's written verdict reflected its ideology of the border: "For purposes of sentencing, it is essential to note that the defendant committed a serious offense against the state order. The permanent guarantee of the inviolability of the GDR border with the imperialist FRG [Federal Republic of Germany] is an unalterable necessity for securing peace in Europe and for the success of the principles of peaceful coexistence. The defendant disregarded this important protective function of the state border." Through a series of letters and visits to state authorities, Werner was able to have the sentence cut in half. Although he had served as "social plaintiff" in the trial, he is still admired by many in the community for his intervention on Martin's behalf.[7]

Werner is hardly aware of this respect and admiration from other members of the community, however. At the time of our conversations, he was mostly conscious of having been labeled "really red," a category he felt had placed him in the same group as Stasi informants and corrupt party officials. Shortly after the Wende, his house, along with six others in the village, was the target of youth vandals who spray painted the facades in red with slanderous graffiti. Later, his name was forged by an unknown adversary in a letter to officials of the Treuhand (the state organization responsible for privatizing former GDR industries after reunification) in Erfurt denouncing fellow factory managers for communist sympathies and, in some cases, Stasi involvement. "Words can kill people, you know! Worse than with a weapon sometimes," he said, raising an issue to which he would frequently return in our conversations. "You can't just say, 'Hey, you or you or you! Since you were a party member, you were also working for the Stasi.' And you don't even have to prove it, it's that simple. This is a dangerous thing."

Also disturbing to Werner was what he perceived to be a general devaluation of the GDR past by western Germany, exemplified by the portrayal of East German factories as "only inefficient and desolate," the discrediting of the GDR educational system, including discussions about whether to honor East German diplomas, the condemnation of all aspects of the socialist system by the victors of the cold war, and above all, the frequent comparison of the East German to the Nazi regime: "Today there are attempts in the press to claim the GDR, in its forty years of existence, was worse than National Socialism. This just can't be done! National Socialism declared war on the world, it cost 50 million people their lives! . . . This isn't how you overcome the past, even school kids know that." Another aspect of the devaluation of the past, he felt, was the dismissal of capable and experienced people simply because they were party members.

> I learned many things through my involvement in the state—anyone would agree with that—but this doesn't mean, just because I was red, that I'm an enemy of the new social order! People want to put us on ice, to brand us and put us to the side and say, "Look, that's them!" If they think they can get along without us then, please, go ahead, but I don't think it's good.

Since the Wende, Werner has not been involved in local politics. Forced into early retirement like many men his age, he largely keeps to himself and concentrates on the new family business.

Ursula Meyer does not fall easily into either category of complicity. Although considered "really red" by many members of the community because of her tenure as village mayor between 1980 and 1990, others perceive her as an opportunist. Several people who know about her church activities see her not as hypocritical, as many do, but as courageous and defiant. In a sense, Ursula is all of these things. After working as a secretary in the mayor's office for nearly twenty years, she was asked by the local party leadership to take over for her boss when he retired. She accepted the job, hoping to help the community as well as to eradicate the mismanagement and corruption she says she witnessed as a secretary. As mayor of a border village, however, she was required to join the SED and was strongly discouraged from attending church. It was a compromise that she was, at the time, willing to make: "I became mayor around 1980, and at the time there was this rule that every mayor in the Schutzstreifen had to be in the party and wasn't allowed to go to church. . . . I thought, well, OK, I'll become mayor—that was certainly a wrong compromise, but I did have a few good intentions. I told myself I could help these people, these little people who are so often treated unjustly." Ursula stopped going to church for years but resumed with the encouragement of a new village priest. Despite Kreis officials' warnings, she was persistent and began participating, although at first secretly, in church council excursions to Czechoslovakia. In 1988, she supplied state materials to covertly erect a crucifix on the community boundary, an act of considerable courage.

When the Wall fell in 1989, Ursula was at the forefront of village festivities. She helped organize a candlelight demonstration calling for a border crossing in Kella; when the fence was opened at the end of December, on her fiftieth birthday, she planned festivities for Kella and its neighboring villages to the west, complete with a brass band, bratwurst, and plenty of mulled wine. She remained mayor until the municipal elections in May 1990, when she ran for reelection "to see whether the people really wanted me, or whether I was mayor because the state chose me." Although she was reelected by a margin of two to one over the second-place candidate, Ursula was later ousted at the first meeting of the new, Christian Democratic Union–dominated village council.[8] "So this is democracy," she remembers thinking, "the candidate favored by the people doesn't win." Then, recalling the pain of that experience, her eyes filled with tears, and she whispered, "When I think about how hard I worked, how I fought for every little thing, how happy I was when I could help. And now to think that was all wrong. Everything I did! For this village! I didn't necessarily want that [communist] system, but simply to help make life somewhat more bearable for the people here." Today Ursula rarely participates in community functions outside the church. When the village put on a parade in celebration of German re-unification on October 3, 1990, Ursula left town. Whereas her doorbell and telephone used to ring frequently while she was mayor, she is now visited only by close friends. She is the first to admit to being oversensitive to outside judgment, and although many residents believe she was treated unfairly by the village council, others believe she was rightly punished. "Ursula shouldn't have kept her support for the church a secret," one villager said to me. "That has hurt her now. . . . I can't forgive her for joining the party."

In their own ways, Werner, Ursula, and even Thorsten have struggled to come to terms with a devalued past. For Ursula this struggle has been intensely personal, burdened by a guilt for having participated in the system at the expense of her religious convictions, yet defensive because a part of her still believes in the ideals it represented and the work she was able to accomplish. Werner has wrestled not with a personal guilt about his own past but with the widespread derogation of the East German experience, which he associates with choices he has made in his own life. Some would argue that Thorsten, through his membership in the FDJ and Kampfgruppe, also helped sustain the system. I frequently heard, particularly from former party members, that "everyone somehow participated," whether by attending town meetings, joining a mass organization, or simply hanging out a flag on state holidays. Or, as one man put it, "everything was spread out to the smallest element [of society]. Each person had a duty that served to strengthen the backbone of the state." The degrees, gradations, and shading of complicity vary from case to case, often with different standards for self and others, often context-dependent. Together, these individual stories reflect the complex and contradictory aspects of the way in which the system was negotiated, interpreted, and reproduced.

CONTROLLING DISSENT

The state's ability to create spaces for dissent, to bound and control it, and finally to force citizens to draw their own boundaries was instrumental in the affirmation of the regime. In addition to engaging a large number of residents from a variety of political backgrounds—from active SED party members to "partyless," church-going women—the regional political structure was also able to give people a sense of having a voice at a local level. In practice, however, the very existence of certain state-sponsored pockets of dissent conveyed an understanding that one's voice was ultimately controlled: in the end, the state had the final say.

Involvement in community decision making is one reason many residents chose to be members of the village council. Although the number of candidates for the seats allotted to each party by the state (majority SED) never exceeded the thirty seats available, and although much of the council's duties entailed formally approving resolutions and plans handed to it by the state, there was some room for initiative and the ventilation of grievances. Special subcommittees dealt with issues regarding housing allocation, building permits, village social activities, and the supply of material goods to the village. When a family wanted to add on to their house, for example, they went to the Committee on Building and Housing for permission. When there were complaints about the quality and quantity of meat available in the Konsum store, grievances were filed with the Committee on Retail and Supply, which then dealt with the proper authorities. Their ability to answer grievances depended on the response of Kreis officials, but frequently they were able to affect change, at least in the short term. The construction of a new community building to house the mayor's office, a day-care center, a hair salon, and meeting rooms, for example, was the initiative of the village council, under both Ursula's and Werner's leadership. Furthermore, members of the village council were responsible for heading neighborhood meetings and for initiating dialogues with neighboring households in order to discuss residents' concerns in a more intimate setting. They were required to inform the village council of their findings, and reports listing the frequency of such meetings and number of participants were submitted monthly to state authorities. Ursula later reflected on the usefulness of such public

forums, particularly in light of the fact that village council meetings today are usually held behind closed doors: "I think that when people
came together [in these meetings] they had a chance to say something
and that this would also be taken into consideration. Today this opportunity no longer exists . . . even the women's [DFD] meetings. We used to
argue and discuss a lot, and what is there today? The hair salon, for example, that materialized because the women sat together and discussed
it and decided how we could do it. People were simply listened to more."
Ursula's comment reveals her sense of having had a voice in local government—a sentiment I heard from other villagers as well. She failed
to see, however, a certain irony in her statement: people were "listened
to more" not only to appease small grievances but also as a means of
control.

Einwohnerversammlungen (town meetings) and the closely related
Eingaben, legally sanctioned complaints, are additional examples of this.
Held on a quarterly basis, Einwohnerversammlungen were generally
well visited; people were concerned that attendance was taken and that
an absence could be punished later by being denied building materials, travel to the West, or permission to receive visits from relatives who
lived outside Kella. After several speeches by regional (Kreis) and community (*Gemeinde*) officials, participants were encouraged to ask questions and/or register complaints. Although most residents do not recall
these obligatory meetings fondly, many do recall—and today miss—the
opportunity for critique. Expressing her feelings of loss and confusion,
one woman complained to a group of friends: "We don't know where
to go anymore when we have problems or concerns. We have to figure
everything out for ourselves, and I think this will take a while to learn."

Complaints at these meetings usually pertained to a lack of building
materials, services, or consumer goods supplied to the village, specific
cases where travel to the West was denied, poor quality of foods, or suggestions for community improvement. As expressions of both dissatis-
faction and loyalty, grievances voiced at these meetings were frequently
submitted as formal Eingaben, although these could be filed through the
mayor's office as well. A typical Eingabe might concern the delivery of a
washing machine: if a family had been allotted a machine but had not yet
received it, they would file a complaint. Eventually the distribution man-

ager at the washing-machine factory would be contacted, and, after several months, the machine would arrive. Many Eingaben in Kella were related to the small factory there. In one instance, for example, the employees filed a grievance to have a flush toilet installed. Other Eingaben, such as requests for a paved road or a street lamp, could drag on for years. Occasionally, residents who filed complaints involving the rejection of visa applications for western travel were able to obtain permission to visit the West. This was rare, however; most decisions regarding travel to the West were final, with no explanation provided by the state.

Eingaben were taken very seriously by authorities.[9] As a means of control (Borneman 1993), they not only kept tabs on petitioners but also underscored the state's ultimate authority. Eingaben thus reflected what Charles Maier has called the regime's principle of governance through rationing and privilege (Maier 1997): by rationing travel to the West, for example, the state made the granting of a pass a privilege. The response to grievances also served to appease residents of the Schutzstreifen, who were given priority for materials and were kept better supplied than were those in communities outside the Sperrgebiet. Furthermore, Eingaben were viewed as a way to win residents' trust and involvement in the regime. As a typical mayor's report in the 1970s stated, "Through the tips, suggestions and Eingaben, our citizens will contribute simultaneously to improving the work of local agencies and to pulling them into the social mass political work in the community. . . . By resolving Eingaben of our citizens we will continue to win people's trust in the state and thereby make our own work easier." Most Eingaben were resolved, and all were responded to even if the petitioner's wishes were not granted. One resident recalled how these Eingaben and gatherings allowed for "open critique" of the state: "In the meetings we would say, for example, 'Listen, we can't meet the production norms if the state doesn't make sure the materials are there.' That was a violent critique."

The fact that this resident viewed complaints about lack of materials as a "violent critique" is indicative of an awareness of certain unstated limits, boundaries that were constantly negotiated in everyday life. People did not submit Eingaben complaining about the border fence or guard tower, for example, but they did file a complaint if travel to the West was denied. Residents did not directly oppose the party or its policies, but they did circumvent overtly political complaints by personally criticizing the officials who embodied them. One man who prides himself on being viewed as "black" in his political and religious orientation explained to me: "I learned to voice my opposition by criticizing individuals rather than the party itself. I couldn't be attacked for that."[10]

This language of protestation was part of a shared knowledge. One town meeting erupted in such anger toward a Kreis official that participants vowed publicly not to attend any more meetings when that particular official was present. "You could actually say anything," another villager maintained. "It was *how* you said it that mattered." Even the simple mention in the *Ortschronik* (official village chronicle) of a curfew extension in 1984 for a village festival could contain an implicit criticism: rather than complaining about the limitations of the regular curfew, the chronicle describes the positive consequences of extending it.[11]

Perhaps the most radical critique of the regime was voiced during Fasching.[12] In a festive setting, participants performed skits, speeches, and songs poking fun at fellow villagers as well as at the regime. Although most performances consisted of largely bawdy humor, including cross-dressing, exemplified by the popular *Männerballett* (men's ballet), or were parodies of village events and residents, there were always a few acts that were explicitly critical of the state. In one song performed in the mid-1980s, two young women lamented the restrictions on mobility imposed on residents of the village:

> I am a girl from the Zone.[13] I live in Kella, where this world ends.
> I have a nice house with a garden, a car and money to spend.
> But despite the town's pub, Kirmes, and Fasching, I feel so alone.
> I dream of the beautiful cities, of Dallas, of Denver, that's where
>   I want to roam!
>
> A prince must come and my dreams fulfill,
> to satisfy my passion for the world, he will!
> In a fancy car he will come this way,
> And in my ear he will quietly say . . . But wait!
> Without a special pass from the state
> he'll never get past Kella's checkpoint gate![14]

Even in this unique space for critique, however, dissent was controlled, delimited, and bounded. In fact, the most politically critical speeches were delivered by party members themselves. Each year that Ursula Meyer, who had a penchant for writing clever and witty rhymes, was mayor, she gave a performance that was one of the highlights of the program. Many of her speeches were critical of things not usually discussed publicly: the need for special passes to enter Kella, the difficulty in obtaining police clearance for visitors from outside the village, the hassles of a planned economy, or the need for bribe money to have an automobile repaired. In one speech entitled "The Dreamer," Ursula portrayed a series of visions that came to her in a dream:

> Then I saw the fence, it was like cotton,
> And nobody thought the border guards were rotten.
> About Braunrode, nobody even had a thought
> Because people went to Eschwege via Eisenach.[15]

In a 1983 skit as the village chronicler, she criticized the village's present situation by comparing it with ancient times. Noting the hassles of daily life that did not exist back then—the border fence, the Sperrgebiet, queues in front of the store, the shortage of consumer goods, the planned economy—she alluded to the existence of informers within the village: "[In these times] people did not tattle or inform, thus creating within the village a terrible storm."[16]

Although critical in tone, these speeches were also about control (and had to be approved by state censors). Complaining about the existence of informers also suggests they were there. Poking fun at attendance at Einwohnerversammlungen reminds people that this was noted. Ursula's skit as village chronicler concluded by stressing how much better things were "at the beginning of the world," a challenge to the frequent reference to Kella as "the end of the world." Like other performances in this socially constituted and state-sanctioned space for dissent, it was both a criticism and an affirmation of the regime.

SUSTAINING THE UNKNOWN

One of the regime's most effective means of control was a culture of secrecy that forced its citizens to test the limits of the possible and thereby aid in setting them. As the carnival celebrations demonstrate, people's actions were both subversive and constraining: they challenged the forms of control while defining the limits of power. In his writings on discipline and surveillance, Michel Foucault has pointed to the mutual dynamic of power relations: "Although surveillance rests on individuals, its functioning is that of a network of relations from top and bottom, but also to a certain extent from bottom to top and laterally; this network 'holds' the whole together and traverses it in its entirety with effects of power that derive from one another: supervisors, perpetually supervised" (1979: 175). His description of Bentham's panopticon also illustrates the function of the unknown in maintaining control: "The inmate cannot see whether or not the guardian is in the tower, so he must behave as if surveillance were perpetual and total. If the prisoner is never sure when he is being observed, he becomes his own guardian" (Rabinow 1984: 19). Rather than viewing the state's power as totalizing, therefore, it may be more useful to conceptualize it as a dialectical interplay between above and below, to explore how daily interaction helped stabilize the state.

In the space between the boundaries of the known, or Zwischenraum, people sought to interpret events that might tell them what the unknown was. Everyone knew, for example, the potentially fatal consequences of an attempted escape over the border. After the arrest and imprisonment of Martin Schneider in 1983, they could also surmise the consequences of an aborted escape. They could even guess the repercussions of criticism of the border voiced in the presence of unknown informants after a local bus driver spent ten months in prison for comparing the border intensifications in the 1970s to the "Warsaw Ghetto." However, residents did not know what would happen if they were caught waving to relatives on the western side of the fence (although they knew it was forbidden), so they pretended to clean windows or to shake out tablecloths. Everyone knew they were supposed to hang out the GDR flag on state holidays, but they learned through experimentation that one could resist this a bit by hanging it out the back door, invisible to the West for whom the display was intended; or they wedged it between windows instead of placing it in the flag post and were secretly pleased when the wind blew the flag onto the window sill. Like the language of shared protestation, such practices were part of a kind of "hidden transcript," a "critique of power spoken behind the back of the dominant" (Scott 1990: xii) that simultaneously tested and contested the authority of the regime. They also reflect what Czeslaw Milosz, in *The Captive Mind*, once eloquently described as *ketman*. An Arabic term and Islamic concept meaning "hidden," ketman entails the simultaneous public affirmation and private deception by citizens under socialism that produces a sense of pride and feeling of superiority over those in power who are being deceived: "Ketman in its narrowest and severest forms is widely practiced in the people's democracies. As in Islam, the feeling of superiority over those who are unworthy of attaining truth constitutes one of the chief joys of people whose lives do not in general abound in pleasures" (Milosz 1991: 52).

An inconsistent use of state power was especially effective in sustaining a sense of the unknown. The state gave no reason for denying requests to travel West, thus forcing applicants to search for one.[17] Had they not attended enough Einwohnerversammlungen? Should they have become involved in the village council? Although state policy may well have been guided by caprice rather than reason, residents' assumption that something knowable was being withheld by state design, ultimately on the basis of "reason," both reflected and contributed to an idealization of the regime's power. The seemingly arbitrary approval or denial of such requests—sometimes different decisions were rendered within the same immediate family—fostered resentment and suspicion among people in the village. (What had someone else done to have his or her request approved?) Suspicion was also raised when a resident was treated leniently on a crime he or she was known to have committed. A common example cited are cases when one person's driver's license was reinstated immediately but another resident's was revoked for two years for the same crime.

Such actions created the perception that everything the state did was calculated, and residents struggled to decode its logic. In one case, a woman from Kella went all the way to East Berlin in search of a reason for the denial of her application to attend her brother's silver wedding anniversary in West Germany. Emma Hauser had been granted a pass to visit western siblings several years earlier and thus could not understand why she was being prohibited from traveling this time. When the six Eingaben she submitted to the mayor's office failed to bring about a reversal of the decision, she appealed to SED leaders in the Kreis administration. On the back of her son's small moped, she traveled thirty kilometers to the county seat of Heiligenstadt, hoping for approval of her application. Her appeal was again rejected, and her son, seeing his mother's despair, resolved to take her to East Berlin that day. For someone who, like the rest of her generation in the village, rarely ventured far from home, this was no small feat; it was the only time Emma had visited the nation's capital.

After an all-night train ride the mother and son arrived in the city, not sure what to expect but hopeful that their appeal would be approved. When they were informed by an official at the Interior Ministry that the decision would not be reversed, Emma asked if it was because of her involvement in the church, adding, for the official's information, that she attended church regularly. As Emma recounted this story to me, her normally cheerful demeanor turned solemn. She slowed her eager and rapid speech as she recalled how the official responded to her: "'Frau Hauser, you don't need to tell me anything. We know everything.'" She and her son left, defeated and certain that she was being punished for her active church involvement. To this day, Emma harbors resentment and suspicions about who in the village, if anyone, is responsible for this decision made nearly ten years ago. It is the one reason she briefly considered applying for access to her Stasi file.[18]

The most critical event to produce fear and suspicion of the regime among villagers was the deportation of several families from Kella in 1952. This action was the result of a politburo decision on May 13, 1952, to create a "special regime on the demarcation line" (Potratz 1993: 60). According to this resolution,[19] the border between the GDR and the FRG was to be additionally fortified through the creation of a security zone consisting of the 500-meter-wide Schutzstreifen and 5-kilometer-wide Sperrgebiet, as well as through the evacuation of residents from the following groups: foreigners; people who were not registered with the police; convicted criminals; and "people who because of their position in or toward society pose a threat to the antifascist, democratic order."[20]

In an action termed "Operation Vermin," more than 8,369 people (approximately 2 percent of the entire Sperrgebiet population) were evacuated from the Sperrgebiet into the GDR interior during late May and early June 1952 (Potratz 1993: 63). Regional police, together with officers of the recently founded Stasi, were responsible for drawing up the lists of those slated for deportation.

Most villagers will now claim that all five families who left that day in the spring of 1952 were forcibly evacuated. In fact, only two families were deported; three others left voluntarily early in the day out of fear of deportation. According to what has now become legend, Heinz Müller, a *Großbauer* (independent farmer with ten to twenty hectares of land and draft animals) from Kella, discovered a note in his stable when he went to fetch his cattle that morning. His son, also named Heinz Müller, recalled what the note had said: "Heinz! You must leave. And quickly." Rumors spread rapidly through the village, and four other families were allegedly warned by the well-meaning mayor, who had received advance notice of the planned deportations.[21] Three of these families, all Großbauern, gathered their members, their livestock, and as many of their possessions as possible and brought them to the other side of the border. Later that night relatives from the village smuggled clothes, bedding, and other supplies to them. Heinz remembers spending the night with his family and their twenty cows, six horses, and a wagon on the Braunrode hill overlooking the village. Like many former villagers, all three families who left voluntarily that day settled in the neighboring western village of Grebendorf, only three kilometers from Kella.

Two of the families who were reportedly warned, the local innkeeper and an especially vocal carpenter, refused to believe the rumor. "'I haven't done anything wrong. They can't take me away,'" a villager remembers one of them saying. Later that day, state officials appeared at their doors, and the families were ordered to leave, taking with them only the things that would fit into the state's truck. They were evacuated to a region near Halle (GDR) and later emigrated to West Germany on exit visas.

It is a day that remains indelibly etched in the memories of villagers. People can remember exactly where they were when they heard the news. Heinz's cousin was a child at the time and remembers returning to Kella with a friend after buying shoes in Eschwege:

> We bought the shoes and then started heading home. In Grebendorf, I remember clearly, the women there who knew me approached us and said, "You Kellsche girls! You're horsing around down here! Everyone in Kella's been evacuated! No one's there anymore!" So we ran up the hill [toward Kella]. Ach! It was terrible. We thought that when we got there everyone would be gone. And then our relatives were sitting up there with their horses and wagon and I asked my aunt if it were true that everyone had left Kella. "Only us," she said.

It is still not known whether the three families who left voluntarily were truly slated for evacuation; nor is it known why the two deported families were forced to leave while other landholders and vocal opponents of the regime were permitted to stay. So the criteria for evacuation, the definition of the people who posed a threat "in and toward society," remained—and remains—unknown.[22] People were left to speculate: several families had been large property owners; one was particularly vocal in their opposition to the regime; one had been a Nazi party member; two others owned private businesses. The uncertainty created by this action encouraged, indeed demanded, acquiescence. As one woman recalled: "That [1952] was the beginning, when people became quiet and thought, 'We'll take everything in stride so that we can stay here.' This is why so many people participated [in the system]."

Although no one was deported from Kella after 1952, there was a similar round of evacuations from the Schutzstreifen, including neighboring border villages, in 1961; the last deportation of a family from the region was as recent as 1978. The expression "up the sand road," referring to the only road leading out of Kella, became synonymous with forced deportation—and with fear. Emma Hauser remembered struggling with this unknown threat, especially during moments of noncompliance: "Here in the Sperrgebiet we were always threatened with having to go up the sand road. And I was always scared." Emma admits that her family was never directly threatened with deportation, but she maintains that the fear was always present. Today she, like several other villagers, is proud to claim they were on "the list" of families to be expelled inland or placed in an internment camp—although to my knowledge there has been no confirmation of the existence of such a deportation list.

A culture of secrecy and publicity was thus produced and sustained by an alliance of the unknown and the highly visible, both united in the all encompassing "them" (die, the term used in referring to any aspect of the state ranging from village party members to Kreis officials to the politburo).[23] This dynamic encouraged people to invest the state with an exaggerated aura of power and knowledge. The existence of monthly information reports submitted to Kreis authorities by the mayor was well known, for example, but people imagined its contents to be much more extensive and damaging than the mundane details of daily life the reports actually described.[24] Similarly, people knew each citizen had a dossier containing letters and reports by work supervisors that passed from employer to employer when a person changed jobs. During the socialist period, these dossiers remained inaccessible to employees and were imagined to contain secretive and damaging detailed material. On receipt of these dossiers with the closing of socialist factories after the Wende, people were shocked at their innocuousness: the majority of files contained little more than a listing of dates of employment and an occasional report on an employee's productivity. Furthermore, many residents believed that the mayor, the embodiment of the state at the most local level, was responsible for decisions regarding western travel when, in fact, this was decided at the Kreis level, probably arbitrarily.

Immediately after the Wende, villagers organized and signed a petition to reveal the ultimate unknown, local Stasi informants, imagining that there was an orderly list readily available on demand and that Kella's mayor had access to it. Revelations in the national press after the opening of the Stasi archives have since demonstrated this could not have been the case. As Verdery has pointed out, the presence of informers and collaborators, as well as citizens' knowledge of the existence of these files, created an atmosphere of suspicion and mistrust that helped sustain state power; the purpose of the files, she writes, was to produce "political subjects and subject dispositions useful to the regime" (1996: 24).

Imaginary lists, empowered mayors, and illusory malicious monthly reports are indicative not only of an idealized state power but also of the way in which people created their own sense of order out of the unknown. Like the boundaries of the possible, this sense of order was negotiated collectively. Most important was the ability to ascertain the "trustworthy" members of the community. As one woman explained, "We knew the people in the village, and those that I didn't know, I never let get close to me. I never told strangers what I really thought. But within the village, you knew the people. The people whose houses were spray painted after the *Wende*, those were the ones we all suspected." Several villagers described a strong sense of community among most residents, constructed and defined in opposition to those suspected of Stasi involvement. "It was, you could say, like a big family against a small family," one man recalled, "You knew who you were up against." How accurate this sense of order was remains to be seen; it may yet be challenged if villagers choose to file for access to their Stasi files.

CONCLUSION

Secrecy, as Michael Geyer has observed, "was more than an attribute of a particular organization. It became a mode of conducting politics in the GDR" (Geyer n.d.). The success of this secrecy was partly the product of the public nature and omnipresence of the regime in all realms of daily life—the product, in a sense, of the state as a symbolic force. Publicity made the secrecy imaginable and thus compelling. It contributed to an idealization of state power and the perception of the state as something that had to be interpreted. A skit performed at carnival, an Eingabe submitted at a town meeting, a flag hung on a state holiday, or a clandestine greeting to a relative across the border are typical of the daily practices, often within the Zwischenraum between the known and the unknown, that not only sought to interpret the regime's power and its limits but also helped define and sustain them. Although this kind of Zwischenraum operated in some form throughout the GDR, it most likely functioned more completely in Schutzstreifen villages like Kella because of the threat of deportation into the interior regions of East Germany. Indeed, the deportations may have been inspired by nothing more than the regime's decision to demonstrate its arbitrary power and thus to instill fear and exercise control. It became the ultimate sanction, for it separated people from their Heimat and all that was imaginable—hence the need for careful, accurate definition of the boundaries of dissent.

There is no question that state-level practices and rituals facilitated the reproduction of socialism and, ultimately, contributed to its demise (Burawoy and Lukács 1992; Kideckel 1993; Verdery 1996; Watson 1994). However, the role of everyday life as a source of simultaneous contestation and affirmation of the regime also deserves consideration, and further exploration, if we are to understand socialist society in the GDR as well as other in other eastern European countries.[25] Indeed, important cultural practices and forms of negotiation emerged out of the interpenetrations of—and spaces between—state and society (Hann 1993; Wedel 1992), public and private, above and below. Such practices and negotiations both helped constitute state power and contributed to its collapse.

3 | The Seventh Station

COMPLEX COMMITMENTS

One warm spring evening in 1991, our neighbor, Hans Becker, invited us to join him on a walk to the Kella chapel (Figure 10). It was Good Friday, and although the priest had preached in church that afternoon against working on a holy day, Hans had spent the day cleaning and remodeling a cousin's home.[1] He dropped by our place to pick up the chapel key, which was temporarily in our care so that we could visit the local pilgrimage site with some guests from Göttingen, and invited my husband and me to join him. During the forty years of socialist rule, the chapel had been inaccessible to residents of Kella. Situated on a hill overlooking the village, it had fallen into the no-man's-land between the border fences, caged 150 yards from daily life, when the inter-German border became impermeable in the 1950s. "I have a special connection to this

Figure 10.   The Kella chapel, restored shortly after the Wende, as it looked in 1992. (Photograph by the author)

chapel," he explained. "I've been working all day, and now I just feel like going to the chapel. It doesn't have to be for long. Sometimes I go alone and just sit there."

As we hiked up the steep, rocky incline, a forested area before the war that had been cleared to improve visibility along the closely patrolled border, Hans pointed to where the alarm fence had once stood, as he had on many previous walks, and reiterated how this area had been off limits for most of his life. He talked about an upcoming trip to Italy with his wife in celebration of his fiftieth birthday, and he confessed to us that he was having second thoughts about these plans—insecure about being alone with his wife for the first time in years, he wondered whether he would rather stay at home and celebrate with friends, as he had in past years when there had been no opportunity for travel—and he hoped that some time at the chapel would help him sort out his thoughts.

Once we arrived at the chapel, Hans proudly informed us that he had been largely responsible for the renovations of the building following the opening of the borders in 1989. After more than thirty years of neglect and abuse (border guards had occasionally used the space and components of the chapel to build fires for warmth), it was in need of extensive repairs. Materials were donated from *drüben* (over there, the term used in referring to the West), he said, but he had organized the labor "here" (in the East). As we entered the building, Hans went up to one of the front pews and, omitting the traditional genuflection, sat down. After several minutes of silence, he crossed himself and approached the altar, where he tenderly, almost lovingly adjusted the embroidered altar cloth, trying without success to make it hang straight. Realizing his efforts were futile because the cloth had been nailed to the altar, he gave up, looking defeated. For a strong, burly man who enjoys a high status in the village as an adept mason and hearty beer drinker, his obvious care for the chapel, embodied in a simple gesture full of emotion, revealed a sensitivity that surprised us, for such emotion is not easily or readily displayed by men in Kella. His behavior suddenly made the forty years of Germany's division and the village's isolation seem particularly absurd: what Hans had missed during the period of socialist rule was not necessarily the freedom to travel or an array of consumer goods, although certainly these had been lacking. What had been painfully absent—precisely, perhaps, because it had been so close—was simply the freedom to walk up to the chapel on a beautiful day, pull his thoughts together, and straighten the altar cloth.

Observing Hans's small ritual that day was in many respects revelatory. In subsequent visits to the chapel with other villagers, I witnessed similar gestures of care: watering the trees at the chapel's entrance, checking the flowers on the altar, making sure the information sheet for visitors was intact. Hans's display of enduring faith, his strong attachment to the chapel, his joy in being able to return there, and his pride in the role he played in its restoration poignantly captured not only particular kinds of local religious practices but also the way in which such practices reflect an interplay among religion, identity, place, and belonging.

My aim in this chapter is to explore this dynamic, particularly as it has been affected by the fall of the Wall. The study of religion during and after state socialism, I suggest, must account for a distinction as well as a dynamic interplay between popular faith and institutionalized religion. During the period of socialist rule in Kella, the interests of these religious traditions converged in opposition to the socialist state. Since the Wende, with the disappearance of this common commitment, they have largely diverged, resulting in a renegotiation and redefinition of religious identities and practices.

I have chosen religion as a category of analysis, as one of many border zones that provide a context for the articulation of different forms of identity, because of its unique role in local history as well as its relationship to other boundaries that have shaped and informed social life and identities in Kella. Although the focus here is on religious behavior and identities, underlying my argument is an assumption shared by many anthropological studies of religion, namely that religion may be viewed not as a distinct sphere of cultural life but, rather, as something that permeates, and is permeated by, complex negotiations of identity within changing political and economic structures.

CHURCH AND STATE UNDER SOCIALISM

Like most communist countries, the East German state hoped to virtually eliminate organized religion and replace it with the secular values of Marxism-Leninism. While there was little direct persecution of religious leaders and believers in the GDR (in contrast to other countries, such as Czechoslovakia), both the Protestant and Catholic churches were subjected to a range of controls and repressions as the state attempted to curtail their role in society. Despite the state's relative numerical success—by 1986, the number of Protestant church members had been reduced by more than 50 percent, from 14.2 million in 1946 to 6.5 million (Ramet 1991)—it was never able to eliminate the church's presence and influence, as demonstrated by the leading role the church played in the protest movements of 1989.

After largely ignoring the church during the early years of socialist rule, the state began to impose restrictions on church activities in the early 1950s. Religious instruction in schools was banned, youth organizations were eliminated, church property was confiscated, and church meetings were subject to control and harassment (Smith 1985: 70). In an effort to establish socialism as a secular religion, the state introduced socialist ceremonies to replace traditional religious rituals. The "socialist name-giving ceremony" became the alternative to the Christian baptism; the "socialist marriage ceremony" aimed to supplant church weddings; and "socialist funerals" were intended to replace religious burials. In the early 1950s the state even proposed celebrating Stalin's birthday on December 21 instead of Christmas, although this suggestion was never implemented.

Introduced in 1954, the most widespread socialist ceremony in East Germany was the Jugendweihe. Local committees throughout the GDR worked with schools, parent associations, and the youth organization FDJ to ensure a high participation rate. In an effort to endow the occasion with special importance, fashion shows representing appropriate Jugendweihe dress were held in Berlin and publicized throughout the country. Performances by youth orchestras and chamber groups, as well as poetry recitations, dances, and singing, added a festive atmosphere to the ceremony. In preparing for the state's rite of passage, students learned about the responsibilities of socialist citizenship, the goals of communism, and the party line about how the antifascist socialist state had overcome the horrors of National Socialism.

This ceremony immediately became a highly contested and symbolic issue for both the Protestant and Catholic churches. Although the Protestant church at first resisted, excluding Jugendweihe participants from confirmation ceremonies, it soon became resigned to accepting the Jugendweihe after the number of confirmations began to drop sharply (Smith 1985: 72). The Catholic church's opposition to the ceremony remained consistent throughout the socialist period, although it never denied church membership to Jugendweihe participants.

The Protestant and Catholic responses to the Jugendweihe issue were, in a sense, reflective of each church's individual stance under socialism in general. The Protestant church's principal strategy was to carve out a place for itself within socialism. In 1969, it split from the all-German Evangelical Church of Germany (Evangelische Kirche Deutschland

[EKD]) to establish a separate League of Evangelical Churches in the GDR (Bund der evangelischen Kirchen der DDR [DDR-BEK]). The decision not only was indicative of a new generation of church leaders but reflected a new attitude within the church itself. Referred to as "the church in socialism," this new phase in Protestant church-state relations was characterized by the church's willingness to reach an accommodation with the state and work within its political framework; in exchange for its loyalty, the church extracted a degree of official acceptance.

A consequence of this new approach was a meeting between leaders of the BEK-DDR and Communist Party leader Erich Honecker in 1978. Emphasizing the common ground between church and state, the meeting was intended to usher in a new era of church-state relations. An agreement reached during the talks granted the Protestant church increased freedoms and privileges, including access to television; permission to erect buildings; access to prisons; help in restoring church memorials; eligibility of clergy and church workers for state pensions; and financial support for church kindergartens and cemeteries (Smith 1985: 74).

Despite an improvement in relations, tensions between the Protestant church and the socialist state remained. As the only official organization allowed to exist independently of the state, the church implicitly remained a site of potential opposition. In the 1980s, with the Protestant church as a refuge, various peace and environmental movements began to emerge in the GDR. United by their opposition to the international arms race, these groups organized peace seminars, church congresses, prayer vigils, and worship services with contemporary accompaniments. They publicly opposed state policies that, in their view, were indicative of an increasing militarization of GDR society, including mandatory military indoctrination and the military draft. Although their protests were often directed against state policy, their ultimate goal of world peace was not inconsistent with the stated values of the socialist regime.

Environmentalist movements similarly emerged in the shadow of the Protestant church. Widespread pollution of the air, water and soil in East Germany was the focus of this protest; the church's participation in these movements was motivated by "scriptural injunctions about stewardship of the earth" (Jarausch 1994: 37). Influenced by the rhetoric of the western Greens and the international environmentalist movement, informal circles gathered (primarily in East Berlin) to discuss ecological issues, and local groups throughout the GDR sponsored public seminars, tree plantings, and ecology days.

The experience of these grassroots groups under church protection—which by 1989 numbered 150, according to Stasi estimates—provided much of the basis for the protest movements that emerged during the fall of 1989.[2] Protestant clergymen were often leaders in the new civic movements, including the New Forum (Neues Forum), Democracy Now (Demokratie Jetzt) and the Democratic Awakening (Demokratischer Aufbruch). Church buildings were important spaces of protest, particularly the Nikolaikirche in Leipzig, with its reformist pastor and Monday evening prayer meetings. By early October 1989, dissenters were beginning to leave the sanctuary of the Protestant church to become a public voice as demonstrations spilled over into the streets of major East German cities (Jarausch 1994: 44; see also Maier 1997).

Despite the important influence of the Protestant church and the involvement of its clergy as leaders of the opposition, however, it never attained the status of a counterhegemonic discourse that Polish Catholicism did in its cooperation with the Solidarity movement (Kubik 1994). The Protestant church in the GDR provided an arena for political opposition; it was not an agent of it.[3]

In contrast, the Catholic church in the GDR had a more quiescent attitude toward the state. Its small numbers—1 million members, or approximately 6 percent of the population (Fischer 1991: 211)—and withdrawal from public life made it much less visible than the Protestant church. Instead of creating a separate church as did the BEK-DDR, the Catholic church maintained its ties to the centralized Vatican. Its primary aim was to maintain the doctrine of Catholicism (Gordon 1990). Until the 1980s, the Catholic church remained skeptical of the Protestant church's "church-in-socialism" approach and largely distanced itself from public affairs. This "minimal-contact policy" meant that the church's activities were generally limited to individual parishes (Fischer 1991; Meyer 1991: 90); as a result, the Catholic church never harbored the kind of organized political opposition to the regime that the Protestant churches did.

With a new generation of church leaders in the 1980s, the Catholic church began to emerge from its isolation to define itself as part of the socialist state. Although by 1988 church leaders and lay members had initiated their own peace movements and were participating in ecumenical conferences, the Catholic church continued to lag behind the Protestant church in terms of political activity. It was late to recognize the decline of socialism and deep crisis within GDR society and only joined the 1989 protest movements shortly before the Wall fell (Meyer 1991).

The relationship between the church and the state, particularly the situation of the Catholic church within the GDR, provided a context for religion and religious activity in Kella. As the remainder of this chapter will show, the situation of the church and religion under socialism was a critical factor in shaping the meaning and form of many religious practices here, both before and after the Wende.

HEIMAT AND GLAUBEN

The Eichsfeld

As we saw in chapter 1, Kella lies not only on the former border between East and West Germany but also on the Catholic-Protestant boundary of the Eichsfeld region. Crossing the border into Kella is thus a passage from West to East and from the predominantly Protestant federal state of Hesse to the almost exclusively Catholic Eichsfeld. This multilayered boundary was marked not only by the former border fence (which was dismantled in the summer of 1993), but also by a wooden crucifix station and a sign bearing the Catholic greeting "Grüß Gott in Kella" (Welcome to Kella), both erected shortly after the Wende.

Throughout the region's history, residents of the Eichsfeld have actively constructed and sustained a strong sense of regional identity. When unity seemed threatened by the division of 1815, for example, the local population on both sides of the new boundary became active in voluntary associations for local historical studies (Heimatvereine and Geschichtsvereine). Similar in form to the Heimatvereine that emerged throughout Germany in the nineteenth century (compare Applegate 1990), these organizations systematically researched the history of the Eichsfeld, emphasizing a common heritage and traditions resulting from centuries of Mainz control (Meinhardt 1986). When the Industrial Revolution in England displaced the once prosperous local textile production, Eichsfelders who emigrated or sought seasonal work outside the region formed similar associations throughout Germany; by the early 1900s, more than eighty Eichsfeld Heimatvereine had been established (Gerlach 1985: 41). Similarly, after the boundary between East and West Germany became increasingly impermeable in the 1950s, eastern Eichsfelders who had settled in West Germany founded new Heimatvereine in order to maintain (and construct) a sense of common heritage. Many of these associations erected memorials to the "divided Eichsfeld" that depicted the region as a microcosm of divided Germany. A 1980s educational exhibit in the western Eichsfeld city of Duderstadt, for example, was entitled "Divided Eichsfeld, Divided Germany, Divided Europe" and featured displays about the regional history of the inter-German border as well as winning entries from a local drawing and painting contest for the best representation of the divided Eichsfeld within the larger context of German and European division.[4]

A particularly active association for people from the southern Eichsfeld (where Kella is located) is the Heimatverein Eichsfeld-Werratal. Based in Eschwege, this group sponsored the construction of a memorial to the Eichsfeld's division on the West German side of the border long before the fall of the Wall. Called "the Eichsfeld Cross," the memorial sits on a hilltop just across from the Hülfensberg, the Eichsfeld's most sacred pilgrimage site, located ten kilometers from Kella within the highly restricted Schutzstreifen zone.[5] Plans were in the works when the Wall fell to erect a chapel near this cross as a "substitute pilgrimage site" for the inaccessible Hülfensberg.[6] After the Wall fell, the Heimatverein helped sponsor renovations of important Eichsfeld landmarks, including the Konrad Martin Cross at the Hülfensberg, a memorial to the native Eichsfelder and bishop of Paderborn, Konrad Martin, who was imprisoned and later died in exile during Bismarck's Kulturkampf. The association also provided substantial financial support for the restoration of the Kella chapel.

In addition to being constructed and maintained both within and outside the region, the boundaries of the Eichsfeld are also the product of an interplay between local identity as Catholics and the Protestant identity of the surrounding region. Eichsfelders are constituted as "others" in a manner that Johannes Fabian calls "modern time/space distancing" (Fabian 1983: 27): they are distanced in time and space by emphasizing religious differences. The superstitions, rituals, icons, and pilgrimages of the Catholic Eichsfeld are perceived as backward by their neighbors in the surrounding region. Often regarded as a separate group, Eichsfelders are the object of some curiosity and the butt of jokes.

Because of the region's history as a Catholic enclave, Eichsfeld identity is often regarded as synonymous with religious sentiment. Local pilgrimages, religious traditions like the Heiligenstadt Palm Sunday procession, or the icons of faith that construct and ascribe meaning to the Eichsfeld landscape are expressions of religious devotion as well as of regional loyalty and identity. The "Eichsfeldlied" (Eichsfeld Song), commonly referred to as "our national anthem," contains numerous references to the religiosity of the region's inhabitants, as the song's last two stanzas illustrate:

> The stove, at which the loyal wife
> rules in faithful modesty,
> and children, like the olive tree,
> fold their little hands in prayer;
> the house, were the Lord our God still matters,
> and not just what satisfies the stomach,
> where unwavering faith
> lifts one's view from the dust.
>
> Eichsfelder with the love of travel in his blood
> and a breast full of song,
> home, home, is where your heart and courage are
> your purpose and your soul,
> home, where the cross towers from the hill
> and tells you of God's love.
> When your last hour arrives,
> may it be on Eichsfeld soil!

Other stanzas of the song are similarly part of a cultural construction and performance of the landscape.[7] The song not only renders the Eichsfeld landscape legible by defining and highlighting critical markers and signposts but also reflects how culture may be reimagined in the landscape (Schama 1995):

> If you have traveled around the world
> on every road and path,
> set up your tent in north and south
> on alpine and beach fronts:
> have you not seen my Eichsfeld?
> With its hills crowned with castles
> and merry residents
> you'll want to sing praises [of the Eichsfeld].
>
> There, where the young Leine [river] flows,
> the Unstrut [stream] wanders to the valleys
> the Hülfensberg greets the Werra
> the Ohmberg its Hahle
> the Wipper flows through the Au
> near and far, what a show
> in valleys and hill ranges
> and tidy villages.

In Kella, nearly every adult knows all five verses of the song by heart; it is sung enthusiastically at community or social gatherings, village festivals, family outings, and group excursions. It is particularly common for people to break into this song while hiking through one of the Eichsfeld's many rolling hills and valleys, a transversal of the landscape that simultaneously inscribes and performs it.

Place, Identity, and Belonging

The "Eichsfeldlied" reflects not only the construction of a meaningful landscape but also the interdependence of religious practices and regional identities. It is, moreover, a ballad of belonging, reflecting the complex, ubiquitous, and emotional concept of Heimat. Literally translated as *the home* or *homeland*, the term *Heimat* refers to a discourse of belonging in which identity becomes grounded in place. As Celia Applegate (1990) has pointed out, the term has no one meaning. It is both inherently linked to notions of Germanness and an imagining of a local community. It has provided emotional as well as ideological common ground for the construction and maintenance of local identities (as illustrated by the Heimatvereine associations throughout Germany, including the Eichsfeld), and it has been the focus of explorations by various writers, politicians, scholars, and filmmakers.[8] Entailing a dynamic interplay between invention and tradition, Heimat, as Applegate notes, "has never been a word about real social forces or real political situations. Instead it has been a myth about the possibility of a community in the face of fragmentation and alienation. In the postwar era, Heimat has meant forgiving, and also a measure of forgetting. Right up to the present, it has focused public attention on the meaning of tradition and locality for the nation itself" (1990: 19).

As the "Eichsfeldlied" and many local religious practices demonstrate, the notion of Heimat in the Eichsfeld is closely associated with religious sentiment, or *Glauben* (faith).The East German state recognized this connection between Heimat and Glauben enough to feel threatened by it: like its attempts to undermine religion and replace it with loyalty to the state, it also discouraged expressions of regional loyalty. The "Eichsfeldlied" was banned from schools, maps of the undivided Eichsfeld were locked away, and Heimatvereine were prohibited.[9] Despite—indeed, perhaps because of—the state's attempts to undermine regional loyalties, many of these traditionally localizing practices continued during the period of socialist rule. Whereas most residents of Kella can sing the entire "Eichsfeldlied" by heart, for example, I was told by residents of the western Eichsfeld that few people in their part of the formerly divided region can do the same.

Immediately following the Wende, many of these forbidden practices in the eastern Eichsfeld were publicly revived: local voluntary associations were reestablished, maps of the entire Eichsfeld, locked away for forty years, have reappeared on schoolroom walls, and thousands have participated in pilgrimages to the sacred sites formerly enclosed by the Sperrgebiet. In the summer of 1990, a small citizen's movement denounced the region's division into several administrative districts and states (the Eichsfeld bridges Lower Saxony and Thuringia) and called for a separate Eichsfeld Kreis belonging to Lower Saxony, in order to "preserve our identity as Eichsfelders."[10] Although this proposal failed, the two Kreise of the eastern Eichsfeld, Heiligenstadt and Worbis, were united into one Eichsfeld Kreis following another citizens' initiative in 1994. Such localizing practices reflect not only the intensity and aura of durability surrounding Eichsfeld identities but also the way in which identity may be grounded in place.

These practices also reflect how processes of localization are very much intertwined with those of nation-building or even globalization (Appadurai 1996; Miller 1995; Morley and Robins 1996). Like many European "traditions," the modern idea of Heimat emerged during a period of rapid social transformation in the second half of the nineteenth century (Applegate 1990: 10). In this context, Applegate continues, Heimat "tried to make sensible at least small pieces of that changing society, brushing them with a false patina of fixedness and familiarity" (Applegate 1990: 10).

The resurgence of local Eichsfeld Heimatvereine after the fall of the Wall may be part of a similar process. Heimat, David Morley and Kevin Robins have observed, "is about sustaining cultural boundaries and boundedness" (1996: 459). As the local Heimatvereine differentiate the Eichsfeld from as well as link it to the re-united German nation (especially in presenting the Eichsfeld as a microcosm of divided and then re-united Germany), these associations and localizing practices may be a way of demarcating and making sense of a small piece of a rapidly changing society since the collapse of socialism. They may also be part of a redefinition and renegotiation of Germanness and German nationhood following re-unification.

The Volkskirche

The history and construction of Eichsfeld identity, expressed and experienced in the concept of Heimat, provides the context for discourses and expressions of place, identity, and belonging in Kella. As Hans's actions at the chapel revealed, there is a strong connection between Heimat and Glauben here.

Like much of the Eichsfeld, this link is both reflected and constituted in the local landscape. Kella's landscape is embedded with markers of the community's religious and communist pasts: the chapel between the fences; the community church near the village center, with its separate bell tower; roadside shrines and crucifixes that mark village boundaries, including one secretly erected in 1988 by the village priest and a defiant mayor; a pilgrimage path leading up to the chapel with the fourteen Stations of the Cross; and a wooden cross, built shortly after the Wende, adorned with barbed wire from the border fence. In a sense, the village is framed by a trinity of religious symbols: a crucifix marks each of the two village entrances (one from the East, one from the West); the chapel between the fences completes the triad.

Although Glauben and Heimat have been a central aspect of Eichsfeld identity as well as key elements in popular definitions and practices of religion, they have not always coincided with the interests or leadership of the Catholic church. In fact, the relationship between Eichsfeld identity and religious sentiment has occasionally been cause for conflict between parishioners and church officials. "The clergy has often reproached us for going to church simply out of local habit," explained Günter Bachmann, one of the few villagers to attend a university and receive a doctorate. "They say Catholicism in the Eichsfeld isn't as genuine as in the diaspora, where people go to church out of religious convictions." As he continued to describe this tension, Günter distinguished between a *Volkskirche* (people's church) in the Eichsfeld and the institution of the Catholic church: "I don't think the church is always in a position to understand what goes on here [in the Eichsfeld]. People aren't necessarily fanatical Catholics, but rather they hang onto the external frame that the Catholic church has provided here for the last 400 years."

According to Günter, the *Volksfrömmigkeit* (popular faith) of the Volkskirche, represented by certain cult-like actions, such as pilgrimages, processions, and roadside shrines, goes deeper than that of traditional Catholicism. This stems largely from the Volkskirche's embodiment of Heimat and Glauben, from its ability to generate what he called an "ethnic belonging" in the region. It was the Volkskirche, Günter argued, that was largely responsible for the preservation of religious faith in the Eichsfeld under socialism: "If people remained true to the church here, they didn't do it because of a particular confession of faith. Instead, I think they clung to the truth of this Volkskirche, to this community." He added with pride that his Volkskirche was not as accommodating to the regime as the orthodox institution had been.

Other residents agree, citing a struggle in the early 1980s between the community and church officials over the future of the pilgrimage chapel. The state wanted to tear it down, and the diocesan provost had approved the action. Emma Hauser, a woman in her early sixties and a "religious virtuoso," recalled:

> The chapel was a thorn in the side of the whole regime. Even though it didn't do anything, it reminded them of religious life here. . . . The provost and our church's high officials, they were cowards. Today they all pretend to be martyrs, they all claim to be political martyrs. . . . At the dedication of the memorial on the Hülfensberg, he [the provost] made a speech. He claimed to be the big resistance fighter, the provost, and then I had to think about the chapel here.

Led by Emma and her husband, Wolfgang, the community success-fully fought the church, and the state, to preserve their chapel. As in-fluential members of the local church council, without whose approval the provost and the state hesitated to authorize the demolition, they were able to convince authorities to leave the chapel standing. "The most con-vincing argument," Wolfgang recalled, "was what it would look like to the West if they tore down the chapel. Everyone would have been able to see that and would have said: look at how awful this state is. It even tears down beautiful chapels." Although inaccessible, they both explained, the chapel had to be preserved, for it was still a "piece of Heimat."

The Kella chapel thus came to be an important symbol of the commu-nity, the church, and religion under socialism. Like the residents of Kella, it was isolated between the fences, cut off from easy and normal contact with the rest of the world. The state's plan to demolish the chapel was similarly emblematic of its efforts to undermine religion and regional identities. Yet, like their religious faith, people kept the chapel alive through sentiments and practices associated not necessarily with the in-stitutionalized church but with their Volkskirche—through a strong no-tion of the interdependence of Heimat and Glauben.

POPULAR AND INSTITUTIONALIZED RELIGION
IN AN AUTHORITARIAN SOCIETY

Heimat and Glauben under Socialism

This notion of a Volkskirche or Volksfrömmigkeit as opposed to the Catholic church reflects an important distinction between popular faith and institutionalized religion. Anthropologists have long recognized this distinction and recently have pointed to the tension and dynamic interplay between the two (for example, Badone 1990; Christian 1989, 1996; Stewart 1991). Challenging monolithic, "two-tiered" models of religion, Ellen Badone defines popular religion "as referring to those informal, unofficial practices, beliefs, and styles of religious expression that lack the formal sanction of established church structures" (1990: 4, 6). In a similar vein, Caroline Brettell writes that popular religion "applies to any social situation where a conflict or dialectic emerges between official religious models proposed by the ecclesiastical hierarchy and 'unofficial' forms" (1990: 55). Popular religion may thus denote practices that are ignored, denounced, or informally sanctioned by the church. It may even entail behavior that is not intrinsically religious but takes on religious meaning in context and practice. Straightening a cloth and tending to flowers, for example, are not in themselves religious acts; yet Hans's tending to the altar cloth or similar gestures I witnessed during visits to the Kella chapel with other villagers acquire spiritual meaning because they are performed at a sacred site and because of their larger connection to religious and regional identities, to Heimat and Glauben. Such local and localizing practices also reflect a crucial interdependence between what Charles Stewart calls "doctrinal religion" and "local or practical religion—the form that religion takes in relation to the life of the community" (1991: 11).

Research on religion in Eastern Europe, however, has largely ignored the distinction and interplay between popular faith and institutionalized religion. Shaped largely by cold-war discourse, studies of religion in Eastern Europe have focused primarily on church-state relations (Osa n.d.). Unofficial definitions and local practices of religion—both sanctioned and denounced by the church—were an important means of opposing the state in everyday life and must also be considered if we are to understand the changing role of religion in eastern Europe.

In Kella, religious practices expressed and affirmed regional identities as well as opposition to the socialist regime. Having one's child baptized, being married in the church, and sending a child to first communion instead of the Jugendweihe were often overtly political acts (compare Nagengast 1991). As we saw in the previous chapter, when church services were prohibited in Kella in 1953 and 1954, villagers walked ten kilometers every Sunday to attend mass in a neighboring village. When the Hülfensberg became inaccessible without a special pass owing to its location in the Sperrgebiet, people applied more than five months in advance for permission to attend pilgrimages there.

In addition to the community church building, an important site and symbol of institutional religious presence in Kella was the Schwesternhaus, a church-owned facility that housed a Catholic kindergarten and a small nursing home and offered weekly office hours for nonurgent medical care. Except for a few loyal party members, who sent their children to a state-run kindergarten housed in the public facility of the village administration building, most parents sent their children to the Catholic kindergarten housed in the Schwesternhaus; it was a small gesture of defiance, a local tradition that people proudly recall today. Built in 1929, the Schwesternhaus is a conspicuous landmark within the village due to its size, unusual yellow exterior, and hillside location. The fact that Franz Iseke, Kella's resident priest between 1901 and 1947 and the driving force behind the initiative to build the Schwesternhaus, was the brother of the author of the "Eichsfeldlied" continues to be a source of local pride, providing the village with an intimate connection to the history of Eichsfeld regionalism. Although not as prominently visible as the village priest, the three nuns who lived in and ran the facility were an important presence in the community. The social services they offered through the Schwesternhaus contributed to the church's self-definition as an alternative institution to the socialist state.

Symbols of Catholicism and popular faith—ranging from roadside shrines to the crosses hanging on living-room walls—similarly represented the way in which a "collective self" was defined in opposition to a "collective other" (the state, bureaucracy, the party) (Nagengast 1991: 140). Many of these sites and symbols have a long history not only as places of resistance but also as sites of a convergence and interplay of popular faith and institutionalized religion.

The crosses that mark the village boundaries, for example, while officially sanctioned by the church, have also been invested with certain legends, stories, and superstitions indicative of a kind of popular faith. Although both crosses were removed in the 1950s, their sites remained important spatial markers in village discourse until they were reerected, one shortly before, the other shortly after, the fall of the Wall. According to local legend, a Soviet army officer who shot once at the crucifix figure on the cross near the East-West boundary accidentally shot himself later in the knee, the same place where the Christ figure had been hit by the soldier's vandalism. The crucifix station on Kella's eastern boundary has a similar story associated with it. A school principal during the Nazi period refused to allow crosses to be hung in the schools, the legend goes, and was killed a few months later in a motorcycle accident just meters before the crucifix station. "He couldn't get past the cross," people say. Such stories and legends not only invest these sites with meaning and memory but also reflect a moral economy of values outside the official realm of institutionalized religion. Although neither sanctioned nor denounced by the church, they are circulated, reproduced and endowed with meaning in the realm of popular faith.

A year before the Wende, these meanings and memories were invoked in an unusual act of defiance and cooperation between the village priest and Kella's mayor, Ursula Meyer. Together with three other villagers, they secretly erected a cross on Kella's northeastern boundary near the neighboring village of Pfaffschwende. The priest secured a life-sized wooden crucifix from church officials in Erfurt; Ursula supplied cement for the foundation. Despite some questioning by the local policeman, who stumbled across the group digging a hole for the structure's foundation one evening, authorities left it standing, reflecting a growing relaxation in state control. The cross was dedicated in a community procession headed by the priest a week later.

Religion, both popular and institutionalized, could thus be a means of testing or contesting state power as well as a reason for resistance.[11] As Emma Hauser explained:

> In socialism, the world view was atheism. That means a world without God. It all happened gradually so we didn't notice it at first, but then we did. . . . When they closed our church here, we went to church in Pfaffschwende. People said "Now we're really going to go!" In wind and rain, old and young, everyone went. . . . A bit later they introduced the Jugendweihe. For me that was a serious crime—I would have seen it as betraying God if my children had participated.

Religious beliefs were cited as grounds for refusing to participate in state activities. As I noted in chapter 2, this affected party membership in Kella. Parents also objected to the Jugendweihe ceremony and mandatory military training camp for ninth- and tenth-grade boys for religious reasons. "It's because the word *Weihe* [dedication] has such important religious connotations," one man explained. Others simply claim that the Jugendweihe was an "atheistic ritual" and thus had to be resisted by true Christians.

Emma Hauser's story of her battle to keep her son from participating in the Jugendweihe reflects how the ceremony was a politically and symbolically charged issue. In 1978, her youngest son, Manfred, was in the eighth grade and thus eligible for the Jugendweihe. Despite being repeatedly called into the principal's office, along with other children whose parents were resisting the ceremony, Manfred followed his parents' instructions and refused to sign the form agreeing to participate. The school then sent a representative to visit the parents in their home. "I was so terrified," Emma recalled, "I wasn't able to sleep some nights. I must have lost ten pounds—just because the teacher was coming to see us!"

Reminding herself that this was an opportunity to demonstrate her faith in God, she prepared diligently for the teacher's visit. She familiarized herself with socialist teachings by reading *Das kleine Wörterbuch der marxistisch-leninistischen Philosophie* (Small Dictionary of Marxist-Leninist Philosophy). She discovered there that Jugendweihe was defined as "an important contribution in the education of youth in the worldview of socialism" and noted from her other experience that the "worldview of socialism is atheism." She memorized and practiced what she would say to the teacher, and she prayed to the Holy Spirit to bless her with the right words.

Emma's prayers were answered, although indirectly, for it was her husband who did most of the talking during the meeting with Manfred's teacher. "'My family and I profess to be practicing Christians,'" Wolfgang said, "'and you can't demand of us that we acknowledge Christ on the one hand while sending our children to an atheistic ritual on the other.'" When the teacher objected, Wolfgang reminded her, as Emma had planned to, of the definition of Jugendweihe in the "Small Dictionary of Marxist-Leninist Philosophy." After the teacher admitted that the "worldview of socialism" was "atheism," Emma recalled, she realized the Hausers were not to be persuaded. She left three hours later, and Manfred avoided the Jugendweihe.

Although active church members like the Hausers were never directly threatened with deportation or imprisonment, they were monitored especially closely and often suffered discrimination in housing, building-material allotments, travel permits, and educational opportunities.[12] The village mayor and her secretarial assistants recall that the most frequent topic of their regular questioning by Stasi officers concerned church activities, participants, and sermon contents.[13] And as Emma Hauser's story illustrates, careful tabs were kept on families with children eligible for the Jugendweihe.

Many residents view these forms of opposition as part of an ongoing local tradition of resistance to an oppressive political system. Indeed, there appear to be important continuities between religious struggles, resistive practices, and the politicization of religion under both Nazi and SED rule. Memories of the Nazi period in Kella are frequently expressed in terms of religious opposition, a local narrative that is both supported and, perhaps, to some extent structured, by the church chronicle that was carefully written and assembled in 1946 by an assistant priest who had served in Kella during the war.[14] After the annual Corpus Christi procession through the village was prohibited by Nazi officials in 1940, for example, the congregation processed along the inside of the church property line. There were similar struggles over religious instruction in the schools until the assistant priest assumed responsibility for this task in 1939. Support for the Nazi party was reportedly limited to a handful of villagers, most notably teachers; this claim is supported by the 1933 election results in Kella, where the National Socialist Party received less than 10.7 percent of the popular vote, in contrast to 43.9 percent nationally and 28.6 percent in the Eichsfeld.[15] The priest's 1946 chronicle describes local opposition to Nazi ideology:

> The regional chairman of the Nazi party for the southern Eichsfeld was the teacher Raubold from Großtöpfer. He worked hard to educate people about his worldview. But he lacked listeners because he mostly railed against the Bible, the Catholic church, and the Papacy. He had to resort to many tricks in order to lure Eichsfelders, who instinctively rejected this violent system, into his meetings. This is how a meeting was advertised in Kella, for example: "Tonight at 8 P.M. there will be an important meeting in the room of the new school. Each family must send one adult member." Because food-ration cards were often distributed in this manner, people naturally came. As soon as they recognized that Raubold simply want to propagandize, they left the room in protest.

Villagers in their fifties and sixties similarly remember their parents' rejection of National Socialism on religious grounds, while some (including clergy) even invoke the period of Bismarck's Kulturkampf. Recalling that, like the socialist state, the Nazi regime instituted alternative life-cycle rituals ("national socialist baptisms" or "national socialist marriages," for example), Emma Hauser remembered how her mother refused to join a national socialist women's organization because it "contradicted her Christian beliefs." Similarly, she recalled her father commenting on the Nazi regime: "A regime that rejects the cross, that rejects God, can't win a war. They may have put a cross on their flag, but as much as you can try and turn it, there will always be a hook on it." In a sense, this notion of religion as opposition is part of a teleology preached by the church and supported by popular discourses about the durability and timelessness of Christianity and local faith. "No matter what the regime," one man explained, echoing a recent pilgrimage sermon, "whether National Socialist, socialist, or capitalist, faith will prevail." As we shall see in the final section of this chapter, however, this assumption is no longer unquestioned.

Heimat, Glauben, and the Wende

The fact that religious practices and beliefs were perceived as resistance and employed in opposing the regime is especially evident in local uses of religious symbols and language at the time of the Wende. During this period of intense and rapid transition, political demonstrations emerged, though belatedly, out of the Catholic churches in the region. Immediately after the borders opened, residents of Kella cut a hole in the fence near the pilgrimage chapel to make it easily accessible. Just two weeks later, they organized a procession to the chapel, still under the scrutiny of border guards, following the fourteen stations of the cross that lead to the pilgrimage site. In preparation for the procession, a local artist helped village children paint pictures for the empty concrete stations to replace the originals, which had been lost long before. And to replace the Seventh Station, which had been totally destroyed when the border was fortified, residents constructed a cross out of tree branches near the border, adorning it with barbed wire and a small piece of the border fence (Figure 11). The barbed wire formed a circular "crown of thorns" around the intersecting branches, while the piece of fencing was affixed near the top of the cross where "INRI" is traditionally placed in Christian iconography. Despite the border guard's insistence that the cross be removed after the procession, villagers left it standing; later they secured it in a concrete base.

The fence, a very real and material symbol of the border, was thus transformed into a religious icon, an expression and interpretation of villagers' experience in their own symbolic terms. Intended as a quick, functional solution to the problem of the missing station, the cross quickly attained enormous symbolic value. A local embodiment of the transcendent and a transcendent embodiment of the local, it has, like all symbols, been invested with a multiplicity of meanings.

In different ways, the Seventh Station symbolizes for most residents the forty years of division, reflecting the ways in which larger historical

Figure 11.   The Seventh Station, a substitute for a
Station of the Cross that had been destroyed by border
fortifications, was assembled immediately after the
fall of the Wall with materials from the former border
fence. (Photograph by the author)

processes are given meaning through local, proximate symbols. "The
fence was our cross to bear," several people told me. Others see it as a
"memorial to what was destroyed by the border" and cite everything
from "Heimat," to the specific stations of the cross destroyed, to families
who were separated by the division. As the cross's designer, Johannes
Schneider, explained:

> I decided to take wood near the station because so much [wood] was cut
> down [to clear space] for the border. And the metal fencing, that was to

represent everything they destroyed here on the border . . . the station, the vegetation, the trees. . . . And then I decided to put the barbed wire around the cross for the people who have suffered on and because of the border. That was my idea, and then I didn't really think much more about it. For me, it was important that a station had once stood there and that this had been destroyed.

Anna Biermann, a woman in her late twenties and a devout Catholic, similarly explained that for her, the cross is less a religious symbol than a kind of memorial:

I didn't have anything to do with [setting up] the cross. . . . I'd heard that they'd put a cross up there, but didn't really think about why, or how. At some point I went up there and said to myself, it's actually quite nice. . . . I saw it simply as a substitute for this [missing] station, and since they couldn't find anything better up there, they took the barbed wire.

Afterwards I thought the barbed wire could stand for the fence. As a symbol, na? Because basically for me, the barbed wire stands for the crown of thorns. And one can see this crown of thorns as pain. When they put the crown of thorns on Christ, he must have suffered. So, too, did the border cause suffering—this fence, this barbed wire.

At the Seventh Station, border residents, Catholics, the Eichsfeld, indeed the divided German nation, are constructed as martyrs, as victims of the border and of the SED regime. This wooden cross remains an important image of suffering in Kella, a symbol of enduring religious faith and identity, of Heimat and Glauben.[16]

Although supported by the church, religious behavior initiated and organized by the community, like the procession to the chapel, the construction of the wooden cross, or the chapel renovation, is typical of the kind of popular religion practiced here. Despite the tension inherent in the relation between unofficial and official religion (Badone 1990: 12) and despite numerous incidents of struggle between parishioners and clergy, the interests of the two interrelated religious traditions remained largely congruent during the period of socialist rule. Referred to as a Zufluchtsort (place of shelter), the church was viewed as an alternative institution preaching against official values of the socialist regime; popular religion, including local legends and superstitions as well as notions of Heimat and Glauben, empowered its position. Ironically, therefore, the socialist state's antagonistic policies toward religion had an effect that was opposite to what it intended.

POPULAR AND INSTITUTIONALIZED RELIGION IN A CONSUMER SOCIETY

Since German re-unification, however, the church has lost much of its appeal and influence. Concomitantly, both popular and official religious practices have lost their meaning as political acts of opposition. As in the rest of the former GDR (as well as in many other post-socialist societies), religious activity has declined dramatically in Kella. Church attendance has decreased, contributions to the collection plate on Sundays have dropped to less than half of what they used to be, and participation in pilgrimages is far below what it was when special passes were required. For residents of Kella, the Eichsfeld, and elsewhere in the former GDR, the church's function as a shelter and forum for opposition to the regime has disappeared.[17] As one man explained, "You can't hide from unemployment under the protection of the church."

As it struggles to maintain its influence, the Catholic church in the Eichsfeld has drawn on a variety of rhetorical devices to make its argument. At times, the language has been strikingly similar to the socialist regime's "anti-imperialist" discourse. The border, for example, which was once referred to by the regime as an "armored shield against the West," is now referred to by the church as having been an "armored shield protecting Heimat and faith." The reason for the decline in Heimat and Glauben, says the church, is the rampant consumerism and heightened individualism inherent in the new capitalist system.

Condemning the *Nachholungsbedarf* ("the need to catch up," a reference to the perceived materialism of eastern Germans following the opening of the borders), local clergy regularly devoted sermons to the dangers of consumerism. In one instance, a visiting priest from Heiligenstadt reprimanded the Kella congregation for failing to attend his parish mission services. Acknowledging and appropriating the interrelation of Heimat and Glauben in the Eichsfeld, he pointed out how both were now threatened as people pursued the "new freedom." "Faith was once determined externally," he argued. "Now this faith must be retained even though the external forces are gone. . . . Right now it's like after the war, when starving people who were finally given food ate so much that they died." Similarly, in a mass honoring the service of nuns in Kella, the local priest, Father Münster, wrote and directed a play about the dissolution of family and community caused by an insatiable appetite for consumer goods: children absorbed in their new Walkmans cease to interact with their parents; a married couple quarrels about a new car purchased in order to keep up with the neighbors. The new threat, the play concludes, is "being separate from another," and this is the result of moral decay caused by consumerism.

Often drawing on messages contained in pastoral letters, Kella's priest warned his parishioners that "consumerism is more dangerous than communism," or "capitalism is just as bad as communism." At one Eichsfeld pilgrimage, Bishop Joachim Wanke of Erfurt conveyed a similar message: "Advertisements promise happiness and joy. With the words 'buy your happiness,' industries try to obstruct peoples view of reality. . . . On the path toward a total consumer society that consists solely of acquiring, using, and then throwing away, not only car wrecks but also human wrecks are left behind." At a dedication ceremony for the renovation of the Konrad Martin Cross on the Hülfensberg, the archbishop of Fulda preached a message along these same lines: "In the last forty years there were clear fronts to fight against. Now the assault of practical materialism is more difficult than that of theoretical materialism. In other words, theoretical materialism has been replaced by practical materialism—and temptation has become strong." In another vein, Father Münster attempted to make his argument using the language of consumerism he thought might appeal to parishioners: "Go shopping at the Aldi of God!" he urged them, referring to the western discount store Aldi, commonly associated with eastern Germans' shopping habits since the Wende.

In presenting itself as the leader in the fight against the onslaught of consumerism, the church has also invoked a glorified memory of its own position and actions under socialism. Local clergymen remind their parishioners of the church's important role in opposing the socialist regime. At the 1991 Heiligenstadt Palm Sunday procession, for example, the presiding priest noted the important "resistance" function the procession had played during the forty years of socialist rule. Although religious practices were often performed as an expression of, or reason for, opposition to the regime, they were rarely defined as such by the Catholic church before the Wende.

Of course, the church's preaching against consumerism is nothing new. In fact, its message of anticonsumerism is not new since the Wende. What is different in this context is the way in which the church has glorified its own past as well as the socialist past. The us-versus-them attitude, with which the church was able to garner support during Communist rule, does not work in a market economy. While residents acknowledge a certain truth in the church's preachings—one of the most common laments since the Wende concerns a loss of community in the village—and many are quick to deplore the decline in church attendance and donations, western democratic political forms and a capitalist market economy are not perceived as being as threatening to religious identity as the socialist system had been. Most villagers maintain they are "still good Catholics," but with their new freedom of individual choice and opportunity for travel they have less time for communal expressions of religious devotion.

With the church now preaching messages its followers do not always want to hear, and with the loss of a common and urgent commitment to religious survival, the interests of official and unofficial religion have, to some extent, diverged. Although an interplay between the two remains, this divergence has forced an individual as well as collective redefinition and renegotiation of the meaning and practice of religion and religious identities. Indeed, it has resulted in new negotiations and contestations of the sacred itself. During the socialist period, for example, the church had been an important means of social control: without any alternatives to the village church, attendance at mass in Kella was closely monitored by both parishioners and the priest. The opening of the borders and increased mobility have created new opportunities and socially sanctioned substitutes for this fundamental measurement of religious devotion. Rather than attending Sunday morning mass in Kella, for example, villagers may choose to go to Saturday evening mass in nearby Eschwege or Grebendorf. In place of Sunday mass, others may simply visit a famous pilgrimage site on a day trip. Similarly, during an excursion to Tirol sponsored by Kella's Heimatverein, several women hiked the hills at dawn on a Sunday morning, repeatedly reciting Hail Marys and singing their favorite hymns. On hearing that they had done this instead of attending mass, Kella's priest reprimanded the women, demanding that they "bring this into the confession." The women, believing that they had expressed religious devotion that day, shrugged off his criticism.

In an interesting sense, such notions and performances of devotion as individual expression suggest an extension of the individualism of the marketplace to religious practice; people come to church and express their faith on their own terms. Individual observance has not necessarily replaced community solidarity, but it may have displaced it.

Not surprisingly, Kella's priest became a central figure in negotiating these changes. A small yet domineering man in his midforties, Father Münster served in Kella from 1982 to 1996. Just as the influence of the church as an institution has declined since the fall of the Wall, so too, did Father Münster's influence and role in the community. Villagers increasingly sought out clergy in other churches for confession, thus severely limiting his control of and access to local and often privileged knowledge.[18] This declining influence and involvement in community affairs were also the product of the dramatic change in circumstances since the Wende, in which all community members have less access to shared information.[19]

Father Münster responded to this challenge by attempting to cling to his control, occasionally through methods and strategies of manipulation.[20] While he still retained a certain measure of authority invested in him as priest, Father Münster remained a fairly controversial figure in the community until his departure in the summer of 1996. According to many villagers, "he changed a lot [after] the Wende." Others challenged his, and the church's, accusations of materialism by pointing to the priest's new Volkswagen Jetta, fax machine, and cellular phone.

Father Münster was most controversial, however, due to his involvement in the charismatic Focolare ecclesiastical movement. Based on an
ideal of "world unity" and "universal love" preached by its founder and
leader, Chiara Lubich, around whom the movement's personality cult is
centered, Focolare is one of the most powerful of the newer ecclesiastical
movements within the Catholic church.[21] It demands of its adherents a
high level of participation and commitment, including regular attendance at local, regional, national, and international gatherings. The opening of the borders in 1989 created new possibilities for travel within the
movement; Father Münster frequently organized trips for the handful of
villagers involved in Focolare activities to meetings in other parts of Germany, Italy, and Poland.

For Father Münster, this was (and, I believe, continues to be) his life's
work. Having grown up outside the Eichsfeld, he had little understanding or patience for many local and popular religious practices.[22] Instead,
he felt that he must devote himself to the Focolare movement. Many villagers resented this, not only because they were skeptical of many of the
ideas and practices of the movement, but also because they believed that
it divided the congregation and detracted from his responsibilities as a
priest to the community, which above all, they argued, entailed presiding over local masses and pilgrimages.

The tension between Kella's priest and parishioners not only supports
the notion that the relationship between priests and parishioners is
"rooted in struggle" (Behar 1990; Riegelhaupt 1984), but also reflects how
the practice and category of religion are subject to, and are the products
of, negotiations and contestations by clergy as well as parishioners. In a
sense, villagers' criticisms of the priest entailed a blurring, indeed inver-
sion, of distinctions between popular faith and institutionalized religion:
it was the parishioners who invoked traditional categories of the church
and roles of the clergy to contest their priest's involvement in what they
viewed as unconventional religious practices outside the realm of institutionalized religion.

Recent events in Kella reflect this continuing struggle, not only between clergy and parishioners but between the church as an institution
and its members as well. In the spring of 1994, the three nuns who had

lived and worked in the Schwesternhaus were transferred out of Kella due to financial pressures on their parent house; its Catholic kindergarten is now housed in the former GDR day-care facility. Several years later, the building still stands empty, slowly showing signs of abandonment and decay with its crumbling facade and broken windows. What was once an important symbol of religious presence and opposition under socialism, particularly in the context of the community's status as a village in the Schutzstreifen, has thus now become for many residents a symbol of loss and betrayal. As one woman told me: "It makes me ill with sadness even to look up there at the Schwesternhaus." The community farewell gathering for the nuns reflected similar sentiments in poems written for and tears shed at the occasion.

This sense of loss and betrayal was heightened by the announcement in the spring of 1996 that Father Münster was to be transferred out of Kella. Most upsetting to parishioners was that the church would not be providing a replacement. Kella was thus not only losing Father Münster but a resident priest as well; the future of the parish rectory, which had recently undergone extensive renovations, was yet to be determined. Because no reason was given by the priest or the bishop for the transfer, people were left to speculate, particularly after Father Münster insisted to inquiring parishioners that he had not requested a transfer. Many viewed his removal as a normal course of events: ten years was an average tenure for a priest in any community, they argued, and this one had already exceeded his. Others pointed to the widespread shortage of priests in the Catholic church and explained the transfer as a product of diocesan reorganization and consolidation. Soon, however, rumors began circulating that the bishop had received letters of complaint from several villagers. According to local gossip, one letter was critical of Father Münster's involvement in Focolare and claimed that he was responsible for creating troublesome factions within the congregation. Another letter allegedly accused the priest of improper conduct in relation to several of his closest female parishioners. There were reportedly no charges in the letter—nor were there rumors in the village—of sexual involvement; rather, the priest was blamed for having created divisions within families and between spouses as a result of his frequent activities and close relationships with several women in the village. Sensing a problematic and potentially disruptive situation, it was speculated, the bishop had determined that it was time for the controversial priest to move on.

Most significant about the local gossip were the changes it reflected in perceptions and attitudes toward the church as an institution. The church had not merely lost the appeal it had under socialism as an alternative institution and forum for opposition to the regime, it had now itself become a power that had to be interpreted, negotiated, and contested. Indeed, I would suggest that certain negotiations and speculations about the church's power were informed and structured by interpretations and negotiations of state power under socialism: a suspicion of the unknown, a sense that something knowable was being withheld by design, a notion of collective negotiation as a means of deciphering the enigma. Echoing similar comments I heard from several villagers, a letter to the bishop protesting Father Münster's transfer stated: "Many [of us] working in the West have learned that those in power care little about the human effects of their decisions . . . is this true in this case as well?"

The loss of a resident priest, and the villagers' reactions to the loss, also reflected an increasing divergence between popular faith and institutionalized religion. Recalling their allegiance to the church during socialism, for which many villagers had paid a price, parishioners described feeling abandoned and betrayed by the church. Of the handful of letters written to the bishop, most mentioned the painful loss of the Schwesternhaus: "The Schwesternhaus overlooks [the village] like a memorial, empty and yawning. . . . Must our rectory also stand empty and unused?" Similarly, another letter argued: "We have defended our faith over the past years. . . . And what has it brought us? We feel abandoned, especially because along with Father Münster we are losing a permanent resident priest." Several parishioners even threatened to leave the church: "Some [people] have even indicated their intention to leave the church," one letter cautioned, "They claim they don't need to pay church taxes in order to believe [in God]."

Anticlericalism, as numerous anthropological studies of religion in Europe have shown, does not necessarily imply a rejection of religion;

nor does hostility toward the church as an institution (Behar 1990; Herzfeld 1985; Mintz 1982; Riegelhaupt 1984; Taylor 1990). However, the anticlericalism and hostility toward the church in Kella are indicative of the kinds of practices that have called into question the very meaning of the church, religion, and spiritual practices in a changing world.

RELIGIOUS CREATIVITY

Both popular religious practices and the interaction between official and unofficial religion are thus being redefined and transformed in relation to the tremendous changes brought about by re-unification. While it is too early to ascertain the impact these transformations will ultimately have on the church's position, on religious sentiment, or on regional Eichsfeld identities associated with the notions of Heimat and Glauben, they do make especially visible the fluid and contested nature of religion and religious practices. The relationship between religion, identity, place, and belonging is always changing and often context dependent. This dynamic is what fosters the kind of religious creativity I witnessed in Kella, a creativity that often emerged from the interdependent spaces between popular faith and institutionalized religion as people struggled to make sense of a rapidly changing world. I am reminded of this borderland creativity each time I glance at the gift that Hans Becker made for us when we left Kella: a cross, made of two pieces of the border fence, adorned with barbed wire.

4 Consuming Differences

One of the more amusing and frequently trying aspects of fieldwork in Kella was learning nicknames. A common feature of European village life, the limited number of family names in the community necessitated the use of nicknames to identify particular individuals.[1] Ethnographic studies of European villages point out how the use and shared knowledge of nicknames can express a sense of communal belonging (Mewett 1982, 1986; Peace 1986). They may also be categories of social classification, the way inequalities are talked about in village discourse.

In Kella, the local nickname for one of the village's most affluent residents under socialism was "J. R.," a name taken from the wealthy, avaricious character in the American television series *Dallas*.[2] Another village nickname, "Alexis," was similarly derived from the American television show *Dynasty*. Transmitted through West German television, whose airwaves easily crossed the otherwise impermeable border even before the official ban on western television was lifted in 1971, both shows were extremely popular in Kella and in the rest of the GDR during the 1980s. The localization of these mass-mediated icons of capitalist excess reflected not only villagers' symbolic positioning of themselves within a larger transnational social space but also an ironic deployment of western cultural forms that contested official versions of a "class-free" socialist society. The nicknames themselves also allude to the importance of conspicuous consumption in the formation of village inequalities under socialism.

This chapter analyzes Kella as a social field, exploring the production and reproduction of inequality in village social relations over time. Like other types of border zones, social boundaries of distinction are fluid, relational, and always under construction. Focusing on the kinds of constructions used to classify social differentiation, my discussion attempts to situate village inequalities in the context of national and regional class formation. The chapter moves chronologically through a series of village events that have influenced the formation of inequalities there. I begin with the pre–World War II period, when property ownership was the principal basis of class organization. I then discuss the first years of socialist rule, when nearly half of the large property owners fled or were evacuated from Kella and the remaining landholders were forced into the agricultural collective. With the removal of the old village elite and the disappearance of traditional economic capital as a means of social differentiation, a largely new group of local elites asserted itself through the social capital of connections. I argue that these new practices of distinction occurred primarily in the realm of the second economy, where social capital was accumulated, exchanged, and displayed. In the interstices of official state production and distribution, consumption became productive in new and strategic ways: it both reflected and constituted difference. The "consuming frenzy" for which East Germans were criticized and ridiculed after the fall of the Wall was, in a sense, nothing new. It was merely an extension, or exaggeration, of a cultural order formed in an economy of shortages. Ironically, commodity fetishism was an integral part of daily life in "actually existing socialism."

SOCIAL ORGANIZATION IN
THE PRESOCIALIST YEARS

During the first half of the twentieth century, village social groups were divided primarily into *Arbeiter* (wage laborers) and *Bauern* (property-owning farmers). The majority of the population were worker-peasants: Arbeiter who cultivated less than one hectare (approximately 2.5 acres) of land, primarily for themselves, through a patronage-labor arrangement with the Bauern. Following in the tradition of Eichsfeld migrant workers (Schnier and Schulz-Greve 1990), which peaked in the mid-nineteenth century when the Industrial Revolution displaced local cottage industries, many villagers were forced by economic necessity to seek employment outside the Eichsfeld region. Except for several women who worked in a cigar factory established in Kella in 1911, most villagers commuted to the neighboring Hessian town of Eschwege. Many others found seasonal employment far outside the region: men worked as construction workers in Essen, Hanover, Mainz, or the Rhineland, while women were employed as seasonal agricultural laborers in Magdeburg or Egeln. As I have previously noted, in 1924 more than 26 percent of the working age population (134 men and 32 women) left the village for extended periods of time as migrant laborers (Müller and others 1966: 11).

Eight Großbauern families constituted the village elite during the presocialist period (1900–1949).[3] The Großbauern's social position was reflected in village spatial organization: their large farmhouses are clustered centrally on the main street and form the core of the village. Due to the practice of partible inheritance that fractionalized landholdings, intermarriage between these elite families became a means of consolidating property ownership and thus a strategy of social reproduction. As David Sabean has argued, the language of class was thereby also expressed in kinship terms (1990, 1998). Even after the collectivization of agriculture, there were still marriages among these Großbauern families.

The Großbauern status as elites derived not only from the size of their landholdings but also from their positions of relative power in relation to other villagers. The majority of wage laborers in the village had small landholdings and no draft animals to cultivate them. In exchange for their labor, villagers would seek out a Bauer as a patron, known as an *Ackersmann* (plowman), to plow their fields. As one former Großbauer, Heinz Müller, recalled, one hour of plowing with a team of horses cost each household approximately seven hours of labor in the Bauer's fields. Women usually fulfilled these obligations to the Ackersmann, by harvesting potatoes and beets or cutting wheat and hay with a sickle and tying them into bundles. Several generations would remain with one family as their Ackersmann. "Every Bauer had his regular people," Heinz Müller explained. "They would come to us and say, 'Can you cultivate my land. I'll help you then.'"

One women whose family had worked for the Ackersmann Peter Kohl did not recall the arrangement quite so fondly:

> We only had half a hectare of land, which we couldn't cultivate ourselves. Everyone had his Ackersmann at that time, and those were the Bauern. And each Bauer had so and so many people whose land he plowed. For that we had to work for them in the fields. It was like a feudalist system! Our family was with the Kohls—my friend Sylvia's parents—for more than forty years. Her father had horses. One could say that in those times, Sylvia was the richest girl in the village. The Bauern always thought they were better than we were. They were the rich people, and we were the poor people. They had a Bauern pride.

Although the village economy was not agriculturally based, agricultural labor was a major part of daily life for most villagers in garden plots, in small fields, or in the larger fields of the Bauern. The number and kind of livestock reflected the size of one's property holdings, the most common measurement of economic capital. Social differences were thus classified in these terms: "We were poor because we only had goats," "They owned a cow," or "They were rich—they had horses" are frequently still used to describe villagers' social and economic status through 1945. One woman, Gretel Schmidt, recounted a story that described earlier village status hierarchies: "We were the little people—not in terms of body size," she added, concerned that her petite figure might confuse me, "but because we hardly had any land. We only had goats." She thought for a minute and then continued:

I want to tell a story about my cousin Katharina. Her family had a
cow, and they thought they were better than we were. Now their oldest
daughter, Anna, had a boyfriend, and his family had TWO cows. And
they imagined themselves to be the big people. And because Anna only
had one cow, his parents didn't want them to get married. When Anna
died suddenly and her boyfriend married another woman years later,
her mother said to us, "We weren't good enough for them because we
only had one cow. But now he has lowered himself even more. He's going to marry someone who only has goats." That's how things were measured—"A cow hides all poverty," that was the saying.

As symbols of wealth through property ownership and patronage, draft
animals like horses and, to a lesser extent, cows, remained categories of
social prestige and inequality until the collectivization of agriculture in
the 1950s, after which, as Gretel later said, "even the richest farmer's
daughter had to go to work in the factory like us, like the little people."

DEPORTATION, EMIGRATION, AND COLLECTIVIZATION

Two events in 1952, often conflated now in the memory of villagers, fundamentally transformed the basis of village social organization and differentiation under socialism. The first was the deportation
and emigration of five families in the spring of that year. The second was
the collectivization of agriculture that forced the remaining Bauern into
the local agricultural cooperative, the Landwirtischaftliche Produktions-
genossenschaft (LPG).

As I noted in chapter 2, it is still not known whether the three
Großbauern families who left voluntarily shortly before the evacuation
of the other two families were truly slated for deportation. It is, however,
quite plausible that these families were on the list of deportees, given the
fact that the majority of those deported were farmers with landholdings
of more than five hectares (Potratz 1993: 63). Regardless of whether they
left involuntarily or at their own initiative, and even though only three of
the eight Großbauern families fled, what is generally agreed on in local

memory is that this day in May 1952 marked the moment when the Großbauern left Kella.[4]

One of the reasons this date is so frequently associated with the removal of the old village elite is that it coincides roughly with the collectivization of agriculture, which drove all landholders, including the remaining five Großbauern families, into the LPG. Kella had not been affected by the initial land reform begun under Soviet occupation in 1945–1949, when the large Junker estates (more than 100 hectares) were split up. In 1952, the state began urging (more forcibly in some areas than in others) voluntary collectivization among all independent farmers. After describing the deportations, one woman's narrative flowed seamlessly into the next major—and, in her mind, related—event: the day the functionaries came to Kella and ordered all the Bauern into the mayor's office.

> That was a grim day, too. The Bauern were all ordered to come to the mayor's office and then they were worked over.[5] . . . What a drama that was with our neighbor, Arnold Hartmann! He had a very small farm, only two hectares, and he didn't want to join the LPG. They [the functionaries] came to his courtyard, where there was a chopping block and an ax next to it. He threw his head down on the block and yelled, "Here! Just chop off my head! I don't want to live anymore! They want to take away everything I've built up!"

She added that the farmers did not know at the time how much less work and worry the LPG would be than independent farming. Later, she said, one of the Bauern wives told her they were doing much better in the LPG than when farming alone due to an easier workload and a higher standard of living.

By 1958, two years before the nationwide accelerated collectivization, only four *Mittelbauern* (owners of five to ten hectares), along with the village's most adamant Communist, Werner Schmidt's father, had joined the local LPG. By 1960, however, all landholders with more than one hectare of arable land had been collectivized, including the remaining five Großbauer families. In the 1970s, as part of state planners' aims to modernize agricultural production on a large scale, Kella's LPG was merged with two farm collectives in the region, and farming was divided between plant and animal production.

Collectivization thus fundamentally transformed agricultural labor and production. Instead of the entire family having to work the fields, as under the previous system of individual family farms, only one member of the household (usually the male in whose name the property was registered or his widow) was required to be a member of the LPG. This membership and its attendant responsibilities was inherited along with the property that had been collectivized. Frequently one or more family members would be employed full-time by the collective, although not all LPG employees were former Bauer.[6] Out of 144 village households, 57 had land in the collective and were thus considered LPG members; all members were obligated to work a certain number of hours every year, depending on the amount of land they had in the collective. Members as well as nonmembers who needed livestock feed (most households in Kella raised at least one pig for slaughter each year) or potatoes for their own consumption worked additional hours for the LPG.

In an arrangement similar to the earlier one with Großbauern, villagers—again, usually women doing stoop labor—fulfilled their obligatory work for the LPG during the spring planting and fall harvesting of potatoes and sugar beets. According to most villagers, the average 100 hours of work per year for the LPG was not as difficult as work for the Ackersmann had been. Indeed, the state seems to have been successful in promoting a sense of collective responsibility in this area. Rather than fulfilling obligations to an individual of power, as under the Ackersmann patronage system, LPG work is often remembered fondly as an easier way of earning livestock feed as well as a way of becoming acquainted with people from neighboring villages who worked for the same regional LPG.

Together, the events of 1952 to 1960—the deportation and emigration of several property holders and the beginnings of agricultural collectivization—essentially removed the village elite through the elimination of private property as economic capital. With the disappearance of this principal means of social distinction, new strategies of social differentiation emerged that produced and maintained a largely new group of elites.

SOCIAL DIFFERENTIATION AND
ORGANIZATION UNDER SOCIALISM

Inequality under Socialism

With the virtual elimination of private property, the collectivization of agriculture and industry, the restructuring of occupational rewards and remunerations, and the increase in occupational mobility, socialist planners in the GDR (as elsewhere) aimed to achieve an egalitarian society under the "dictatorship of the proletariat." Scholars of Eastern Europe have long recognized that this goal remained illusory and have pointed to the creation and evolution of new hierarchies in socialist systems. While most researchers agree that the new hierarchy was different due to the elimination of wealthy entrepreneurs and large landowners, opinions regarding the nature of inequality in socialist societies have differed. Concerned with the parallels between the capitalist property-owning class and political bureaucrats under socialism, Milovan Djilas's classic study argued that a "new class" had been formed in socialist societies, comprising those with "special privileges and economic preferences because of the administrative monopoly they hold" (Djilas 1957: 39). In this view, the bureaucracy became the locus of political power and social reproduction under socialism; positions of power in the bureaucratic state apparatus were a principal means of maintaining privilege (Cole 1985).

Scholars who acknowledge the formation of a political ruling class have pointed to the role of the intelligentsia, either as separate from the political class (Baylis 1974; Ludz 1972) or as a dominant subcategory of it (Konrad and Szelenyi 1979). Particularly in post-Stalinist Eastern Europe, intellectuals became a critical part of this new elite as planners, or "redistributors of the social surplus" (Konrad and Szelenyi 1979: 145; see also Verdery 1991) and as members of the party bureaucracy. Other studies of inequality in Eastern Europe have focused on occupational strata (Connor 1979; Kolosi and Wnuk-Lipinski 1983) as an index of social stratification. Taken together, these studies argue that a new hierarchy of intellectuals and bureaucrats, followed by workers and then peasants, formed the basis of social differentiation in socialist societies (Cole 1985: 250).

Social organization and differentiation in Kella took place within this broader context of hierarchy formation at the regional and national level. Party officials and bureaucrats were viewed as privileged due to their higher incomes as well as preferential access to certain goods and services, housing, and special stores. Although this was less true for village party members, they, too, were regarded as—and often resented for— having certain privileges associated with their status. In addition to their perceived political connection with the state regarding matters like the allocation of housing and building permits, certain party officials were responsible for the allotment of specific goods and services, particularly building materials, within the village.[7] Factory managers, who were almost always SED party officials, were similarly responsible for assigning coveted union vacation homes: whereas unconnected workers often waited years for an assignment, factory managers were often able to take regular vacations.

Although political bureaucrats in the GDR did enjoy a privileged status and lifestyle—indeed, villagers often claimed that national and occasionally county party officials belonged to another social stratum —this was not the principal means of social differentiation and organization in Kella. Theories of class formation under socialism may be useful for providing a context for the structuring of local hierarchies, but they are less adequate for theorizing inequality at a microlevel, as more recent anthropological analyses have shown.[8] Rather than delving into the complex and often contradictory arguments of class theorists in order to question whether or how social classes were constituted in socialist societies, I prefer to employ a more dynamic notion of distinction, hierarchy, and differentiation.

Although some scholars of eastern Europe have cautioned against importing certain concepts of western social theory in the analysis of socialist societies, I find Pierre Bourdieu's theories of distinction and forms of capital a particularly useful way of conceptualizing social differentiation under socialism.[9] Bourdieu argues that traditional Marxist theories of class (which have been most frequently used to analyze inequalities in socialist societies) are inadequate because they reduce the social world to an economic field alone. He extends the Marxist notion of capital to include symbolic and cultural goods, thus collapsing a traditional economic-noneconomic dichotomy. Wealth and power are determined not only by the possession of economic capital like money, property, means of production, and other material assets (Wacquant 1987: 69) but also by other forms of capital. Social capital, for example, consists of the "aggregate of the actual or potential resources which are linked to possession of a durable network of more or less institutionalized relationships of mutual acquaintance and recognition" (Bourdieu 1986: 29). Social capital would thus include resources like social connections, whereas symbolic capital is "the form the different types of capital take once they are perceived as legitimate" (Bourdieu 1987: 4). A family's honor, reputation, and prestige would all be considered symbolic capital. Cultural capital, Bourdieu argues, is accumulated primarily through education—"academic qualifications are to cultural capital what money is to economic capital" (Bourdieu 1977: 187)—and can be used to generate wealth, privilege, and income.

Instead of discussing objective class boundaries, then, Bourdieu employs spatial and economic metaphors to elaborate a notion of social space, which is in many ways itself a metaphorical conception of the social world. Sociology becomes "social topology" in Bourdieu's work. Agents are distributed within the social space according to the volume and composition of capital—"fundamental social powers"—they possess. When agents occupy neighboring positions in the social space, they tend to be endowed with similar dispositions and interests that generate analogous practices, behavior, and representations. There are no clear-cut boundaries between social groups, he argues; positions within the social space are defined in relation to each other.

This concept of social space is also crucial to Bourdieu's conceptualization of the maintenance and reproduction of power relations. Objective structures of this space are internalized, and social distances are inscribed onto the body through strategies that may not even be conscious. Ranging in form from timidity to arrogance, these strategies produce a "sense of one's place" within the social field: "It is this sense of one's place which, in a situation of interaction, prompts those whom we call in French *les gens humbles,* literally 'humble people'—perhaps common folks in English—to remain 'humble,' and which prompts the others to 'keep their distance' or to 'keep their station in life'" (Bourdieu 1987: 5).

Objective power relations are thus reproduced in symbolic power relations, as Bourdieu argues: "The space of objective differences (with regard to economic and cultural capital) find expression in a symbolic space of visible distinctions" (Bourdieu 1987: 11). Taste, a form of symbolic capital as well as a culturally inculcated disposition, is an example of such a distinction that both structures and is structured by one's habitus and position within the social space (Bourdieu 1984).

While Bourdieu's discussion of the forms of capital may cause confusion by describing them "in ways that overlap" or seem "inconsistent" (Smart 1993: 393), this, I believe, is his intention. Indeed, by theorizing the different forms of capital as intersecting, converging, and overlapping, Bourdieu seems to allow more possibilities and freedom for a subject to move within the social space. In a sense, his metaphorical, multidimensional conception of the social world—in which boundaries are blurred, multilayered, and fluid—is a more accurate depiction of the flux and ambiguity of social organization and differentiation.

Following Bourdieu, therefore, I see social distinctions not as fixed objective boundaries but rather as relational concepts produced and reproduced in practice. Different forms of capital, particularly social and symbolic capital, as well as other practices like gift exchange and consumption, were critical elements in the production and reproduction of social organization and differentiation under socialism. Although forms of capital other than economic had been part of village social organization in the presocialist period, they took on new meanings and value under socialism. After the virtual elimination of private property and other forms of economic capital during socialist rule, social and symbolic capital became particularly salient in determining an individual's position in the village social field. As Bourdieu's theory suggests, in practice these forms of capital often overlapped, intersected, or were convertible into each other. These overlappings and intersections are particularly relevant in considering the second economy under socialism.

The Second Economy

Just weeks after I arrived in Kella, my neighbor told me the following joke, which was widely shared on both sides of the border following the Wende: "What is the most difficult [adjustment] for the Ossis since the Wall fell? Having to survive without connections." Even though I did not really understand the joke at first, I politely laughed along with my neighbor, nodding my head in feigned understanding, and recorded the conversation in my field notes that evening. Not until months later, when Michael Schmidt, a young man from the village was trying to describe a recently deceased villager, did the joke make sense. "You know who he is," Michael told me. "He's the one who worked in his garden down the street. I used to feel sorry for him. He was nothing, of no use to anybody—he had no connections [*Beziehungen*]. Unlike the carpenter Thomas Baumann. Now, HE had connections."

Michael had brought to my attention not only the identity of the man whose funeral procession I had witnessed that day but also the way in which people had categorized social differences and inequalities under socialism. The notion of "connections" or "networks" refers to a classification that, as the joke indicates, has a different meaning today. Yet it was extremely important in the GDR, as in other socialist societies, where social connections were the principal means of obtaining scarce consumer goods and services. Not only were such networks an integral part of the second, or informal, economy, they were also central to the way in which social relations were organized and reorganized during socialist rule.

The political economy of socialism was based on a logic of centralized planning, the aim of which was to maximize the redistributive power of the state.[10] With its emphasis on the accumulation of the means of production and the central appropriation and allocation of surplus, socialism's locus of competition made success dependent on socialist firms' ability to bargain for and procure materials (Verdery 1996: 22). Not only did this "work of procuring," as Verdery writes, generate "whole networks of cozy relations among economic managers and their bureaucrats, clerks and their customers" (p. 22), it also encouraged (indeed necessitated) the padding, hoarding, hiding, and bartering of materials and labor that unavoidably produced what Kornai (1992) has famously called "economies of shortage."

As in other socialist societies, the second economy in the GDR arose in response to the chronic shortages of goods and services resulting from these consequences of a planned economy.[11] Based on networks of family or kin groups, ties of friendship, groups of common ethnic or territorial origins, or arrangements among patrons, brokers, and clients, this informal sector depended on the exchange of goods, favors, and services to obtain scarce resources. In acknowledging its existence, the state often claimed that this sector was left over from peasant times; yet, as several scholars have pointed out (Altman 1989; Cole 1985; Sampson 1986), this fails to explain its persistence under socialism. The kinds of connections formed in socialist societies differed from informal networks found in other societies because under socialism they were vital for day-to-day existence (Sampson 1986: 50).[12] Although the activity within the second economy was largely illegal, it functioned outside as well as within bureaucratic contexts. Indeed, an important and dynamic interplay existed between these official and unofficial spheres of economic life.[13] In the GDR (again, as elsewhere), the state came to rely unofficially on activities in the second economy to counter the shortages of goods and services present in the first. Thefts of materials or the illegal use of tools from the workplace in moonlighting work brigades were commonplace, for example, and significantly increased the number of homes that could be built or renovated. As Verdery notes, "The second economy, then, which provisioned a large part of consumer needs, was parasitic upon the state and inseparable from it" (1996: 27).

Public and private spheres, often viewed as a corollary to the first and second economies, must similarly be viewed as interrelated phenomena (Lampland 1995: 273–74). In East Germany, this traditional opposition corresponds to Günter Gaus's famous description of the GDR as a "society of niches," the private sphere of friends, family, and coveted belongings to which citizens retreated for their "real" lives: "What is a niche in the society of the GDR? It is the preferred place for people over there, the place in which the politicians, planners, propagandists, the collective, the great goal, the cultural legacy—in which all these depart so that a good man, with his family and among friends, can water his potted flowers, wash his car, play [the card game] Skat, have conversations, celebrate holidays" (Gaus 1986: 117, quoted in Maier 1997: 29).[14]

Certain details and practices of everyday life under socialism reflected and constituted this pubic-private divide of the "niche society": the intricate red-and-white wrought-iron fences and gates, quintessential GDR style, that defined and enclosed the private space of households or gardens; birthday celebrations that turned into slumber parties because of the strict Schutzstreifen curfew; evenings spent crafting bricks out of homemade mortar to be used, perhaps years later, in building a new house; weekends spent retiling a bathroom with tiles laboriously obtained through a friend of a friend who had purchased them in Czechoslovakia.

Yet, as these examples illustrate, the various spheres of economic and social life—first and second economies, public and private domains— were closely intertwined and interdependent. This interdependence was particularly visible in practices of exchange and display, facilitated by the social capital of connections accumulated largely in the realm of the second economy, that crisscrossed these various spheres. Furthermore, as material from Kella illustrates, such practices of exchange and display were an essential means of social distinction under socialism.

The importance of exchange as a richly symbolic as well as economic activity has of course long been recognized by anthropologists. Marcel Mauss's classic study (1954) pointed out the importance of gift prestations in the creation and maintenance of social relations. For Mauss, the obligation of reciprocity inherent in the gift is its most distinguishable character; countergifts must be both deferred and different in order not to constitute an insult or a refusal. Extending this argument, Bourdieu points out that manipulation of timing makes possible a "misrecognition," the denial of the obligation involved in gift exchange. For Bourdieu, this use of timing and misrecognition is a critical element of the gift (Smart 1993: 395). More recently, critiques of traditional exchange theories in anthropology have noted an exaggerated distinction between gifts and other forms of exchange (Appadurai 1986; Carrier 1994). All forms of exchange may have a calculative dimension (Appadurai 1986: 13); indeed, gift giving can be strategically used to obligate the other (Beidelman 1989; Smart 1993). Thus, as Smart has argued, misrecognition entails not the inability of participants to see through the content of gift exchange but their refusal to acknowledge it: "The form of gift exchange is not dependent on an absence of awareness of the possibility of instrumental use, but rather on the need to exclude explicit acknowledgment of such goals from the performance" (Smart 1993: 395).

It is not my intention here to enter debates on a classic topic in anthropology; rather, my aim is to draw on several insights gained from these discussions in order to explore the nature of social relations and inequalities established through exchange in the second economy under socialism. In Kella, as in many socialist societies, the exchange of favors, goods, and services for scarce resources was heightened during the difficult World War II and postwar years. Some connections established during this time continued to thrive under socialism, but most informal networks in the region originated during the socialist period. Referred to as "Vitamin B" for Beziehungen, connections to people with access to resources were more important than money. "You could earn lots of money," people told me, "but if you didn't have any connections, you were a poor swine."

Anyone with access to scarce resources was thus in a privileged position. Several villagers served as brokers by providing access to resources via networks (Sampson 1986: 47).[15] A good relationship with a high-ranking party member, for example, might ensure a call to the director of the cement factory who could deliver much-needed building materials. Friends, relatives, and acquaintances of the three private trucking businesses in Kella might be guaranteed access to goods from factories throughout the GDR serviced by the truck driver.

Other villagers with direct access to resources became patrons. Three self-employed tradespeople in the village—a plumber, a mason, and a carpenter—were each allocated scarce building materials by the state, which they occasionally sold or traded, sometimes along with their services. Patron-client relations, no longer based on property ownership and draft power, were thus now dependent on access to resources. As one woman explained, "[under socialism] the elites were the people that you needed because of materials—the carpenter, the plumber, the mason. We were dependent on them."

Networks of friendships, acquaintances, and associates were created and maintained through gift exchange, bribes, and barter trade. Gifts, exchanged among kin, friends, or acquaintances, were often used instrumentally. In Kella, the reciprocity inherent in the gift was an essential element of its form. This was not merely recognized by recipients; it was frequently acknowledged openly: "You'll get this back," was a common utterance, often expressed before "Thank you," on receiving a gift. Such statements referred not to a return of the actual gift but to a comparable countergift. In trying to explain this expression to me, still used during the time of my fieldwork, one villager remarked: "It's stuck in us from earlier. It's very hard to accept something without feeling the need to return the favor." Another woman explained:

> Whenever people gave us a present of clothing, food, coffee—especially something from the West—I would always make sure to give them something in return. Even if they told me not to. Otherwise I wouldn't have been able to accept their gift. Sometimes it would take a while, but if they gave us some children's clothes, for example, eventually I would send one of the children down with something special like coffee or chocolate as a thank you.

Gift giving was usually distinguishable from other forms of exchange by the manner in which the gift was offered. Although instrumental goals may have been recognized by both parties, a gift was presented unconditionally, without the explicit expectation of reciprocity. A bribe, on the other had, was understood by both parties as being solely instrumental. Slipping the local grocery clerk an extra twenty marks or a western chocolate bar meant that she would probably set aside a few bananas or green peppers under the counter whenever a shipment of these or other coveted fruits and vegetables came in. A homemade wurst could guarantee being bumped to the top of the waiting list at the driving school. One young man recalled that in order to have his automobile repaired after an accident, he slipped the mechanic 100 West German marks and 520 East German marks. "And it still took six months," he said. "After a while I sent a card that simply said, 'Many greetings from Peter Hartmann.' The mechanic knew what I meant." As Steven Sampson has pointed out, the privilege to buy was more important than money; the price of obtaining access could be more expensive than the product or service itself (1986: 57).

Other exchanges were presented in the form of gifts but understood as bribes: "You always remembered the Trabi repairman's birthday or the electrician's son's first communion [with a gift of money or something scarce]," a once well-connected woman explained, "so they would be there if you needed them." She smiled and continued, "Money actually did help you: it helped maintain the connections! But the connections were most important."

Sometimes bribes could establish an ongoing relationship based on the exchange of mutual favors. If a sales clerk at the local store did not need money or homemade wurst, for example, but knew or discovered that the person paying the bribe installed heating systems, she might agree regularly to set aside particular products in exchange for his services. If she needed some plumbing work done, however, and the heating installer knew a plumber, then access to his connections might be sufficient guarantee that she would set aside some bananas for him. The products of these arrangements were called *Bückwaren* (goods for which the store clerk had to "bend down"). In Kella, the frosted pastel porcelain owned by many households reflected not their plenitude in the GDR, I learned, but exactly the opposite. "Precisely *because* they were *Bückteller* [bend-over plates]—because they were so hard to obtain—is why everyone had to have them!" one villager explained.

While bribes and money transactions were most frequently reserved for people who did not know each other, barter, the most common form of exchange in the second economy, was usually among friends, acquaintances, and distant kin.[16] Trust was of paramount importance. "These kinds of connections were never among strangers," one man told me, "so that you didn't get smeared. Back then you didn't care if friends made money off you. If you needed something, you were just happy they could provide it."

Barter in Kella involved the exchange of favors, goods, and services among networks established and maintained through such transactions. "Everyone scratched each other's back," a young man explained. "I'll repair your furnace if you repair my car. That's how it worked." Villagers trained as masons, carpenters, roof layers, or electricians were able to establish connections by providing their services in exchange for other favors, particularly after renewed nationalizations in the 1970s created a shortage of craftsmen in the GDR (Maier 1997).[17] A mason employed at the local factory plastered with stucco the hospital director's home in the nearby city of Heiligenstadt. In return, his family was given preferential medical treatment when they needed it. Another mason built stairs in a mechanic's home in exchange for prompt service whenever his automobile needed repair. One villager trained as a heating installer and employed as a mechanic in the local factory had a small side business installing heating systems, often using materials allegedly stolen from the factory, in exchange for access to other goods and services, as well as cash. "His wife never wore the same thing twice," a villager told me.

Cash played a role in this unplanned economy, but a minor one. Money could be important, but one needed connections in order to spend it. Building materials and other desirable but scarce items, like porcelain, tiles, or western clothing, could be purchased with cash, but only if one knew where, or through whom, to find them. Villagers with relatives or friends in the West often received packages filled with items that could be traded or sold. Others returned from visits to the West with panty hose, jeans, coats, or electronics to be sold or traded, often after using them first. People joked about the heavy suitcases of retirees, those able to travel freely to the West, full of things requested by the younger generation.

This barter economy significantly altered consumption practices.[18] A *Hamsterkauf* (a hamster, or hoarding, purchase) was the purchase of desirable goods for the purpose of later trade or sale. "If you were shopping and saw something like a bunch of towels," one woman explained, "you said, 'I'll take all of them,' because you could use them later to trade or sell for other things." People often stocked up on such items during trips abroad. Czechoslovakia, for example, was well known as a place to buy tiles and porcelain. As one man recalled, "One time we returned from Czechoslovakia with a Trabi full of tiles. We were able to get rid of all of them." Hoarding was also a regular practice in households. Women would begin stockpiling for holidays or special occasions more than a year in advance; one woman recalled, still with dismay, how a ham she had carefully arranged to obtain had gone bad before it could be used for her son's first-communion celebration.

Gifts, barter, and bribes were thus essential in the circulation of particular goods as well as a means of constructing and maintaining social relations. While I disagree with the overly dichotomous distinctions between "instrumental" and "sentimental" friendships often found in the anthropological literature on patronage (Sampson 1986: 58; see also Loizos 1975; Wolf 1960), I would argue that these practices of consumption and exchange fundamentally transformed the character of social relations and organization under socialism. Not only was there often a strategic element in social life, but social relations themselves became an important form of capital. Connections replaced property as an indicator of social status.[19]

This social capital, like other forms, was expressed in the realm of visible distinctions. A nicely stuccoed house, a flush toilet, a pair of western jeans, a living room with modern furnishings, or a wall unit full of crystal and porcelain neatly arranged on crocheted doilies, represented wealth through access to connections. These goods were not only symbolic markers of objective differences; they were a form of capital in themselves. They could be used for trading or for gifts, and they symbolized the ability to trade for other people. The frequently used term *weiterschenken*, for example, referred to a practice of passing on a gift. Because of the scarcity of most consumer goods, it was not uncommon or considered rude to recycle gifts. We frequently received items carefully packaged and wrapped that we recognized as coming from friends' walls or cupboards. To borrow a phrase from Arjun Appadurai (1986), things in Kella often had long and complex social lives. Consumption became especially productive under this system: in exchange or display, consumption practices were both reflective and constitutive of difference.

The Politics of Consumption

In the context of an economy of shortage, consumption became deeply politicized (Verdery 1996). The socialist "ideology of rational distribution"—conveyed in school propaganda, mass organizations, and factory-brigade "production rituals"—defined the centralized appropriation and distribution of surplus as being in the common interest of all citizens (Konrad and Szelenyi 1979). The fact that the promise of redistribution was rarely met was a critical factor in the "politicization of consumption" under socialism (Verdery 1996: 28). Not only were the dust-free displays of rare crystal or the wearing of western jeans in Kella markers of distinction, they were also political acts. Similarly, a blue Aral gasoline bumper sticker pasted on the inside a cupboard, or a red-and-green adhesive packaging peeled from a West German wurst and stuck underneath the kitchen table, entailed what Verdery has described as the forging "resistant political identities" through consumption (1996: 29). From the shadows of private life, visible only to those in the know, these acts of consuming were also part of a "hidden transcript" (Scott 1990), similar to the languages of shared protestation described in chapter 2, that constituted a critique behind the back of the regime.

Consumption was also politicized under socialism by the regular promises and measure of the regime's success in material terms, reflected especially in the SED's well-known slogan alluding to West German post-war progress and abundance: "Outdistance without catching up." A booklet on local history published in 1966 to honor Kella's 825th anniversary, for example, boasts in typical socialist language of the number of locally owned cars, mopeds, washing machines, television sets, and refrigerators as evidence of the regime's achievements: "This list demonstrates that the residents of our small community have developed into prosperous citizens under socialist conditions" (Müller and others 1966: 32). Such measurements of success and frequent assurances of imminent improvements in the standard of living, combined with constant deprivations in daily life, stimulated consumer desire (Borneman 1991; Verdery 1996). As Verdery writes, "Socialist ideology defined consumption as a 'right.' The system's organization exacerbated consumer desire further by frustrating it and thereby making it the focus of effort, resistance, and discontent" (1996: 28). In the GDR, consumer appetites were further frustrated with the opening in 1974 of Intershops to East Germans, where western goods could be obtained for western currency; this was followed several years later by the introduction of exorbitantly expensive Exquisit shops that sold western goods as well as high-end East German products (made for export) for eastern marks.[20] This combination of deprivation and stimulation, as John Borneman points out and as we shall see in the following chapter, structured much of East Germans' behavior as consumers after the fall of the Wall: "Socialism had trained them to desire. Capitalism stepped in to let them buy" (1991: 81).

In this context, many everyday products became luxury goods. Defined by Appadurai as "goods whose principal use is rhetorical and social, goods that are simply incarnated signs" (1986: 38), luxury goods in Kella included all things western as well as other scarce commodities.[21] As one woman with a closet full of clothes from western relatives explained, "That's where the boundary was drawn. Not in terms of who earned the most, but who had connections in the West and wore western clothing. Kids in eastern clothes were made fun of at school."

The tremendous symbolic value of such commodities was demonstrated in their display. Kitchens were decorated with neatly arranged packages of coffee and cocoa; bathrooms were adorned with evenly-spaced, unopened boxes of western soap and hair products.[22] Deodorant and shampoo from the West were reserved only for special occasions: their display value was their most important attribute. Like luxury goods, such seemingly simple commodities were capable of signifying "fairly complex social messages" (Appadurai 1986: 38), including the successful pursuit of wealth, power, and social distinction through exchange. In describing kula exchange in Gawa, for example, Nancy Munn writes, "Although men appear to be agents in defining shell value, without shells, men cannot define their own value; in this respect shells and men are reciprocally agents of each other's value definition" (1983: 283). While it may be pushing the boundaries of good anthropological taste to equate kula exchange with the circulation of commodities under socialism in Kella, the notion of reciprocal definition between objects and people is applicable here. "We are little people," Emma Hauser assured us the first time we visited her home, "we don't have any carpets."

Those who did have carpets—or other valuables—were often the objects of much envy within a community whose isolation under socialism tended to exaggerate certain qualities of village life. Envy, in a sense, might be viewed as a form of symbolic capital here: who was envied, and why, was—and remains—an important category of social classification. In describing who in the village she thought was privileged under socialism, one woman explained: "Now, Ulrike Braun, she was often envied. She always seemed to have nice things from the West. I remember once there was lots of discussion in the village about an anorak she had. She was envied because of that jacket."

Another form of symbolic capital, a family's honor or reputation, was also an important category of social classification under socialism (and remains so today). One indicator of this status, both under socialism as well as since the Wende, is the election of two church advisory boards. Every four years members of the congregation elect fifteen people to each committee. The parish council, whose members include both men and women, is responsible for community social service: care for the sick and elderly, an annual advent celebration for retirees, and birthday visits to villagers living alone or over the age of eighty. Members of this council tend to be regarded as among the most pious in the community. The all-male church board of directors, on the other hand, deals with matters pertaining to church administration: building upkeep and repairs, finances, and the like. Members of this council tend to be highly respected members of the community, including several of the self-employed tradespeople who have allegedly sometimes used their position for financial gain. The carpenter on the board of directors might be called on to do the altar renovations, for example, or the plumber might be engaged to repair the pipes in the priest's home. Under socialism, of course, the church needed these tradespeople and their access to materials as much or more than the tradespeople needed the work. Being contracted to do a job for the church, however, also placed one in line for state-allotted materials, which could always be useful. As with many group memberships, therefore, belonging to one of these councils, particularly the board of directors, was an effective means of establishing and maintaining connections during the socialist period.

Symbolic capital could thus generate other forms of capital, and vice versa. Although this is not unique to socialism, it took on different forms and meanings under this system. When a villager's status was enhanced through the prestige of connections and the symbolic display of this wealth, his chances of being elected to a church council increased, thereby expanding as well the potential for accumulating additional capital. On the other hand, a villager's reputation could translate into a

living room full of prestigious gifts for a twenty-fifth wedding anniversary or the ability to recruit members easily for an evening work
brigade.[23] This is not to say that all forms of capital were convertible
or overlapped; my point is simply that the volume and composition of
capital is what largely determined a person's position in the social field
of the village.

In the following section, I seek to illuminate the village as a social field
by focusing on a few individuals and families whose stories illustrate
various aspects of social differentiation and organization under socialism. Their situations depict the transformation from a largely property-
based system of inequality to new strategies of social distinction, as well
as how new means of differentiation were interpreted, negotiated, and
constructed in everyday practice.

"J. R.," "Alexis," and Other Notables

Most village nicknames in Kella tend to stem from some identifying characteristic: a spatial marker like "Corner Elizabeth" (*Ecken
Elizabeth*) for a woman who lives on a corner; a family hobby like "Hare
Siegfried" (*Hasen Siegfried*) for a man whose ancestors once raised rabbits; or an unusual family name like "Heckmanns Joseph" (*Heckmanns
Jupp*) for a villager whose great-grandmother married someone named
Heckmann and the name has stuck with the family despite its current
more common last name. Other nicknames reflect a sense of humor,
while some can be undeniably cruel.

One nickname encompassing both these characteristics belongs to
"J. R." His son was called "Bobby" after J. R.'s brother in the show, and occasionally women in the family were also referred to with *Dallas* names.
Like other nicknames, they were used only in referring to these particular individuals, not in addressing them; unlike other nicknames, however, they were not used in the "Dallas Family's" presence. This rule was
once broken during a traditional carnival skit in which a story or joke is
told about each of the eleven men who make up the Fasching planning
committee. When it came to "J. R.'s" turn, the commentator was silent.
Just as the audience was uneasily beginning to wonder whether a mis-
take had been made, a faint hum of the *Dallas* theme music could be

heard coming softly from the stage. As the band grew louder, people recognized the tune and burst into laughter. "J. R." was furious.

When I asked people what the Müller family had done to deserve such ridicule, most villagers would explain that "all they cared about was money." "J. R.," or Gregor Müller, stems from one of the few Großbauern families who did not leave Kella in 1952, and his financial success under socialism was due to his ability to adapt to new strategies of social differentiation. Unlike several of the other former Großbauern, who went to work in factories or the LPG and whose earnings and other holdings dropped to those of most other villagers, Gregor worked hard to establish different kinds of connections throughout the GDR.[24] He joined the village council, and although he was never a member of the Communist Party, he was in good standing with village party members. At the toy factory in neighboring Pfaffschwende, he headed the tool-making division, the largest in the factory, and was able to establish connections with other factory and division managers throughout the country.

Most of his wealth, however, was earned as a middleman between the state and villagers during the fruit harvest. Kella's unique lime soil made it one of the only villages in the region that could produce substantial amounts of marketable cherries and apples. For centuries a source of supplemental income for villagers, the larger orchards were destroyed in order to clear space for the expansive LPG fields. Many gardens remained, however, and people were permitted to retain ownership and/or lease from the LPG small (half a hectare) household garden plots for their own use. Many of these plots, particularly those with fruit trees, produced not only food for villager's own consumption but substantial supplemental income as well. In a good year, many villagers earned an extra 800 to 2,000 marks—twice an individual's monthly income—through fruit sales. During the fruit harvest, Gregor collected and purchased the harvested fruit from other villagers, which he then sold to the state for a commission. "It was hard work for him," one woman recalled, "and although people resented him for it, they never really stopped to think how hard it would have been for them to get rid of their fruit if he hadn't done it for them."

"J. R.'s" money and connections enabled him to own one of the largest, most modernized homes in the village. Situated among the other large farmhouses of the former Großbauern, his house stood out as the "whitest" house on the street—an unusual feature in the GDR and Kella, where most of the houses were "unfinished" owing to the difficulty in obtaining plaster materials and, especially, white paint. The family owned two automobiles, and as one woman told me, "They were able to take trips abroad that we could only dream of." These trips, like other luxuries, were made possible not only by Gregor's money but also by the connections necessary in order to spend it.

Another, though more mean-spirited, village nickname also derived from an American television show. One of the best-connected people in Kella, "Alexis," or Maria Botling, was named after the manipulative, greedy, and promiscuous Joan Collins character in *Dynasty* because of her wealth and, according to malicious village gossip, her lifestyle. As one woman explained, "You could say that back then [in GDR times] that Maria stood at the top in the village. First of all, she earned lots of money. Second, as the head bookkeeper for the factory, she traveled extensively and was able to build up connections that way. When she saw something she wanted, she could get it. She was especially able to get things abroad, like porcelain or tiles from Czechoslovakia." Maria's immaculate home was full of the most modern furnishings and decorations; her cupboards overflowed with porcelain and crystal pieces collected during years of travel and bargaining. Another woman recalled: "She went all over the place and was able to get things that no one else could. Like that super furniture—no one else could get that." More than any other villager, her home and possessions reflected her wealth in connections and ability to trade for and with others—which, according to many villagers, she did.

Maria's obsession with material goods may have its origins in an impoverished childhood and difficult young adulthood. Her father was killed in World War II when Maria was a small child, and her mother, like other war widows, received no compensation from the socialist state. The family had never belonged to the local elite; their house, built in the early 1920s, was situated on the periphery of the village. As soon as she was old enough, Maria went to work long hours in the fields to earn extra income for her mother and younger sister. After she was married and working as an accountant, she lost two of her three children in infancy to a rare degenerative illness. Fifteen years later, Maria was widowed when her husband died suddenly of a stroke at the age of forty-three. I often had the sense that her material possessions were the only sense of stability and comfort she was able to obtain in her turbulent life.

Two years before the Wall fell, Maria made the ultimate social and economic connection: she married a wealthy westerner and moved to West Germany. Her husband, a cantankerous spice salesman who rarely keeps his opinions about "lazy Ossis" to himself, has been derisively, but with typical local humor, nicknamed "The Pepper Prince" (*der Pfefferprinz*). The couple owns a large home in Eschwege, complete with a sauna, a tanning booth, and a three-car garage. His Porsche turned heads whenever the couple visited Kella, and her more modest Audi was instantly recognized by all. The first time I visited Maria in her Eschwege home, she gave me a tour of the house and then, as if to explain, or even apologize for, her new affluence, remarked, "You know, I served my time in Kella."

Just down the street from Maria's old house in Kella live Hans and Barbara Becker. Hans is one of the few villagers to be graced with two nicknames (although neither is from an American television show): one alludes to an old, unusual family name in his heritage, while the other, "The Heavy One" (*der Schwere*), affectionately alludes to his burly physical build. The Beckers' story illustrates the interplay and convergence of symbolic, social, and economic capital in the social field of the village. Neither Hans nor Barbara stems from one of Kella's elite families. Their capital is largely symbolic: as members of the church board of directors (Hans) and the parish council (Barbara), they are generally regarded as some of the most pious and "good" people in the village. Despite a daily schedule that begins at 5 A.M. and usually ends around midnight, Barbara attends church daily and is one of the priest's most devoted assistants. She is always available to tend the sick and elderly, and her exquisite pastries are a feature of nearly every communion or wedding celebration in Kella. She is commonly viewed—and, to some extent, views herself—as a self-sacrificing nurturer. Ever since her elderly mother fell ill with an unusually aggressive form of senility, for example, Barbara has tended to her lovingly and patiently despite the scratches and frequent verbal abuse she receives from her. She is regarded, with good reason, as one of the most generous and thoughtful members of the community. One day when the electricity was cut off on our street, Barbara appeared at noon on our doorstep with a warm meal cooked over a gas stove in her garage.

Hans is similarly involved in community and congregational activities: he has been a leader in numerous church-related renovation projects, is a member of the carnival club's planning committee, and may often be found enjoying a beer with other village men (although he does not belong to the crowd that regularly frequents the village pub). They are revered not only for their individual activities and personalities but also because they represent an ideal of a village couple in which domestic and social duties are divided along traditional gender lines. Because of this status, their rebellious children have often been granted more leeway in village gossip than are children from less reputable families.

During the socialist period, this form of symbolic capital came to be reflected in other forms of capital as well. Because of their popularity and honorable reputation, Hans was readily able to assemble a private brigade of village men trained as masons to do moonlighting work on homes in the area. This moonlighting produced not only substantial supplemental income but also established important connections throughout the region. Employing his brigade and materials acquired through connections, Hans was able to maintain one of the whitest, most modern house facades in Kella—an important marker of wealth and good character (hard work) within the village as well as a feature highly valued and rewarded by the state.[25] In fact, Hans was the recipient of a GDR state award for having the most beautiful house.

Barbara's activities were also rewarded with the repayment of debts incurred through her material and spiritual gifts.[26] While it would be wrong and invidious for the villagers—or, indeed, for me—to suggest that her actions were motivated by the expectation of reciprocity or that she utilized her symbolic resources for economic gain, a certain amount of remuneration was the practical consequence of her accumulated symbolic capital. For the Beckers' twenty-fifth wedding anniversary, for example, they were lavished with an exorbitant amount of gifts, reportedly far more than the usual amount for such an occasion. While they could never be counted among the village elite—their clothing and home decor were quite modest—their symbolic capital of reputation, along with the other forms of capital it generated, nevertheless placed them in the upper echelons of the village social field.

My final story involves Edgar Koch, a master craftsman and self-employed mason. Like other independent craftsmen, Edgar was allotted building materials by the state. During the socialist period, his services as a mason and his access to scarce resources and numerous connections throughout the region could have placed him, like the other self-employed craftsmen, among the village elite. But when villagers recite the names of elite families, his is never among them. People often stress his friendly and generous character ("He'd give you the shirt off his back") and recall how he was willing to lend villagers materials and equipment; at the same time, however, they commonly note that he never did anything with his various forms of capital.

Edgar's case illustrates the importance of display and conspicuous consumption in the organization and structuring of village inequalities. His house, among the shabbiest in the village, was given a white stucco finish only when his son, Joachim, long ashamed of his family's dilapidated home, completed the job himself after the Wende. "Since my father was a master mason, we should have had one of the nicest homes in the village," he once told me, "but he was too busy with other things." A few months after refinishing the exterior of the house, Joachim felt he was being treated differently, as if his own social standing in the village had improved. To illustrate, he told me about a recent interaction with a former classmate's parents: "I saw Annette's parents the other day. They are much nicer to me now. They had a nice, big, timbered house, whereas we lived in a disintegrating hut. Somehow I had the feeling [back then] that I wasn't good enough for her. Now I have done something and also have a nice house, and it's almost as if they're saying, 'Now you could marry our daughter!'" Although neither Joachim's nor his father's social or economic capital had been altered through the remodeling of their house, their symbolic capital—and particularly Joachim's—had increased. Joachim's gesture will probably not significantly alter the family's standing within the village hierarchy, but it may have affected his own. By refinishing the house, Joachim displayed virtues long appreciated in village life: initiative, effort, hard work, responsiveness to his neighbors' values, and a certain degree of social malleability (unlike his father). In Kella, as elsewhere, the social value attributed to these traits transcends different regimes and are especially appreciated by potential in-laws, as Joachim's own example revealed.

Joachim's actions and the resulting display carried a different meaning, however, from what it would have under socialism because the remodeling project was undertaken after the Wende, when building materials had become readily available and less expensive. Instead of symbolizing access to scarce resources and connections, therefore, the Kochs' new house facade became one of dozens of home renovations completed by villagers as part of an urgent Nachholungsbedarf after the Wende. We now turn to these emergent strategies and categories of distinction.

SOCIAL DIFFERENTIATION AND REORGANIZATION IN A MARKET ECONOMY OF STRUCTURAL UNEMPLOYMENT

The second economy, along with many of its elaborate networks that had been cultivated and maintained under forty years of socialism, largely disappeared, almost overnight, with the fall of the Wall. This entailed the erosion of not only many social contacts and the concomitant sense of community these networks had engendered but also the social capital of connections that had been so important under socialism.

Former elites like the independent craftsmen are now scrambling for business, much to the delight of many villagers who used to be at their mercy under socialism, and many have had to give up their small businesses for wage labor in the West. Tragically, the failure of one local business appears to have been a factor in a recent (1997) suicide of a man in his mid-forties. Postsocialism in Kella has been a transitional period somewhat reminiscent of the expropriation and collectivization of the 1950s, when the foundations of the village elite were essentially pulled out from under them. The influx of a market economy has brought with it a return to economic forms of capital as a primary means of social distinction, as well as new practices and meanings of consumption.

My intent in this final section is not to provide a definitive account or argument about the transformation of village social organization and hierarchies under a capitalist market economy, for that would be premature. Instead, I suggest how this transition has produced new categories and strategies of social distinction, and I explore how these emergent forms are being negotiated, assimilated, and contested in everyday life.

During my fieldwork I witnessed how the reappropriation of products according to a cultural order shaped by an economy of shortages gave way to new cultural meanings of these same commodities in a market economy. I noticed, for example, that western soaps and shampoos left the domestic display shelf as they were transformed into items for everyday use. I observed how representations of formerly scarce and coveted western products—Chiquita Banana stickers on the front of television sets, Tschibo coffee stickers on automobiles, Aral bumper stickers on the inside of a cupboard—lost their initial meaning as novel display objects and were gradually peeled off. Now available to all, these everyday western products, as well as representations of them, ceased to be status markers and thus were no longer displayed.

This is not to say that consumption ceased to be definitive and constitutive of difference. Indeed, as income disparities widen within the village, consumption remains an important marker of status. However, rather than signifying indirect access to consumption through access to connections and/or the ability to trade for others—including the objects themselves as capital for trade—consumption in a market economy signifies a return to the economic capital of income, other monetary resources, and direct consumption. It is the resources and their availability that have changed—and, concomitantly, the meanings and practices of consumption.

One of the major resources that has changed, of course, is the acquisitive power—indeed social meanings—of money. "Being able to afford" something has become a more frequently used phrase and category of distinction. A new automobile, heating system, furniture, kitchen appliances, clothing, or home renovations now represent disposable income rather than access to scarce resources or connections. After a promotional gathering sponsored by a dubious West German health-products firm in which several villagers purchased the extravagantly priced products (500 marks for a twenty-one-day supply of nutritional supplements), one woman explained to me, "That's the way it is now in the village. One person buys it, and people think 'if they can afford it then we can afford it, too.'"

Another woman related a similar story: "I was shopping in Heiligenstadt the other day and overheard a woman say to her daughter: 'No, we can't get that. We can't afford that.' You never would have heard that before [in GDR times]." The transition to a market economy in which "money rules," as many say, has brought with it new frustrations. A former janitor turned salesman explained to me: "Earlier [in the GDR] we lived simply. It wasn't always nice, we didn't have much, but it was enough. . . . Now we can have everything but nobody has the money, and that's driving people crazy."

Employment, particularly in the West where wages are higher (although in 1992 still 20 to 30 percent lower than those of West German coworkers), thus became a new category of differentiation in a society where full employment used to be the norm. Much time at social gatherings was spent sorting out who in the village had found work, and where.[27] The importance of employment was reflected in frequent responses to greetings, as one woman explained: "You can tell how important work is when people ask you how you are. If you say 'good,' then they respond, 'then you must have work.'"

Time became an important marker as well. As Borneman has pointed out, German re-unification entailed a "reordering of spatial and temporal categories" on both sides of the former border (1993: 41). In the context of what Borneman has identified as an experience of accelerated time in the former GDR after the fall of the Wall (1991, 1993), "having time" in Kella revealed one's lack of employment—which is one of the reasons people were careful not to be seen taking a midday stroll or relaxing in the garden on a warm spring afternoon. There were instances when people were outright defensive about "having time," as the following story related to me by an unemployed young woman illustrates: "I was down at Konsum this morning and ran into a woman I used to work with who is also unemployed now. When it came time to pay, I said, 'Go ahead, we both have time.' And she snapped back: 'Maybe you enjoy being unemployed, but I don't!'" Paid employment was thus valued for both its monetary rewards and its social and personal merits, reflecting the importance of a worker identity that had been inculcated during forty years of socialist rule.[28] Income disparities and the resulting inequalities, however, became the real outcome of differences in employment status.

New categories of distinction and lines of division emerged through the negotiation of these growing discrepancies. "Sure, there used to be differences before," one man told me, "but now the differences are getting bigger. It's not the same anymore when some people earn so much more than others." In a comment that echoed similar sentiments voiced by other villagers, another man said, "When one of us has work and the other doesn't, we can't sit together at the same table anymore. It just isn't fun now to be together, to sit next to somebody who's unemployed."

This notion of "being able to sit together" is part of an increasing nostalgia and romanticizing of community and "togetherness" under socialism. Characteristic of what Michael Herzfeld has called "structural nostalgia" (1997: 109), one of the most frequently voiced laments throughout my fieldwork involved the loss of community. "The togetherness, it's not what it used to be. I miss that," one man told me. Or as Hans Becker explained, "We used to all sit in the same shit. But now when one of us earns nineteen marks and the other only eight marks an hour, there are problems."

The loss of community is attributed to many changes since the fall of the Wall, especially the increasing income differences and resulting envy. "Envy has gotten really bad," one young woman commented. "It's all my parents talk about." Another woman explained, "Envy is really bad now. All the couples in our clique had about the same: they earned the same, they had the same furniture, etc. Now I feel as if people resent us because we're doing so well." And in a similar comment, a man from the same circle of friends told me after one couple from the group bought a new automobile: "I never thought it would happen to our clique. I've watched it happen to others. Nobody gets together any more. But I didn't think it would happen to us. But look, it has." The disappearance of the numerous networks and connections formed under socialism has also contributed to a sense of a decline in community.

Not only are income differences and employment status perceived as destructive forces; products themselves are viewed this way as well. Such products especially include items highly visible to the rest of the community (and among the first western purchases of East Germans): automobiles, clothing, and exterior home renovations. They also include less public things like appliances, electronics, and furniture, visible only to those who enter the private space of the home but known to others through local gossip. "We have to learn now to draw our own boundaries," one woman commented to a group of friends. "These products are driving us apart." Ironically, therefore, some of the very products that helped sustain elaborate networks of friends and contacts under socialism are seen to be "driving us apart" in the new market economy.

As easterners struggled to acquire a certain cultural fluency in western consumption, a notion I shall discuss at length in the next chapter, another category of distinction, already familiar in the West, began to emerge: the culturally and market-constructed associations between brand names or stores and their particular positioning in class or status hierarchies. When the Wall fell, all things western seemed equally good because of the symbolic value of western goods under socialism. Anything purchased in the West had to be better because it was not from the East. People would return from a first visit to West Germany with inexpensive cassette players or gold-plated bracelets, for example, only to have them break or tarnish weeks later. Discount stores like Aldi or Lidl were so packed with East Germans that in border regions, their very names became synonymous with Ossis. Since all products had been uniformly priced by the state under socialist rule, people puzzled over why butter cost more at Edeka than at Aldi and why the imitation Birkenstock sandals were half the price of the brand name.

Such topics dominated conversation, particularly during the first two years after the Wende. Women would talk for hours at a dinner party about the quality and prices of everything from coffee to mattresses.

Children could recite the price of a loaf of bread from three different bakeries. These discussions and collective negotiations of new cultural practices of consumption became part of a bonding ritual that replaced the "them" of the state with the foreignness of a market economy, a notion that "we" have to figure out how "they" work in order not to be taken advantage of. Yet this ritual could also ultimately be divisive: in discussing the cost and quality of certain products, one may also reveal—even boast—that one can afford them. "I've learned that it's worth it to spend the extra money on good shoes. I recently had to spend 100 marks on a pair of shoes for Kerstin [her daughter]," one woman told her group of friends.

As people began to acquire a cultural fluency in consumption ("learning where to shop," as one upwardly mobile young woman put it), they also began to uncover the cultural meanings of certain consumption practices. Several villagers with good jobs in the West abandoned Aldi for the more prestigious grocery stores frequented primarily by western Germans. Others began to pay careful attention to brand names of electronics, appliances, and clothes.

More than a year into my fieldwork, I witnessed an exchange between two women, Marianne and Ilse, over their children's clothing that brought this to my attention. Marianne had taken the children shopping and bought them each a pair of footless tights as "leggings." When Ilse's daughter, Marika, happily showed them to her mother, Ilse was upset, not only because she had told Marika to wait until her birthday for a pair but also because they had been purchased at Woolworth and, she inferred, were a cheap imitation of "real leggings." After Ilse had left, Marianne, who had bought herself a pair as well, commented as both a reassurance to herself and as a question to me, a westerner assumed to be practiced in the art of consumption: "It doesn't always have to be the best—does it?" A few weeks later, Ilse bought her daughter a pair of more expensive leggings from a more prestigious department store, and Marianne's daughter lamented to her mother, "Now Marika has a pair of *real* leggings." A year ago, I thought to myself, Ilse would have been thrilled with the leggings from Woolworth; when I first arrived in Kella, she frequently shopped there. The incident reflected how much her thinking and practice in relation to consumption and differentiation had changed.

Taste, an important manner in which consumption expresses distinction (Bourdieu 1984), thus began to enter into the construction, experience, and expression of difference in Kella. This field of play is largely new here: under socialism, when commodities and clothing were either uniform or scarce, people took whatever they could find. Most villagers' taste in clothing, for example, was determined by the hand-me-downs sent by western relatives. "I used to wear that dress every day," one woman recalled, pointing to an old photograph of herself, "just because it was from the West. Now, of course, I know they just sent us the things they didn't want any more." While people creatively used their limited options to shape different styles and expressions of distinction under socialism, the range of possibilities—and the meanings of those possibilities—have changed.

CONCLUSION

While it is too early to ascertain whether or how a new group of village elites will assert itself, new and emergent categories of differentiation—most associated with a consumer market economy—are becoming visible. The return to landed property as a means of differentiation has not been a factor, at least not yet.[29] Like other areas of social life, particularly in this moment of historical transition, social organization and differentiation are in a state of intense flux. It will likely take many more years for village hierarchies to sort themselves out in a market economy.

Nevertheless, some conclusions may be drawn about the changing nature of the village as a social field. Although an individual's position within this field remains highly relational, both to those in other fields (like religion or gender) and to others within the same field, many bases for that position have been transformed as the values of different forms of capital have changed. Under socialism, the interactions (or lack of them) between the carpenter, Thomas Baumann, and the now deceased villager who was described by Michael as having been "nothing" due to his lack of connections—as well as other villagers' consciousness of such relationships—were part of a process through which objective structures and social distances were internalized and reproduced in everyday practices. Such practices under socialism also included gift giving, bartering, and bribes—practices whose meanings in an economy of shortages have been lost in a market economy of abundance.

Today both the discussion between Marianne and Ilse about Woolworth leggings in Ilse's affluent home and the different behavior generated by this interaction entail practices that are reflective and constitutive of social distinctions—even if temporary ones. While the shift from the social capital of connections under socialism to the acquisitive power of economic capital and the symbolic capital of taste in a market economy may eventually result in the formation of new village hierarchies and status distinctions, the dynamic processes through which these distinctions are internalized, negotiated, reproduced, and transformed in everyday practices transcend the political and economic system of which they are a part. Although different in context and content, both socialist and capitalist societies share not only certain similarities in the structures of these processes but also central elements of their form: consumption as production. We shall return to this theme of productive consumption in the next chapter.

5 | Borderlands

Ossi to Wessi: "We are one people!"

Wessi to Ossi: "So are we."

Post-Wende joke told on both sides of the
former border, especially in western Germany

This popular joke, one of many such witticisms to be circulated nationally and locally after the Wende, poignantly captures the heightened tensions between East and West Germans after re-unification. Drawing on the slogan of the demonstrations in the fall of 1989, "We Are One People," it expresses both the hope of unity and an increasingly common perception of two emergent (and divergent) German identities. It also reflects the asymmetrical nature of inter-German relations: while the Ossi strives to be "one" with his western neighbor, it is the Wessi who is empowered to deny this unity. Germany may be unified into one state, the joke says, but its citizens remain two separate people. The Grenze has had a haunting afterlife.

My focus in this chapter is on the border and the kinds of borderland identities it has engendered. This Grenze, a literal concrete border as well as a symbolic construction whose meaning has changed over time,[1] has created a border region that is both a "privileged site for the articulation of national distinctions" (Sahlins 1989: 271) and a transitional zone where identity can be particularly fluid; it is a place of intense clarity as well as complicated ambiguity. This, I suggest, is the paradox of the borderland.

One of my principal aims in this chapter is to explore the creation of a literal borderland and its relationship to the borderland concept as a symbol of and metaphor for the "transition." I thus explore the development and experience of the border under socialism, noting how, over time, it came to be invested with meaning and memory. I describe events surrounding the opening of the border in 1989, the subsequent invention and maintenance of a cultural boundary between East and West, and the construction, invention, and assertion of new forms of identity. Borderland residents may be Ossis or Wessis; at times they may appear to be both. In examining such contradictory and complex aspects of identity, I explore how people negotiate and manipulate a liminal condition created by the collapse of this significant frame of reference.

FROM BORDER CROSSERS TO SCHUTZSTREIFEN RESIDENTS, 1945–1989

The "Green Border," 1945–1952

Despite the boundary fortifications that were put in place soon after Kella was transferred to Soviet rule in July 1945, the border remained more or less permeable in the immediate postwar period.[2] A single barrier across the road leading to Eschwege, along with a few signposts and sentry boxes, were its only demarcations. Continuing a prewar trend, regional economic ties were directed toward Hesse as villagers who were unable to secure employment at home were forced by economic necessity to seek work elsewhere. Permits to cross the border enabled locals employed or with arable land in the West to travel back and forth relatively freely. Those without passes were often able to bribe Soviet border troops or crossed the boundary illegally through the surrounding hills. One woman would place a pillow in the window facing west as a signal to her son, who worked and lived in Eschwege, that it was unsafe to return home for a visit that Sunday. Residents devised different "disguises" to avoid calling attention to themselves as they headed in the direction of the border: one might carry a saw or an ax, for example, as if heading to the hills to collect firewood. Punishment if caught usually meant spending the night in the cellar of the Soviet commander's "station." In Kella this was the house closest to the border, where the Soviet troops stayed during their occupation of the village until 1949; its basement walls are still covered with the names and graffiti of apprehended border crossers. While mild compared to the life-threatening consequences of a border crossing after 1961, an undercurrent of anxiety during this period was an important component of the fear and danger associated with the border.

The following story reflects this perception, for it captures the impact of the border on everyday life during the transitional period of Soviet occupation. Told to me by Gretel Schmidt, who was in her late teens at the time, it is typical of many villagers' recollections of the early years of the border.

> While the Russians were here, it was easier [to cross the border]. Sometimes it was better to go through the valley, sometimes over the hills. It all depended. But we were always afraid. . . .
>
> I remember how my sister [who worked in Eschwege] was so homesick and wanted to come home [for the weekend]. We used to put on plays in the [public] hall here—my mother was the manager—and my sister wanted to come. While we were having our dress rehearsal a child came into the hall behind the stage and said to my mother: "Aunt Marie, the Russians have Annie!"
>
> My mother dropped everything and went to see the commander. My sister, she wasn't so afraid. She wasn't yet familiar with the facts of life. . . . My mother came in, and the commander said—he had a lot of nerve—[he would let her out] "for a bottle of Schnapps." We didn't have anything, but my mother borrowed the money—a bottle of Schnapps cost 100 marks back then—and offered it to him so she could buy my sister's freedom. But he said, "No."
>
> As my mother left she saw the cook—he was a soldier—and he said, "Poor Fräulein. Commander devil." He was a good guy, and my mother said, "Two bottles of Schnapps?" He said, "Maybe."

Mother went to get two more bottles of Schnapps from the restaurant while the cook kept the commander occupied. She put them on the kitchen table, sneaked in, and opened the basement door and yelled, "Come on, Annie!"

They ran home, and mother yelled, "Close all the doors! I stole Annie from the cellar!" I gave my sister my dress—I remember it as if it was yesterday—I was wearing a blue checkered dress. Suddenly they were knocking on our door—like thunder! My sister was so scared she ran into the closest room. My brother was there, too, and he told her to jump out the window! And it was pretty far up, that window. So she jumped out the window—and landed right in front of people who were going the see the play! She hid behind the stage in the hall.

[They questioned us]—I was crying from fear—and then went to look for my sister in the hall. It was packed with people. But it couldn't start until we arrived. My mother said to my brother: "Go get her and bring her over [the border]. The air is clear now because they're all down here [in the village]." So my brother fetched her and brought her back to Eschwege that night [over the hills]. . . . That must have been in the winter of 1947.

Border crossers included not only locals employed in the West but also refugees and evacuees from the Sudeten region and Silesia, among other areas. Villagers who were able to navigate the hilly terrain and/or negotiate with Soviet border guards served as guides for these illegal border crossings, often for a hefty fee. Other locals smuggled goods across the border; the sale of produce, eggs, and homemade wurst in the West was a way of earning a little extra income in difficult economic times. Stories of thieves and rapists lurking in the woods, which were confirmed by the arrest of one sex offender in a neighboring western village who had posed as a border guide, added to the sense of the border as a place of danger and fear.

As the cold war intensified and its front line became increasingly demarcated, the inter-German border grew less permeable. With the founding of the two separate German states in 1949, Soviet border troops yielded their authority to the newly formed East German People's Police. According to older villagers, the introduction of German efficiency (or "Prussian thoroughness") made it much more difficult to cross the border illegally.[3] Many villagers employed in West Germany chose to stay there permanently, leaving behind close friends, family, and, in a few instances, even young children. Between 1945 and 1952 Kella lost one-quarter of its population.[4] Others returned only on weekends under the cover of darkness after border police officers had abandoned their posts for the night. Parents began sending their children to smuggle goods or people over the border because children were not punished if caught. Many villagers' childhood memories are thus full of border tales: of crouching behind trees in the snow to avoid being seen by passing patrols, of feigning illness to support a story about having to get to a hospital in Eschwege, of whispering repeated Hail Marys to ease their fear of the dark woods. One woman, assigned the routine task of delivering belongings to relatives at the border, recalled defecating in her pants when she realized that a Soviet army officer might catch her with a baby carriage full of bedding.

The Border Becomes Impermeable, 1952–1961

When the border became largely impermeable in 1952, many villagers say they were relieved. "As bad as it was," one woman recalled, "people said, 'At least it means that it's finally over with this [back and forth].' While it was still open there was always the temptation, but once it was closed, no one could go anymore."

The year 1952 is indelibly etched into villagers' memories, even those not old enough to have experienced it. Not only was it the year in which two families were deported and three families fled from Kella, as we saw in chapter 2; it was also a turning point in the fortification of the border. On the same day that West Germany joined the European Defense Community (May 26, 1952), the GDR Council of Ministries issued an order for the "Regulation of Measures on the Demarcation Line between the German Democratic Republic and the Western Occupied Zones of Germany" (Hartmann and Künsting 1990: 369). This state directive created the five-kilometer-deep Sperrgebiet zone as well as the highly restricted 500-meter Schutzstreifen. It invalidated all permits to cross the border and resulted in the evacuation of thousands of border residents during May and June of that year. The demarcation of the increasingly fortified border began that summer with the creation of a ten-meter-wide "control strip" along the boundary line; it was cleared of all vegetation and filled with carefully groomed sand. Shortly thereafter, a barbed-wire fence was installed along the entire length of the inter-German border.

In Kella, as in other border villages, men from the community were employed in a work brigade to assist in the construction of the control strip. One man from the village recalled: "The tree stumps were blown up, and there wasn't enough soil left over so they had to carry dirt up [the hill] in baskets. They also had to bring all sorts of gardening tools with them. The ten-meter strip was made into something like cultivated garden soil—so that you could see every footprint, every impression. And it was patrolled regularly . . . usually by three [officers]."

Despite the tightening of control, there were still isolated incidents of border crossings. In the memories of most villagers, however, 1952 marks the date the border became impermeable. "After '52, nobody went [back and forth] anymore," many older villagers told me. The growing impermeability of the border encouraged several village residents who had been employed and living in the West to return permanently to Kella in order to avoid being cut off from Heimat and family indefinitely. Records in the village archives indicate that more than twenty-five people had returned to Kella by 1961. "These were people who came from here," one man explained, "who said [to themselves], 'Go home. Mother and father have property that I'm supposed to inherit.' . . . An Eichsfelder is very attached to his Heimat."

By the time the Berlin Wall went up in August 1961, the fortification of the inter-German border was nearly complete. In 1957, the passport law of the GDR was changed to characterize any illegal border crossing as "Republikflucht," punishable by imprisonment. A year later, the state instituted Grenzhelfer, a means by which civilians could assist in boundary maintenance and patrol. Border police were armed with assault guns and tank gunners by 1958. In the years before the building of the Berlin Wall, there were an estimated eleven to fifteen fatalities on the inter-German border.[5]

After the erection of the Berlin Wall, the state put up an additional border fence at the foot of the hills surrounding Kella. A guard tower was built and guard dog runs installed to assist in surveillance. Because of its hilly terrain and the "stability" of its population (determined by the relatively low number of attempted and successful Republikfluchten), the village managed to avoid the planting of trip-wires and land mines that fortified much of the inter-German border. Kella also escaped a second wave of Schutzstreifen evacuations in 1961, although its residents were aware of deportations from neighboring villages. Furthermore, the intensification of controls along the border was accompanied by a tightening of control in other spheres of daily life: curfew ordinances, control checkpoints, and the proliferation of mass political organizations were evidence of growing state power and presence.

In many respects, the years between 1952 and 1961 were a transitional period in which the reality and materiality of the border became a part of everyday life. Except for those who departed or returned permanently, border crossings ceased. By 1961 the barbed-wire fence at the base of the woods signified to residents of this Schutzstreifengemeinde not only the sharp division of Germany into two separate states but also, I was often told, that Kella had become the place "where the world ended."

Boundary Maintenance and Normalization, 1961–1989

In the next decades leading up to the fall of the Wall, the Grenze and its fortifications became increasingly intensified and normalized. Two new rows of iron fencing and a concrete road for army jeep patrols were added in the mid-1970s; the more eastern of the two fences, in many places located within yards of villagers' homes or gardens, was armed with an optical and acoustic alarm system as well as multiple rows of barbed wire. A sand strip, carefully groomed and regularly patrolled by border guards as well as Grenzhelfer, lay directly in front of this alarm fence on its eastern side (Figure 12). Villagers grew accustomed to the flashing lights and sirens usually set off by rabbits, cats, or wild animals until the army cut holes at the base of this alarm fence to prevent small animals from setting off the alarm. The second fence, which ran along the base of the wooded hills rising west and southwest of the village, was three meters high and was topped with barbed wire (Figure 13). The immediate area around this fence was cleared of all vegetation, often with toxic exfoliants, while the no-man's-land between the fences was maintained by the collective farm as a grazing pasture. Only

Figure 12.   The alarm fence in Kella, with the sand strip, 1989. Behind it is one of the Stations of the Cross leading to the chapel. (Photograph courtesy of Gisela Lange)

LPG employees with spouses and children in Kella (who were thus considered at low risk to attempt an escape) were permitted into this area.

In order to hinder escapes by citizens outside the Sperrgebiet, all road signs directing traffic to Kella were removed. "Pointing in the direction of Kella was essentially telling people where the border was," a villager explained, "and the state didn't want that." Kella was no longer featured on most East German maps for the same reason; publishers often conveniently placed the map's symbols key or alphabetical listing in the spot corresponding to Sperrgebiet villages. Thus Kella was, in the words of many locals, "on the arse of the world."

In GDR state rhetoric, the border was a "protective shield against the western imperialists," or a division between "workers and imperialists." The state justified the institution and maintenance of the Sperrgebiet and Schutzstreifen by claiming that the borderland was dangerously close to the enemy. As one man recalled, "We were simply told that because we

Figure 13. Kella as seen from the western side of the border through the three-meter-high fence, 1991. (Photograph by the author)

were here in the immediate proximity of the enemy, imperialism, we needed to have peace and order here. That one needed exact information about who is moving about here and where." He added, with emphasis, "but the barbs were pointed at us, not toward the other side." The direction of the fence's barbed wire was often pointed out to me as evidence of the state's attempts to deceive its citizens; it also suggested a certain degree of the state's own self-deception. "We all knew they just wanted to keep people from escaping," one older woman explained.

Nevertheless, the state was often successful in inculcating its border ideology into the younger generation. As one woman in her late twenties, Anna Biermann, recalled:

> For me, the Wall was built between the workers, who had all been in concentration camps, who wanted their freedom, the little people, and the big ones on the other side . . . capitalists, Nazis. That's how I understood it back then. That's how it was explained to us in geography or his-

tory. . . . By the time I was eighteen or nineteen, though, I didn't really see it that way any more. By that time I realized people there [in the West] were just people too.

The children of the villagers whose childhood memories are full of border crossings thus grew up with a different view of the Grenze. Once, when the wind carried sounds of drums and fanfare across the border from the western side, for example, some children assumed it meant war. Because of incessant antiwestern propaganda in the GDR, an apparent West German military exercise that was visible from Kella in the mid-1970s was terrifying to many villagers, especially children. "The entire village was in a panic," Anna remembered, "because the tanks' gun barrels were pointed toward Kella. [The teachers] told us in school the next day that they [the West Germans] just wanted to scare us and show off their fighting power, that they probably wouldn't shoot at us."

For many children born in the 1970s and 1980s, too young to have experienced such cold war confrontations or the intensification of the border's fortification, the Grenze was simply a fact of life. "I never even asked why we couldn't go to Eschwege," one teenager told me, "I didn't know anything else. The border was something totally normal." In many cases, children only began to question the existence and purpose of the border after hearing stories of their parents' or grandparents' border crossings.

On the western side of the border, the boundary was being maintained in a different fashion. West German Federal Border Police erected boundary markers and warning signs to visitors to keep out of GDR territory. More important was the creation and designation of a viewing point on the Braunrode hill from which westerners could gaze down on and ponder the Otherness of the East. A parking lot large enough to accommodate several tour buses was installed, and a restaurant was opened in an adjacent house. Referred to as the "Window to Kella," this site, like other viewing points along the Grenze, was nearly as important in demarcating the boundary as the fence itself. It not only provided a place for former residents to look to, often through binoculars, in the hope of recognizing a familiar face but also turned Kella and the socialist East in general into a spectacle, a tourist site to be viewed from the "safety" of the West. It was part of what Borneman has called a "mirror imaging process" in the construction of two German states and identities (1992); it was also the beginning of the construction of Otherness on both sides of the border.

As a result of this visibility, the state attempted to turn Kella into a kind of Potemkin village. It offered extra incentives and provided scarce building materials to modernize house facades visible to the West, for example, and subsidized community-improvement projects like the renovation of the village cemetery. As with East Berlin, the state granted this area certain preferential treatment, when possible, in supplying it with consumer goods. "They wanted to keep us quiet," one villager explained. "Our Konsum sometimes carried beer, wine, or fruit that people outside the Schutzstreifen didn't get."

The peculiar physical isolation of Kella's borderland location could not fully hinder the influx of a variety of external influences. The border, for example, was porous to the airwaves of West German television and radio. Western radio was usually the sole source of music and was eagerly but poorly reproduced on low-quality East German cassette tapes. Western television, watched by most villagers throughout the socialist period despite the fact that it was not officially permitted until Erich Honecker became Communist Party leader in 1971, provided a source of entertainment (and village nicknames, as we saw in the previous chapter), as well as information about and a connection to the West. American television shows like *Dallas* and *Dynasty* competed with East German reports on crime and homelessness in the United States. Although both were exaggerated representations, people tended to reject the East German reports as propaganda and accept American television fairly uncritically. Similarly, West German news was regarded as "real" news, whereas East German news was only watched if children were required to report on it in school.[6] Advertisements and commercials were regular and painful reminders of the superior quality and availability of consumer goods within walking distance on the other side of the border. "The commercials made a big impression," one woman told me. "We'd learn about how every year there was a new car model [in the West] while our Trabis stayed the same." A common joke told in the GDR reflected this influence: "Marxism would work if it weren't for cars."

More than anything else, western television helped maintain the illusion of the "Golden West." Western goods, which crossed boundaries in *Westpakete* (packages from western relatives), in stuffed suitcases of returning retirees, and later in the state-run elite stores, seemed to confirm the images on western television. "It was like Christmas," one woman recalled, "every time Grandma returned with her suitcase full of things. We couldn't believe everything they had over there." Just on the other side of the border was a world where "everything shines," a paradise that, if attained, could solve most every problem.

Over time, the presence of the border was routinized; it was an irritating, mysterious, and potentially dangerous fact of daily life. Although a genuine element of fear surrounding the border remained, particularly for parents with teenage boys (those most likely to attempt an escape), in daily life the border and its restrictive regulations were usually regarded more as nuisances than as the sources of pain and suffering that the border came to symbolize after the Wende. Depending on the degree of state control, which fluctuated largely in response to local behavior,[7] social gatherings had to end by an 11 P.M. curfew; lovers were forced to say their good-byes at the control checkpoint because passes were not available to nonfamily members (even for an unmarried father of a child living with its mother in Kella); dances and other festivities in neighboring villages had to be missed when villagers were required to be home by sundown.

People experienced and negotiated the spatial and temporal reconfigurations of the border in a variety of ways. Spatial practices were transformed as villagers sought new paths through woods or gardens after curfew. New routes outside the Schutzstreifen were discovered for Sunday walks. Weddings and other large family gatherings were held in Heiligenstadt or Erfurt so that relatives from outside Kella could attend. People working in their garden plots near the border would hope, imagine, or pretend that the figures they noticed but could not recognize or acknowledge on the other side were long-lost western relatives. Others who did recognize the onlookers through the lenses of binoculars, or who were expecting a "visit" from a western relative, would wave by washing windows or by shaking out tablecloths.

Then there were people like Ralf Fischer, a border crosser of the imagination and a traveler of maps. In the comfort of his living room, whose windows offered one of the best views of the border and the Braunrode hill in Kella, Ralf spent hours pouring over maps of worlds inaccessible to him as a GDR citizen and resident of a place that was not even featured on most maps produced in his own country. While stationed in East Berlin during his army service, he would wait outside a bookstore starting at 4 A.M. on the day he knew they were to receive a shipment of new and often illicit maps. With these maps and the power of his imagination, he journeyed through Asia, South America, and, most frequently, across the United States. He was so well traveled, in fact, that his knowledge of U.S. geography was far superior to mine. When my husband and I once explained to him that we had attended colleges in different cities before we were married and could only visit each other on semester breaks, he astonished us by observing, "Oh, then you must have taken I-80."

Border Stories

In addition to being a fact of life with which, like the system itself, people struggled to make their peace, the border was also the stuff of stories and legends.[8] Border crossers from the immediate postwar era related their experiences to the younger generation and, in the presence of peers, often tried to outdo one another's horror stories (several of which have been recounted here). Legends circulated about illicit border crossings, like the one about a man who was able to cross the newly formed ten-meter sand strip by attaching pig's hooves to the bottom of his shoes, thus leaving only the footprints of a wild boar. Even within families, stories could be so transformed in their telling that they had become legends, indeed fictions, by the time they were repeated several generations later. In one instance a young girl, Cornelia, had been left to live with an unmarried aunt when her parents decided to remain permanently in the West in 1952. According to several older family members, as well as Cornelia herself, the parents had opted to leave their daughter in Kella: "They already had two children and one on the way," an aunt explained, "and Aunt Marie had no children, so they left Cornelia with her." When Cornelia's younger cousin in Kella first related the story to me, however, the family had nearly been caught fleeing Kella and was unable to return to retrieve the missing child. According to this narrative, the family had been victimized by the dangerous and evil nature of the border and those who guarded it. In a manner similar to the imagined "lists" and monthly reports discussed in chapter 2, an imagined past and perception of danger not only embellished border stories but also endowed the border with an aura of evil and danger even during times when it may have been unwarranted.

In addition to an aura of danger, stories of escapes over the border similarly invested it with a sense of mystery. After 1961, according to archival sources as well as recollections of villagers, there were approximately ten to twelve incidents of Republikflucht in Kella. They included two young women whose friendship with a border guard worked to their advantage when they persuaded him to join them; a young man whose despair at not receiving his choice of apprenticeships prompted him to seek a new life in West Germany; a young man who left as he saw the alarm fence going up; and Cornelia, the child abandoned by her parents in 1952, who crept over the border with a friend one night in 1969. There were no fatalities on the border near Kella. Most escapes took place during the 1960s, before the erection of the two metal fences made it nearly impossible to leave without being caught.

The most celebrated escapes are those that occurred after this final fortification. The last Republikflucht from Kella was in 1986, when a young man in his midtwenties, Dieter Lenz, successfully dismantled the signal fence's alarm system and surmounted the second three-meter barrier. A trained electrician, Dieter had been planning his escape for a long time. He watched the border for months, taking careful notes on when and how it was patrolled. With materials obtained from his workplace, he constructed hooks to use in scaling the three-meter fence. His electrician's knowledge and awareness of certain functions of the border gained from service in the army several years earlier—it was not totally uncommon for young men from Kella to serve as border guards elsewhere—provided the information he needed for disarming the alarm system. Over a period of days, he slowly cut a hole in the alarm fence, snipping away just inches at a time, and concealed the spot with a pile of bushes and branches when he was finished. According to several accounts of the story, he did such a good job of hiding this spot that border guards had a difficult time locating it after he was gone. Dieter's best friend, who declined at the last minute to join him, was the only other person aware of his intentions. His mother learned about the escape on the next morning's (West German) television news.

The story I was most frequently told concerned the attempted, or rather aborted, escape of Martin Schneider, the youth mentioned in chapter 2 who was sentenced to a year in prison for tossing his jeans over the alarm fence in 1983. Perhaps this tale was recounted so often because, more than any other, it illustrated for residents the potential danger of the border, its relation to state power, and, most importantly, the possible consequences of transgressions. Despite daily contact with and observance of the border and its operations, much of the border remained a mystery. Like the system itself, it was something that had to be deciphered and interpreted as well as negotiated. Border stories were a means of doing this.

Whatever the narrative's content, stories and legends of the border invested this intensely symbolic space with meaning and memory.[9] With each telling, a story became embedded in a culturally constructed landscape. Edward Bruner's description of the relationship between stories and sites helps explain a similar interaction here: "Names may construct the landscape but stories make the site resonate with history and experience. Stories introduce a temporal dimension, making sites the markers of the experiences of groups and historical persons, not just markers of space. In spite of the inevitable changes that occur with each retelling of the story, the now culturally constituted landscape, in its solid materiality and sequentiality, authenticates the story" (1984: 5).

Together with the border's constant presence in everyday life—the effects of which ranged from the extraordinary to the mundane—border stories were a process through which the very materiality of the Grenze was physically impressed on the consciousness of border dwellers; the border was a primary means through which state power was inscribed onto space and bodies. The presence of the border in everyday life was so internalized by people living here, in fact, that a year after the Wall fell some people were still taking their feet off the gas pedal or reaching for their identity cards when they approached the site where a Schutzstreifen control point used to be located.

Like other symbols, therefore, meaning is not inherent in boundaries but is invested in them through cultural practices. In this sense, the border and its stories are an instance of what James Fernandez has described as "the conditions that make practical artifacts and arenas, and the signals and signs of coordinated human interaction, into evocative symbols with historic resonance" (1990: 95). As these border stories demonstrate, territorial borders may take on cultural meanings beyond their political purposes. They may even generate meanings that did not exist before their construction,[10] and their disappearance may be so destabilizing as to generate new cultural practices and identities. We now turn to the creation and expression of such meanings.

FROM BORDER DWELLERS TO BORDER CROSSERS

The opening of the border on November 9, 1989, created opportunities to invest this culturally constructed space with new meanings and memories. Tellings and retellings of border stories, both old and new, often entailed a complex and dynamic interplay between cultural representations and lived experience. The border and its impact on everyday life became a central aspect of a local identifying narrative, a reference point for people to tell themselves stories about themselves.

The following section discusses the events surrounding the Wende and the opening of the borders near Kella.[11] I explore how, amid the euphoria surrounding the fall of the Wall, initial border crossings both reflected and established the dynamics of East and West German post-Wall relations. These border crossings also initiated certain practices as rites into the new society, particularly in the realm of consumption, where differences between East and West were most marked before and immediately after the fall of the Wall.

The Wall Falls

Unlike the majority of border crossings throughout Germany on November 9 and 10, most of the first crossings for Kella were from West to East. For days after the Wall fell, the village was full of curious

West Germans who were anxious to see up close the place they had often peered down on from their side of the fence. Western relatives on an emotional return to their Heimat were also part of this influx of visitors. The euphoria in Kella, stemming not only from the elimination of travel restrictions to the West but also from the end of the village's isolation as a Schutzstreifengemeinde, paralleled the feelings and expressions of elation throughout the country: strangers embraced spontaneously on the streets, villagers invited visitors into their homes for coffee and conversation, and siblings and cousins were reunited at the highly symbolic *Elternhaus* (home of one's parents).[12] For western border crossers, a trip to the East was often a nostalgic journey into the past: "It reminds me of my childhood"; "I haven't seen anything like this for thirty years"; or "Look! Remember these?" were frequent remarks of westerners.

Similarly for East Germans, crossing the border into the West was like going back to the future. The modern houses, paved roads, elaborate shop windows, and bountiful supply of coveted western products held promises of what might have been, as well as of what might be. The West was a giant curiosity cabinet; with the 100 marks of *Begrüßungsgeld* (welcome money) offered to each East German citizen by the FRG during a first visit to West Germany and spontaneous gifts from West Germans— in the days following the fall of the Wall, it was not uncommon for West Germans spontaneously to hand out ten or twenty marks (or more) to perfect strangers from the GDR—it seemed both oddly distant and almost free for the taking.

The following letter, written just days after the fall of the Wall, captures and conveys the excitement, euphoria, impressions, and experiences of many first-time border crossers. It is from Thorsten Müller, a young man in his midtwenties, and is addressed to his cousin and her husband, who were living in West Germany.[13]

13 November 1989

Dear Hildesheimers!

Warm greetings from Thorsten and Katje![14] I've been wanting to write you for weeks, but the events have occurred at such a rapid pace that one couldn't even think normally. The culmination of course happened this weekend. Whenever I think of it I still get tears in my eyes. I don't even know where to start.

[I remember when Christoph [15] was still here and we would go up to our garden where we would always look to the West—which seemed so close and yet was unreachable. Only once to be able to see Kella from the other side seemed as unlikely as being able to fly to the moon.

Then on Thursday I watched the "opening" of the Wall and the whole confusion on TV until 2 A.M. It was impossible to believe. . . .

Friday morning it was announced on the public-address system that the Sperrgebiet had been lifted. The joy here knew no boundaries. . . .

But I didn't want to go [the West] right away. To be honest, I was scared to see everything. And I was totally irritated at how everyone was after the 100 western marks. . . . It's humiliating to get rich from your tax money. If we could at least have exchanged for it. . . . Maybe [the West Germans] will destroy the GDR this way. It's like an investment. They buy the GDR citizens (their sympathy), and then they won't want to remain GDR citizens anymore. . . .

Anyway, I didn't want to go over to the West right away, but Katje talked me into it, especially when we heard that another border crossing had been opened near Heiligenstadt. We filled up the tank and left around 1 P.M. After four hours of stop-and-go traffic we came to the GDR control point, where they let us through without having to show our identity card, even without stopping. For us it was unbelievable. After a few hundred meters we came to the provisional western control point. It was absolutely insane. It was already dark, and still there were people standing at the border shouting for joy. We honked and yelled. It was simply unbelievable. I was shaking so much I could hardly drive. People waved and greeted us more warmly than I've ever experienced. I had to fight back the tears.

It was great to drive on the western streets. We kept wondering what we should do. . . . I wanted to come to Hildesheim, but I was afraid we wouldn't be able to find you. . . . We decided to go to Göttingen . . . where we stopped at a rest area. How the parking lot was laid out, the neon signs, all the amazing cars. I walked around as if I were drunk.

Katje absolutely wanted to go to a McDonald's restaurant [located at the rest area]. She stormed in, and I stood outside just opening my eyes as wide as I could. I was shaking so. It was all so modern, white and made of glass, the windows were so amazing, the roof was constructed in a way that's only familiar to us through western newspapers. Katje pulled me inside. I felt like a lost convict who'd just spent twenty-five years in prison. Katje had some money that we used to buy a Big Mac.

I'm sure we behaved in such a way that everyone could see where we came from. Above all, I was in such a state of shock that I was stumbling over everything.

When we were back in the car and heading for the city center we passed numerous car dealers. It's a miracle I could still drive. We went for a walk downtown where all the shops are. It's good that the shops were closed because we wouldn't have known what to do. . . .

Traffic wasn't so bad on the way home. At the border crossing there were still FRG people standing, waving and shouting as we yelled good-bye. It was an amazing experience, and I hope it was a step forward in history. Let's hope the mandatory [currency] exchange is abolished for you, or even better that the whole border will disappear . . . but that's probably too much to ask for. In any case, you're welcome to visit us any time now, . . .

See you soon!
Thorsten!

Thorsten's euphoric letter not only captures his own experience as a first-time border crosser and resonates with the elation experienced and expressed throughout Germany during this time but also addresses several important themes and issues surrounding the fall of the Wall and its aftermath. His discussion of the Begrüßungsgeld, for example, highlights some of the early power dynamics of East-West relations. Long before the fall of the Wall, of course, there existed a power imbalance between the East and West. The exchange of people for western currency, loans, and even Westpakete were reflective of this; the Begrüßungsgeld from the West German state as well as spontaneous gifts of cash from individual West Germans was a continuation of the trend (Borneman 1993; 1998). As gifts that could not be reciprocated, these gestures accentuated the discrepancies between East and West and placed westerners in the dominant position of gift-givers. As one villager explained: "I found the Begrüßungsgeld embarrassing. It made me feel like a beggar. And when a westerner tried to hand me 20 marks, telling me to buy something nice with it, I tried to give it back. I was so ashamed."

More than a year later, these power dynamics resulting from uneven exchanges still informed many encounters between eastern and western Germans. While shopping in Eschwege, for example, a young woman from Kella, Helga Schneider, ran into a woman who for years had sent her family gifts from West Germany. The wife of an old friend of Helga's grandfather, the woman was well dressed with heels, light but noticeable makeup, and a fur coat. I noticed Helga's instant awkwardness and nervousness on greeting her. After listening to Helga's brief update on the family in response to her inquiry, the woman said, "We may have some more things to pass on to you, but I'll have to check with my son first. But now you don't need them as much as you used to." Helga, whose face had turned crimson with embarrassment, thanked the woman profusely for the offer but assured her this would not be necessary. "I'll look—I think we might have something," were the woman's departing words. Once out of earshot, Helga, still visibly flustered from the encounter, informed me how embarrassing this woman's charity was to her, however well intentioned. "They think we are so needy and dependent," Helga said, "I wish she wouldn't only talk about giving us things."

Like this brief encounter, Thorsten's letter also reveals an implicit assumption—shared by westerners and easterners—of western dominance defined by economic prosperity and material abundance. The notion of a time warp, prevalent in West German discourses and reflected in Thorsten's statement of feeling like a convict entering society after twenty-five years of imprisonment, also underlined the superiority of the West. It was clearly up to East Germans to catch up with, adapt to, and later simply adopt this system.

Certain initiation rites thus became part of East Germans' entry into the new society, and Thorsten's letter reflects the beginnings of several such rituals. Above all, he alludes to the centrality of consumption as an organizing category and metaphor for East-West distinctions. He is disgusted by his countrymen's "consuming frenzy" and lust for the almighty D-Mark, yet he marvels at the fancy automobiles, flashy advertisements, and elaborate shop windows of the West. His first stop after crossing the border is at McDonald's, a potent symbol of western capitalist expansion and consumption.[16] The fact that he and Katje did not know what to do at McDonald's reveals the lack of a certain cultural fluency in consumption that made them easily identifiable as East Germans— a marker that would become increasingly significant in the months to follow.

The centrality of consumption in Thorsten's letter echoes both media representations and other individual accounts of the events surrounding the fall of the Wall. One of the most pervasive images at the time was that of East Germans possessed by a cargo-cult mentality on a frenetic collective shopping spree.[17] As depicted especially in the West German press, the triumph of capitalism and democracy was reflected and confirmed in their lust for all things western. Local as well as national newspapers carried numerous photographs of East Germans gawking at western products. As one headline read: "Waiting, Marveling, Buying." The first thing most villagers note in recollecting their first visit to the West—whether before the Wende on a special pass or after the fall of the Wall—is the "huge offering" of products. "The stores!" one young woman recalled, "I didn't want to leave them!"

Finally, Thorsten's letter hints at a ritual unique to the borderland and cherished in Kella. He mentions how he had dreamed of being able to view Kella from the other side of the border—which, just days after writing the letter, he did. "One of the first things I did after the borders opened," he later told me, "was to go to Braunrode. I looked for the exact spot where my western relatives would have stood when they came to look at Kella. And when I found it, I couldn't fight back the tears." Thorsten was repeating a ritual already established by villagers who had been to the West on special passes before the Wende. During a brief visit for his uncle's seventieth birthday, for example, one villager recalled the view from the "Window to Kella": "I will always remember this impression. I looked through the binoculars and could see my son coming home, my wife outside the house. That was only three years ago. Here is where the world ended."

A Border Crossing in Kella

The creation of a border crossing in Kella on December 30, 1989, was the final step in ending the village's physical isolation, the day when Kella officially ceased to be "at the end of the world." Until then, villagers had to go to the Katharinenberg crossing, approximately eleven kilometers away. Soon after the borders opened in November, residents began to demand the creation of a border crossing near their village. In the security provided by the regime's open demise, between 150 and 200 villagers took to the streets in a candlelight procession on November 22.[18] Shouting spontaneous chants like: "For forty years we've been dead, to Braunrode now, we want to head!" and, "This is where a crossing should be! We in Kella long to be free!" they marched to the alarm fence that cut across the path where the road to Eschwege had once been. On the other side, "on Braunrode," residents from western border villages gathered in support of their demands.

Following a rapid trend all along the inter-German border, an opening was scheduled for Kella at the end of December. Under the supervision of the still operational but nearly defunct NVA border guards, volunteers from East and West spent three days clearing the brush, cement slabs, and fencing that had made the once frequently traveled road to Eschwege unrecognizable. Residents from both sides gathered to watch the long-anticipated first cut in the fence on December 27. "That was the most interesting moment of the whole opening," one participant observed: "Even though the official opening wasn't until the thirtieth [of December], the newspapers had announced we'd be cutting through the fence that day. It was absolute chaos. Even the Eschwege brewery set up a booth in the Braunrode parking lot! I tried to maintain some order so we could get our work done, but I finally gave up when a colleague said, 'Today the people rule!'"

The official opening was attended by hundreds of people from East and West (Figure 14). Funded by donations from nearly every household in Kella, festivities began with speeches by government officials from Heiligenstadt and Eschwege (including the newly elected district president, a former resident of Kella[19]) that stressed the importance of "coming together"; the speeches were followed by a procession though the new border opening led by a brass band from a nearby western village. The village place-name sign that once read "Kella, Kreis Heiligenstadt" (Kella, District of Heiligenstadt) was temporarily replaced by a West German one that read "Meinhard, Ortsteil Kella" (Meinhard, Subdivision of Kella). A gift from a western village mayor, the sign included Kella within the West German municipality of Meinhard and was intended to assure villagers that they "now belonged to the West."

In an atmosphere of spontaneous communitas (Turner 1979), villagers

Figure 14.   Opening a border crossing in Kella, December 1990. (Photograph in the collection of the author)

and their guests sought to extend the euphoria of the initial fall of the Wall. Residents handed out food and drink prepared for days in advance to a packed house of festival participants. "People were just amazing in those days," one woman recalled. "We really tried to make them feel welcome here." Or as another villager, Peter Meyer, remarked with surprise and irony while watching a videotape of the border opening more than a year later, "Look! So many people from East and West—and they get along!"

"THE WALL IN OUR HEADS"

Borderline Conflicts

In the borderland, as throughout Germany (and as Peter's remark indicates), the euphoria surrounding the fall of the Wall soon subsided.[20] The welcoming, emotional embraces of the early days were replaced with animosity, resentment, and in many cases aggression. West

German discourses began projecting East Germans as inferior, backward, and lazy. A host of legal, political, and discursive practices reflected a systematic devaluation of the East German past that challenged some of the very foundations of easterners' identity and personhood. Such practices included the selling of East German factories to western companies by the Treuhand, occasionally for next to nothing;[21] the discrediting of the GDR educational system, particularly the restructuring of the universities;[22] the renaming of schools, streets, and other public buildings; the removal of socialist memorials and monuments; the trial of Berlin border guards; the dissolution of East German media such as local newspapers and the television station DFF; the restructuring and rebuilding of urban and rural spaces following western models; and comparisons in dominant West German discourses of the socialist state with the Nazi regime.

Such devaluations of East Germans' work, values, indeed life experience, affected many villagers on a very personal level. Commenting on the village renewal plan, modeled after West German designs, for example, the former mayor of Kella, Ursula Meyer, lamented: "Everything we did [under socialism] was wrong. The streets we built were wrong, the trees were planted were wrong, even the roses we planted were wrong!" Her remark was intended metaphorically as well as literally: after the Wende, village streets constructed under socialism were repaved, while several trees and even roses planted by the village socialist administration were cut down or removed. In a similar vein, another villager remarked: "Are we supposed to say now that everyone who went to school in the GDR was an idiot? Or that all the factories in the GDR were just deadbeats? It's simply not true!"

Tensions mounted as West Germans complained about East Germans taking away their jobs by working for lower wages, while East Germans lamented the salary inequities. Villagers reported being yelled at for taking away parking spaces or for emptying stores shelves of yogurt, kiwis, and, above all, bananas. A few of the villagers who found employment in the West were refused service at their factory canteen; others had their cars sabotaged.[23] Many endured regular harassment from West German coworkers ranging from verbal attacks ("Shut up, Ossi! You don't have anything to say! You haven't done anything for forty years!") to more subtle forms of aggression such as delegating the least desirable work to easterners or humiliating them by assigning easterners tasks requiring knowledge of unfamiliar western machinery.

Many villagers employed in the West were also subjected to numerous Ossi jokes told by their western German colleagues. A key indicator of mounting East-West tensions, many jokes entailed a reworking of classic ethnic stereotypes and prejudices in the German context.[24] More uniquely German, the affectionate Trabi jokes told immediately after the Wende became outright hostile, focusing no longer on the cute little car but on the driver and passengers.[25] Similarly, the banana became the subject of many jokes and thereby part of a discourse of Otherness that depicted East Germans as dirty, uncivilized, and apelike. "How do they know that Ossis descended from apes?" begins one joke. "The banana shelves are always empty after they've been there." Another banana jokes asks, "How can a banana act as a compass?" "If you put it on the wall the side that's bitten off is the one pointed toward the East."

Banana jokes contributed to the fruit's status as a key symbol of the events surrounding re-unification. Hours after the Berlin Wall opened in November, for example, a West German stationed himself on his side of the Wall and handed out bananas to East Germans as they crossed into the West for the first time (Darnton 1991: 317). Rarely available in socialist countries, bananas were one of the first things East Germans bought when they arrived in the West. For months after the borders opened, fruit stands and store shelves were recurrently depleted of their banana supply. West Germans began to complain about the banana consumerism of their Ossi neighbors, sometimes deriding the GDR as a "banana republic." Leftist critics in the GDR, on the other hand, began to view the banana as a symbol of their country's sellout to capitalism.

Like other symbols, therefore, the banana has been invested with a multitude of meanings that have changed over time. Initially a symbol of the defeat of communism and of the triumph and promise of capitalist abundance, it has come to represent the disillusionments and failed aspirations of re-unification itself. When the Leipzig Monday demonstrations briefly resumed in the spring of 1991 to protest rising unemployment and a growing sense that the East was being "colonized" by the

West, I witnessed one demonstrator carrying a long stick over his shoulder, at the end of which dangled a bunch of dark, rotten banana peels.[26]

Another key indicator and major cause of East-West tensions were disputes over property ownership in the former GDR.[27] In Kella, property claims were filed by several of the families who had left the GDR in 1952, as well as by western relatives who were asserting their claims to family inheritances. As in the rest of eastern Germany, such claims not only stalled much-needed investment in the region but also often severed family relations far more drastically than the Wall ever had.

The experience of the Hauser family provides a particularly poignant illustration of a family sundered by property disputes. Emma Hauser, the youngest of six children, returned to Kella in 1952 after working in Eschwege for several years. Two brothers had been killed in World War II, and the remaining siblings opted to stay in the West. Emma recalled a discussion with her sister just before her return to Kella: "'We can't leave mother and father there [in Kella] to die alone,' I told her, and I remember what she answered as if it were yesterday: 'I don't want to throw away my whole life for the few years they have left to live.'" Emma returned the village to take care of her parents and the family property— a small house and a large garden. Gardening became her passion, she told me, and many of her happiest hours have been spent amid the cherry trees, strawberry plants, and rosebushes in the family garden plot, a five-minute walk from her home.

A year after the Wall fell, at Emma's sixtieth birthday party, two of her three surviving siblings informed her that they intended to keep their portion of the garden rather than accept the monetary compensation she had offered them earlier. Her oldest brother held to his initial promise to forgo the inheritance. A half-brother, to whom she had offered her portion of the garden in exchange for the family house that would have been his inheritance had he remained in Kella, also demanded his share. Together, her siblings' claims threatened to take away all but her oldest brother's portion of the garden.

As tensions mounted during the ensuing months, Emma's siblings began to remind her of the debts she had incurred over the years through their gifts of coveted Westpakete. She, in turn, reminded them that if she

Figure 15.   Mowing "our" (Emma's) side of the garden, 1992.
(Photograph by the author)

had not returned to Kella, the property would not have been there to
fight over in the first place; it probably would have been confiscated by
the state after their parents died. In her own dramatic way, Emma described her feelings of hurt and resentment: "I went from freedom into
bondage in order to take care of my mother and father so they wouldn't
die alone. And now they [my western siblings] won't recognize that anymore. I'm afraid of the cold war that is now about to break out!" Except
for contact with her oldest brother, the families stopped communicating.
"We were always so close," Emma said. "These are my own siblings! And
especially my brother Frank. They have such a huge house, eight rooms
just for themselves. They only see the money." Emma and her husband
ceased caring for her siblings' portions of the garden, allowing the grass
to grow wild and the fruit to rot on the trees (Figure 15). Echoing the now
common phrase, "the wall in our heads," Emma's husband told me: "The
border has disappeared but the rifts have become much deeper. We were
more united with the border there."[28]

The Afterlife of the Wall

The "wall in our heads" is the product of a process through which the former political boundary that once divided East and West Germany has been replaced by the maintenance—indeed, invention—of a cultural one. This has occurred largely through practices of identifying and constructing Otherness on both sides of the former border. Taxonomies of classification, of identifying who is an Ossi and who is a Wessi, have become part of everyday life in the German borderland. While the dynamics of these taxonomies and distinctions may vary in different milieus and contexts (rural versus urban for example), practices of identifying and constructing the Other most frequently entail the reading of bodies.[29] In the first years after the fall of the Wall, the most visible signs of difference were identifying markers: clothing, dialect, grooming, complexion, and even odor were subject to scrutiny and evaluation. According to a discourse of Otherness in the West, Ossis could be identified by their pale faces, oily hair, poor dental work, washed-out formless jeans, generic gray shoes, and acrylic shopping bags. They smelled of body odor, cheap perfume, or, as one West German told me, "that peculiar disinfectant." Wessis, on the other hand, were recognizable by their stylish outfits, chic haircuts, Gucci shoes, tan complexions, and ecologically correct burlap shopping bags. They smelled of Estée Lauder or Polo for men.[30]

As certain visible markers of difference have diminished through easterners' adaptation to western standards of style and dress, mannerisms and demeanor (or "mentalities," the term most frequently used in local, national, and certain social scientific discourses [Gebhardt and Kamphausen 1994, for example]), continue to be primary identifying characteristics. Ossis, western Germans say, tend to be shy and insecure and to travel or shop in groups. One villager's story about an encounter with a Wessi revealed her awareness of these stereotypes as well as her own perceptions of East-West distinctions:

> Ossis just have a different mentality. My brother-in-law [who works
> in the West] backed into a trash can that had been placed behind his
> garbage truck after he'd gotten back inside. When it happened he got

out and exclaimed, "Oh my, what have I done?" The woman who had placed the can behind the truck yelled at him for running over it, and then she said, "You come from over there." My brother-in-law was surprised and answered, "How do you know that?"

"Any West German," she told him, "would have yelled back and told me how stupid I was for putting the can behind the truck in the first place."

According to a discourse of Otherness in the East, Wessis are miserly, arrogant, and self-assured. They always "think they know better," hence the common label "*Besserwessi*" (know-it-alls). One man now employed in the West explained: "They just *are* different. You can say what you want, but they can't be changed. They all act like salesmen, as if they want to sell something."

Consumer Rites

This comment about "selling something" reflects the centrality of consumption as a central organizing category and metaphor for the dynamics of East-West relations, a realm in which and through which distinctions between East and West have been experienced, expressed, negotiated, and contested.[31] The lack of a certain cultural fluency in consumption quickly emerged as a key marker of an Ossi.[32] The stereotypical insecure Ossi, for example, walks with her head down and asks the store clerk not where a certain product is but, "Do you have it?"—a practice stemming from an economy of shortages, when the issue was not where a product might be but whether the store even had it. Whereas West Germans could refer to certain products by their brand names—such as Tempo for a tissue, Tesa for adhesive tape, or Uhu for glue—East Germans would describe their function. When people described differences between East and West Germans, they frequently pointed only to consumption practices. "Ossis compare prices," I was often told; "Wessis always know what they want to buy." It was usually during shopping trips in the adjacent western town of Eschwege that people would recriminate themselves for behaving like an Ossi. "Now she probably knows I'm an Ossi," one woman whispered to me about the bakery clerk. "I didn't know what that bread was called." Standing in line at a department store a teenager similarly scolded her mother: "Don't say that. They'll know we're Ossis!"

These women's self-recriminations were largely responses to West German discourses that condemned the materialism of East Germans as well as their ignorance of western consumption practices. As tensions between East and West mounted on both sides of the former border, insults and complaints directed at easterners frequently focused on a stereotype of materialistic Ossis ignorant of western consumption practices: "Stupid Ossi! They don't know how to shop!"; "See the packs of Zonis [East Germans] who are shopping again today?"; or "Look at them! They're shopping again! Don't they have anything better to do?" After the currency union in July 1990, when easterners overwhelmingly opted to buy western products with their newly acquired western marks, Ossis were projected as ignorant and foolish by western German discourses for being seduced by the fancy packaging of western goods. A common example cited was that East Germans were buying western milk while farmers in the East were forced to dump out the milk they were unable to sell.

Easterners' ignorance of western consumption practices was not only ridiculed and berated but was also exploited. As throughout the former GDR, numerous villagers were the objects, and occasionally the victims, of various mail-order gimmicks, door-to-door charlatans, and company-sponsored Werbefahrten (commercial shows or trips). Some villagers sent in money after receiving notice in the mail they had won a house; others purchased items from door-to-door salesmen that were never delivered; and most villagers over the age of forty (and many younger ones as well) have participated in a Werbefahrt.[33] These trips, lasting usually from one to three days, appealed to easterners' budgets and insecurities: for next to nothing, companies provided travel, meals, and guided sightseeing in exchange for customers' participation in a three- to four-hour-long product-promotion show that companies used to push their products. Organizers would often refuse to continue with the trip until enough items had been sold. Villagers frequently returned from these excursions with kitchen gadgets, pillows, and woolen blankets.

Just as unfamiliarity with western consumption practices was a key marker of an Ossi, then, acquiring a certain "cultural competence" (Bourdieu 1977: 186) in consumption became a central rite of initiation into the new society. Eastern Germans had to learn not only how to navigate their way through new structures of consumer credit, domestic finance, and money management but also where and how to shop after having only experienced an economy of scarcity with standardized products and prices. If, as Appadurai has suggested, we view consumption as the "principal *work* of late industrial society," Ossis, it could be said, had a great deal of work to do (1993: 30; emphasis in the original).

Through personal experience, collective negotiation, and even more formal instruction, they soon became well versed in product names, prices, advertising strategies, and fashion messages. Social gatherings were often dominated by conversations and debates about product choices, quality, and prices. Comparison shopping became an acquired skill and recreational activity. Even the new grade-school textbooks, read by children and parents alike, contained lessons on the aims and functions of advertising. Advertising, one textbook teaches, "serves to provide information; attempts to move us to buy something or to awaken interests in us; serves the buyer and the seller as well as the producer."[34] "Advertisements lie," a ten-year old child told me, "we've now learned that."

A product-promotion show in Kella eighteen months after the Wende particularly captures these dynamics of East-West relations as well as the centrality of consumption as an organizing principle, initiation rite, and metaphor for the experience and expression of East-West distinctions. Invitations to this gathering were distributed to every village household: "Your personal invitation," they read, "to our informative lecture on the topic of health and vitality. . . . Each participant will receive a hearty meal, a drink of choice, and a gift worth 40 marks." Genuine curiosity as well as the enticement of free food and gifts drew more than 150 villagers to the community hall where the "lecture" was given.

The evening began with an introduction by the speaker, a well-dressed yet sickly looking woman in her midforties with smokers' teeth, bleached-blond hair, and prematurely aged, yellowish skin (apparently the result of years of tanning coupled with a heavy smoking habit). She presented herself as a nutritionist with a practice in Bavaria and explained that the firm she worked for manufactured health products. After the audience had received its promised (although meager) meal, she informed us that a drawing would be held at the end of her presentation for a free trip to Spain. Murmurs and mumblings of approval filled the room as she explained: "We want *you* to be able to see Spain, too." Her tone was both paternalistic and patronizing: "we," the Wessis, want to provide "you," the poor Ossis, with opportunities only we have been able to afford. As it turned out, the trip was not entirely free (only transportation by bus was provided), but the suspense of the drawing held people there for the entire three hours of her presentation.

She then began her "lecture" on health and nutrition. According to a "renowned" nutritional society, she explained, one would have to drink more than thirteen liters of milk to receive the necessary daily allowances of calcium, eat two kilos of beef for the requisite amounts of iron, and consume a jar of honey a day to build up one's immune system through bee pollen. "Our health and our bodies are also forms of capital," she informed her listeners. "In fact, they may be the only form of capital we possess. We need to invest in them, like money in the bank." To eliminate the need for such huge quantities of food, she was offering a course of treatment of tablets, powders, and vitamins that would clear arteries and reduce cholesterol within thirty days. Although the "treatment" usually sold for 964 marks, she announced, the first ten buyers would receive it at half price. For those villagers who were unemployed or retired, the full price of the "treatment" nearly equaled a month's income.

Throughout the evening, this saleswoman drew on a variety of strategies to promote her products. Above all, she presented herself as an educator, invested with authority as a nutritionist and as a westerner. She was there to teach not only about nutrition and health but also about the rules and values of the new society. "Invest in yourself," she urged the audience, invoking the languages of production and consumption while privileging the values of western individualism, "You always have money enough for the grandchildren, but now it's time to do something for yourself." Her frequent references to the body as capital were another aspect of her presentation's "educational" function.

Like many marketing strategies, her pitch also played on the fears and insecurities of the audience while pretending to identify with and understand its situation. When people did not respond to her offer at first, she drew on stereotypes and images of materialistic and spendthrift

Ossis: "There's always money for renovating the house, or for buying a western car," she reproached them. After this play on people's guilt, she managed to sell several more "treatments." She similarly invoked a theme of "lost trust," referring to the mounting tensions and suspicions between East and West Germans (ironically through people and practices like her). "We want to restore trust," she said, holding up a West German advertisement in an eastern newspaper that looked like a news report. "That is sheer deception. Today I want to restore trust. You don't even have to pay me until the end of my presentation." Many participants nodded in approval, and several more "treatments" were sold. "I want to help you, and I will be back," she promised/threatened, "because I am firmly convinced by these products."

In the end, this saleswoman was able to sell ten "treatments," as well as numerous other products ranging from rugs to pillows to garlic pills. While several villagers expressed skepticism at her claims, and a few were outraged by people's gullibility, most enjoyed the presentation. Before leaving, some even thanked her personally for such a nice evening.

At the time, the presentation was like a collective initiation ritual: its western German sponsors hoped to profit from "educating" their eastern neighbors about health, nutrition, and consumption. By linking their products' purported benefits to the rules, values, and the spirit of capitalism, they were also selling access to, or entry into, the new society. The evening was in many ways a revelatory incident that highlighted several aspects and dynamics of East-West relations: the Besserwessi lecturing those she portrayed to be poor, ignorant Ossis; the references to easterners' materialism and spendthrift consumption; and the allusion to "lost trust" between East and West as a selling tactic.

Over time, however, the presentation came to be one of many similar initiation rites into consumer society. The meaning of the evening changed as residents became increasingly familiar with (and wary of) certain sales strategies. It became one of many stories of encounters with Wessis; when told and retold, such stories became part of a shared knowledge and common experience, a new genre of border stories.

Many border stories have since acquired the status of legends.[35] One story, also focusing on consumption practices, concerns a woman driving a Trabi who was forced off the road by a BMW. The western driver stopped, walked over to her, and reportedly yelled: "Shitty Zoni! Are you going shopping again? What are you going to buy today?" Although told to me by a villager as fact ("this happened to a friend of my sister-in-law"), it appeared in different versions and in different contexts all along the former border.

Just because the event may not have happened, however, does not mean there is no truth to the story. Stories are expressions and interpretations of lived experience, not necessarily depictions of actual reality. The telling and retelling of stories, including legends, may identify sentiments and describe experience.[36] Once such stories are told—in media representations, at village social gatherings, or both—they become part of a shared knowledge; they may be transformed into cultural narratives that are internalized and reproduced as individual lived experience. The stories of encounters with the Other are also part of an ongoing construction of East-West distinctions.

This new genre of border stories not only is another aspect of boundary maintenance, but also reflects how the construction of Otherness on both sides of the former border entails a complex and dynamic interplay between cultural representations and lived experience, between real and invented distinctions.

Borderland Identities

The construction of Otherness in both East and West has thus resulted in the reformulation of images and categories of the Other as well as in the creation of new forms of identity. On the one hand, there is a Nachholungsbedarf, a need to "catch up" and "blend in" with the Wessis. In this endeavor, villagers have discarded their East German clothes, changed their hairstyles, and undertaken extensive home improvement as well as community renovation projects. When possible, in the first years after the Wende men registered their new western automobile at a West German friend's or relative's address in order to receive the coveted West German license plate, thus making them unidentifiable as Ossis when driving. "People want to blend in," one man explained; "they don't want to be identified as being East German."

Even though they may strive to imitate the West, however, people in

Kella also resist it. This paradox is not inconsistent; it reflects the complex and contradictory aspects of identity in the borderland. Rather than accepting passively the dominance of the West—until recently a prevalent image of East Germans in both eastern and western German discourses—many people have challenged it, both individually and collectively, in overt as well as very subtle ways. These challenges initially involved a simple questioning of western hegemony: "I used to believe everything in the West was golden," one woman in her twenties told me. "If a westerner pointed to something that was red and told me it was blue, I would have nodded and said, 'Yes, yes, you're right. That is blue.' Today of course I wouldn't do that anymore." Other contestations may entail a more explicit rejection of things West German: rather than responding, for example, with silence or tears to West German projections of inferiority, laziness, or incompetence, as many did in the early stages of East-West tensions, people have challenged or even played with western images and stereotypes of Ossis. In once instance, a woman from Kella stopped her Trabi at a stoplight, where a few men exchanged jokes and comments about the automobile. On overhearing their remarks, she rolled down her window and said loudly to her daughter so that the men could hear, "Look, Sabine! They say that everything in the West is better. And it's right. Even the dumb people are dumber!"

Over time, villagers began proudly referring to themselves as "Ossis" or "Zonis." During Heimatverein excursions, for example, club members frequently asserted that they would "rather travel with Zonis." The period of socialist rule came to be called "in our times." In these constructions and assertions of new forms of identity as eastern Germans in opposition to West German discourses, the reappropriation of these derogatory labels has invested them with new meanings. As Sampson has noted, "Unification wiped out East Germany, but created an East German consciousness" (1991: 19).

An emerging consciousness and counteridentity has been constructed, expressed, and asserted in a variety of ways. Village women resumed wearing their East German *Kittel* (smocks) after nearly two years of relegating them to the back of their closets because they were not considered "modern" in the West. In another instance, a family chose to drive their Trabi instead of their western Opel to a dinner with West Ger-

Figure 16. With amusement and rediscovered affection for the Trabi, villagers help restart one. (Photograph by Anne Baldwin)

man relatives, thus consciously highlighting, indeed magnifying, the distinctions between them (Figure 16). "We took the Trabi," they proudly told me, "and parked it next to their 68,000 mark Mercedes!" Similarly, a group of men decided to drink East German beer and commented on this after a year of its being nearly taboo to serve it socially; women resumed buying the eastern German laundry detergent, Spee.

In the last few years, such subtle tactics of symbolic resistance have become widespread cultural practices throughout eastern Germany (see also Merkel 1994). Often called the "renaissance of a GDR *Heimatgefühl* [feeling of belonging or GDR identity]," these practices are part of a discourse of nostalgia and mourning—a "hazy beautification of the past" — that has contested a general devaluation of the East German past by dominant West German legal and discursive practices (Huyssen 1995: 47). A disco in East Berlin, for example, seeks to reconstruct GDR times with East German drinks, music, and the old cover charge; a cinema or regional television station shows old GDR films that are watched by more people now than they were during the socialist period; a self-described "nostalgia cafe" called "The Wallflower" is decorated with artifacts from the socialist period and serves "traditional" GDR fare; a bar in Leipzig called "Trabi-Inn" serves drinks named "FDJtler" on tabletops made of old Trabants; flea markets are littered with socialist paraphernalia for people who have begun collecting objects of the vanished state; and several supermarkets specialize in or at least carry East German products, including one in eastern Berlin whose name seems to reflect a now common sentiment, typical of "nostalgia's stubborn implications of loss and desire" (Ivy 1995: 56): "Back to the Future."[37]

In this business of "Ostalgia" (*Ostalgie*), East German products have taken on new symbolic meaning when used the second time around. These recuperations are both gestures of defiance toward and an ironic play with images and stereotypes of Ossis. And they entail the manipulation of culturally provided forms of resistance within the context of a market economy: consumer choice. Contrary to one of Kella's initial lessons in western consumption, then, Ossis investing in themselves or their "bodies as capital" has entailed not the consumption of pills, powders, and vitamins but the acquisition of cultural capital in knowing how to consume.

However, now stripped from their original historical context of an economy of scarcity or an oppressive regime, these products also recall an East Germany that never existed. Thus while there may be nothing new in the strategic use of consumption as oppositional practice,[38] what is unique in this context is the way in which memory shapes, and is being shaped by, the consumption and reappropriation of things. These products have, in a sense, become mnemonics, signifiers of a period of time that differentiates Ossis. They also illustrate not only the way in which memory is an interactive, malleable, and highly contested phenomenon but also the process through which things become informed with a remembering—and forgetting—capacity. There is not merely a tension but a dynamic interplay between nostalgia and memory here, and one of the key links is consumption.

This rememorization of trivialities is also part of a process through which consumption practices and the meaning of things have contributed to the creation and reification of a temporal and spatial bound-ary. "Ostalgic" and similar practices are not only part of a dynamic of boundary maintenance and invention between East and West; they have also helped create a division between before and after "the Fall." Thus the items purchased with welcome money connect personal biographies to a nationally (indeed, internationally) shared historical moment (the fall of the Wall). Yet they are also what Susan Stewart has called "sou-venirs of individual experience" in connection to a rite of passage (Stew-art 1993). The inexpensive cassette recorders that broke within months of their purchase or the gold jewelry that turned one's skin green are, in a sense, material signs of many easterners' first lesson in western con-sumption. They have come not only to represent easterners' transforma-tion into more knowledgeable consumers but also to symbolize the loss of an illusion of the "Golden West." And the loss of this illusion has been one of the most formative and disorienting aspects of re-unification.

In a 1993 magazine article identifying the emergence of such opposi-tional practices throughout the former GDR, the former East German writer Monka Maron is quoted as ridiculing the notion that anyone who buys "Bautzener mustard or Thüringer wurst is a resistance fighter" ("Wehre Dich Täglich" 1993). While the issue of whether and to what ex-tent such consumption practices may constitute political resistance is an important one, such practices are, I would suggest, both reflective and constitutive of important identity transformations and negotiations in a period of intense social discord.

The annual Fasching celebrations in Kella provide further illustration of these processes. The traditional humorous skits, speeches, and songs at Fasching festivities have served as an interesting barometer of East-West relations since the fall of the Wall as well as a forum for the con-struction and expression of new forms of identity. In the first two years after the fall of the Wall, Fasching performances catered to the western German visitors who attended the village celebration. Rather than con-taining endless references to people and events in the village, as they had in the past, the performances consisted of generic jokes (usually copied from joke books) in order to have a broader appeal. "The westerners wouldn't be able to follow the show if we talked about things from the

Figure 17.   Poking fun at the broken promises of re-unification in a carnival song, 1992. (Photograph by the author)

village like we used to," one participant explained. Furthermore, in the 1990 and 1991 skits and speeches, there were no references to the events, effects, or tensions of re-unification.

In 1992, however, there was a noticeable turnaround. Although there were still fewer references to village affairs, several speeches returned to the often brutal teasing of fellow villagers that required detailed local knowledge in order to be understood. Performances, consisting largely of original material and delivered with an assertive self-confidence that had been absent the previous year, offered commentaries on current events and politics ranging from the rising costs of living to the Stasi files. One speaker made fun of the villagers who had purchased the health-products "treatment course" for 500 marks; another pointed out how "over there [in the West] an Ossi has no rights." In one song, written to the tune of the popular German game-show theme "Das ganze Leben ist ein Quiz" (All of Life Is a Quiz), a group lamented the broken promises of re-unification (Figure 17). After describing the delay in the installation of telephones in Kella and the mysteries of the Stasi files, the song continued:

> The Treuhand's poker game is especially bad.
> The Wessis make a killing, while we end up being had.
> Only between us should our property be split
> Because we're the only ones who have a right to it.
> [Refrain]:
> All of life is a quiz
> And we are only the candidates.
> All of life is a quiz
> And all we can do is postulate.
> We don't understand, but question we must:
> Have we let them make total asses of us?[39]

Such assertions and references were by far the most popular performances of the evening (besides the much-loved Männerballett). Screams of laughter and thundering applause greeted, for example, the following joke from a "school class" skit delivered with careful precision and timing:

TEACHER: I hear your father is working in Eschwege now.

STUDENT 1: Yes.

TEACHER: And does he like it?

STUDENT 1: Yes, but they always call him Udo.

TEACHER: Udo? But his name is Franz.

STUDENT 2: Don't you know what Udo means?

STUDENT 1: No.

STUDENT 2: You don't know?!

STUDENT 1: No!

STUDENT 2: Udo means "our dumb Ossi"!

This trend of defining, expressing, and asserting an identity as eastern Germans during Fasching performances has continued. In 1994, one song about East-West tensions reflected a recognition, even acceptance, of the ongoing division as well as an affirmation of eastern German identities and values:

> Now we see that we don't agree
> with your civilized world.
> Here honesty and courage still prevail,
> for these are values we still hail.
> But over there, where you reside,
> Money's the only value by which you abide.[40]

Although not intended as such by the writers, another song about a garden fence in town was widely interpreted (and applauded) by the audience as referring to putting "the" fence back up. In 1995, a participant dressed as a border guard roused the room to hearty applause with a bit of eastern "people's wisdom": "The fox is clever but stupid he'll play; the Wessi does it the other way."[41]

The purpose of these ethnographic vignettes is to illustrate a process of identity negotiation and construction, a process that is occurring throughout re-unified Germany but that takes on particular significance at the (former) border. For it is here, where the border was once physically inscribed on the space and indeed the bodies of its dwellers, that identities are especially fluid and distinctions are articulated, especially in such moments of social upheaval. This borderland consists of boundary-maintaining practices through which identities and distinctions are constructed and expressed. However it is also an interstitial zone, a place betwixt and between cultures. As Debra Castillo writes, "The border sets up a position for both living and thinking, one involving a sense of place as well as implicit displacement. It suggests a space that is both neatly divided and, in the crossover dreams of its inhabitants, disorientingly confused" (1995: 18).

Residents of the German borderland thus may strive to avoid being identified as Ossis while asserting an identity as East Germans. They may drive to the West in their Volkswagen Golf with western plates, for example, yet decide to work in the East for less money because they'd "rather be with Ossis." They may date a West German to rebel against their father who "hates Wessis," yet confidently declare, "I'll never become one of *them*." They may rise to the defense of Ossis yet distinguish themselves from the rest of eastern Germans, as did the following speech from Fasching in 1992: "They also say that Ossis are lazy, but accusing Kellans of this would be totally crazy." In more extreme cases of interstitiality they may become *"Wossis"*: Ossis who take on exaggerated characteristics of Wessis.

Similarly, people may manipulate their liminal position empowered by newly acquired knowledge of consumption practices. In order to distinguish themselves from other Ossis, for example, some residents began to shop at the more prestigious western German department stores. In a similar vein, one villager was especially proud to be the only one of four eastern Germans not to be recognized as an Ossi at a western restaurant; yet at her workplace in Eschwege, she refused to conform to the demanding dress code of her western German coworkers. "I never want to become one of them," she claimed.

As with most borderlands, this one is characterized by an uneven and asymmetrical intersection of cultures. In this site of cultural confrontation, struggles over the production of cultural meanings and contestations of social values occur in the context of such asymmetrical relations. Although borderland residents may be in-between cultures, both geographically and metaphorically, the hegemony of the West conveys a sense that they are, or should be, moving in a particular direction. As one man from Kella explained, "The West demands that the people here in the East be exactly like they are [in the West]. They presume to know everything, [as evidenced] in their way of presenting themselves and in their demand that our people [in the East] don't have anything of our own to preserve."

Contrary to certain border theories, then, residents of Kella are not "halfway beings" (Castillo 1995). Nor are they, as many popular and academic discourses would have it, passive East Germans who have accepted and internalized western projections of them as inferior.[42] Instead, through a dynamic and subtle interplay of imitation, resistance, and *Eigen-Sinn* (one's own sense, or one's own meaning), these borderliners are creating and articulating new forms of identity and alternative notions of "Germanness."[43]

BORDERLINING

To conclude, I turn to a series of revelatory incidents, all of which occurred at a single family gathering. Together these incidents illustrate the liminal condition of the borderland as well as the ongoing construction of porous boundaries after the collapse of impermeable ones. The occasion for the gathering was a child's first holy communion, and the assembled family members included aunts, uncles, cousins, and grandparents from eastern and western Germany. Throughout the day, conversations about unemployment, government subsidies for the former GDR, and the recent surge in violence against foreigners repeatedly came to an abrupt halt in order to avoid further escalation in familial tensions. "You people need to learn how to work," "You'll never figure this system out," and "A normal person can only shake his head at what goes on over here" were frequent comments of a western relative. Family members from the former GDR, on the other hand, accused West Germany of exporting xenophobia to the East ("We got that from *you*—that didn't exist here before!"), staunchly defended their work habits, and confided to me on the side how hurtful their western relatives' accusations were.

After dinner, several members of the party decided to undertake what has now became a ritualized practice in Kella: a walk along the border leading up the "Window to Kella," where, instead of peering down on the Otherness of the East, as westerners had once done, residents assess the condition and status of their village. This walking ritual reflects the incorporation of the former East-West boundary into a local identifying narrative of multiple and layered boundaries; the ritual is also a spatial practice that defines and reinscribes the boundary. Sunday walks regularly follow this path; people often point out not only the former ten-meter strip but also the former boundary stones between Prussia and Hesse (and hence between the Catholic Eichsfeld and its Protestant surroundings), along which the postwar occupied zones were demarcated. A year after the Wall fell, in fact, one resident took it on himself to repaint these stones—a literal reinscription of a multilayered boundary.

Once we had reached our destination, a recently renovated "Window to Kella" with benches and wooden railings sponsored and erected by the Heimatverein, the group gazed down quietly and contemplatively at the village. With its spring dress of cherry blossoms accentuated by the setting sun, Kella had never looked better. "Nothing stands in the way of Kella looking like the West," one woman from Kella proudly exclaimed. "In a few years it will be as good as any western village." Another village woman agreed: "The inland area [of the former GDR, farther to the east] is supposed to be much worse."

The women's comments reflected the notion, mapped onto the social space of the borderland as well as the minds of its inhabitants, that Kella was somewhere between East and West. Although it may be in this literal borderland that its in-betweenness is most visible, the borderland may also be viewed as a metaphor for "the transition" itself. Indeed, the women's remarks suggest a sense of liminality combined with a particular trajectory, as revealed in their implicit acceptance of the hegemony of western standards as the goal toward which Kella should strive. Yet there is also an unstated recognition that these standards remain distinctly Other. From the in-betweenness of the borderline, the women acknowledged both their liminality as well as their identity as easterners.

The group's quiet observations and contemplations were interrupted just a few minutes later when a cantankerous western relative loudly and only half-jokingly asserted: "I was up here first! I was here before all of you!" There, standing directly on the former border, he was reminding members of the group which side each of them came from, and where each of them belonged. He was also implying that he had been—and still is—somehow ahead of his eastern German relatives.

This ritual of walking the border thus highlighted the dual nature of the borderland as a place where identity is both especially articulated and uniquely fluid.[44] The comments during our walk were uttered in the context of the day's conversations as well as that of mounting tensions between East and West throughout the country. The remarks were part of an ongoing process of boundary maintenance and construction as well as of a process of manipulating, and perhaps sustaining, a liminal condition.

Designing Women

A year into my fieldwork, several women from the village began to paint silk together (Figure 18). Although they met only six or seven times, these women were attempting to renew a community that had been lost when the factory in which they worked was closed. "This is like women drüben," one woman commented. "They have their bowling clubs, their crafts courses. They have to keep busy." Before long, however, the women recognized that they were not like women drüben. As we began to paint our scarves, women moved from project to project, picking up a paintbrush or glitter and adding whatever they saw fit to each other's artwork. At first taken aback by this and protective of my own scarf, I soon realized that a sense of collective production was at work here—a stark contrast to the individual projects in my West German silk-painting course. It was something our West German instructor

Figure 18. Painting silk, 1991. (Photograph by the author)

did not quite know how to deal with. In noting this difference, one woman from the village explained, "In the West it's every man for himself" (which in German has a less gendered connotation: *jeder für sich*). Other women agreed: "It's nicer our way, isn't it?"

At the time, this revelatory incident captured the heightened social consciousness of these women, who were re-creating for themselves, if even for a brief moment, a gendered space after their factory closed. The incident also illuminates and contextualizes some of the issues I explore in this chapter: the production and negotiation of gender identities, the simultaneous imitation of and differentiation from the West, and the gendered nature of East-West distinctions.

My principal aim in this chapter is to examine several ideological and practical tensions that informed the construction and negotiation of gender in Kella before and after the Wende.[1] The most obvious and transformative of these is a tension produced by the influx of western images and ideologies of womanhood that have challenged forty years of women's experience under socialism as workers and mothers. I explore this tension in the second half of the chapter, and I argue that it and the social transformations of which it is a part are both deeply gendered and gendering: the real and invented distinctions between East and West are often structured in gendered terms. National identity may thus be viewed as a gendered phenomenon.

Before discussing this recent turn of events, however, I explore aspects of social life under socialism that were tension-laden in respect to gender roles and gender identities. During the socialist period, I argue, women negotiated contradictions in the state's own gender ideologies: the official proclamation of gender equality, on the one hand, and pronatalist policies that encouraged traditional women's roles, on the other. In Kella, the socialist state's ideology of gender equality was also often in conflict with the strong presence of the Catholic church and its traditional views on women. Since German re-unification, these traditional views have also been challenged by a different set of competing gender ideologies: western feminist ideas.

These diverse tensions have been, and continue to be, negotiated and contested in very subtle ways, both individually and collectively. An examination of these tensions may not only illuminate the heterogeneous production, representation, and negotiation of gender in postsocialist societies and elsewhere, I argue, but also serve as a reminder that women's experiences of socialism and the transformations since the collapse of socialist rule have been highly differentiated.[2]

MAKING CLIPS

In Kella the boundaries of gender continue to structure and organize much of the community's religious, social, and domestic space: in church, women and children fill the downstairs pews while men sit in the balcony; most social and village gatherings are similarly separated along gender lines; and domestic labor and space are divided largely according to traditional gender roles.

As in the rest of the GDR, the workforce in Kella was largely segregated by gender during the socialist period.[3] Ninety-nine percent of vil-

Figure 19. Women working in the Kella clips factory in the 1960s.
(Photograph courtesy of Elizabeth Henning)

lage women were employed outside the home, and more than half of
them worked in the local factory maintained by the state exclusively for
the purpose of providing employment for women in this isolated Schutzstreifengemeinde.[4] Reopened in 1953 as a cigar factory, as it had been in
the decades before the war, the facility was taken over by the VEB Kleinmetalwerk Heiligenstadt in 1966 for the production of suspender clips
(Figure 19).[5] Managers from the factory headquarters often conceded
that this work could have been done more effectively and efficiently by
machines, but the state was committed to employing women locally and
thus kept the plant in Kella operating.

In addition to being a convenient place of employment, the clips factory provided an important space for daily contact among village women
and for the dissemination of local gossip and shared knowledge.[6] Affectionately called the "gossip factory," it was a place where local folklore,
stories, gossip, and even songs were transmitted and transformed. As
one woman in her late twenties explained, "You always learned the latest
news there [at the factory]—everything that had happened in the village.

Everyone knew something, and they exchanged information. Some mean-spirited people used to say that if a woman worked there seven hours a day, she needed at least two hours to tell others [in the village] what she'd learned there. You came together there with people; it was familiar, you know?" Many village women spent the majority of their working lives assembling clips together. Mothers encouraged their daughters to join them when they reached working age. As throughout the GDR, brigade and factory parties, excursions, and seminars highlighted as well as reiterated the social and educational function of the workplace. For many women, the annual factory-sponsored day trip was one of the few opportunities to travel away from the village.

This focus on the importance and centrality of the socialist workplace was a critical aspect of the state's effort to promote its ideology of worker-mothers. In many GDR factories, including the toy factory in neighboring Pfaffschwende, the day-care center, the Konsum store, and even a doctor's office were housed on the factory grounds. In Kella, many of these facilities were within yards of the clips factory. A central kitchen provided a standardized meal for all workers, students, and day-care children in both villages. These policies and practices were not only a way of making it easier for women to work outside the home but also part of a process through which the state attempted to supplant certain roles and functions of the private sphere—child rearing, family meals, and so forth—with the public sphere of the socialist workplace.

The guarantee of paid employment was thus among several rights and privileges accorded to women in the GDR.[7] The East German constitution granted not only formal legal equality but also equal pay for equal work. Throughout the GDR, working mothers were assured of day-care services for their children that included nurseries for infants, kindergartens for preschool children, and after-school programs for pupils up to the fourth grade. All pregnant women were guaranteed pregnancy leave as well as a one-year leave at full salary after the birth of a child. In addition, women were given the right to an abortion after the state passed a law in 1972 legalizing the procedure during the first trimester of pregnancy. As part of the "mirror-imaging" process in the construction of two German states, the GDR abortion law aimed to underscore the socialist state's commitment to women's rights in response to the unsuccessful proabortion battle in West Germany (Borneman 1992; Funk 1993b).

Participation in the political sphere was also part of women's rights, privileges, and obligations under socialism. The state's efforts to integrate women into party political work involved them in a variety of political functions.[8] Socialist gender quotas required that 30 percent of village council members be women; women formed the majority of members in certain state and local mass organizations like the German Red Cross or the senior citizens' People's Solidarity League; and women's organizations like the DFD aimed to involve women by explicitly addressing what it perceived to be, and defined as, women's concerns. The DFD was one of several channels of mediation that sought to convey the party program as well as the socialist state's gender ideologies to its female population; its diverse programs reflected the state's often contradictory images and philosophies of womanhood and women's roles. DFD meetings, at which attendance in Kella ranged from four to fifty women, addressed political topics like "The Woman in Socialism," dealt with local concerns such as renovations of the child-care facility, and offered instruction on various homemaking questions.

Other mediators of the state's gender ideologies included the educational system, work collectives, and state publications like a handbook given to newlyweds. Entitled *Unsere Familie: Ratgeber für Jung und Alt* (Our Family: A Handbook for Young and Old), this handbook was owned by most families in Kella; after the Wende, some women continued to use it as a reference. It stresses the importance and advantages of "the working woman" and offers advice and guidance for transforming "relations between the sexes" in order to facilitate women's paid employment. It urges couples to share housework and emphasizes the role of parents in creating and maintaining good "socialist family relationships" as well as in cultivating a "socialist personality" in their children.[9] Despite its emphasis on equal rights and women's paid employment, however, the images of women conveyed in this handbook remain tied to traditional roles: the only photographs of women are as brides or mothers, whereas men are pictured solely in the workplace.

The GDR women's magazine *Für Dich*, read sporadically by women in Kella during the socialist period, similarly emphasized women's dual role in the socialist state as workers and mothers, or worker-mothers. Yet, as Irene Dölling has pointed out, the magazine's frequent photograph caption reflecting this role, "Our mommies work like men," also conveyed a message that as "mommies," women were always second-class workers (1993: 169–71). Even stories of successful and ambitious women were tempered by the perpetuation of stereotypes like "motherliness, caring, and selflessness" (p. 174). The magazine thus reiterated what was being conveyed to women in many contexts: they were expected to combine motherhood, housework, political activism, and paid employment.

This state ideology regarding women's roles, reflected and internalized through the everyday practice of paid work, factory production rituals, political involvement, and traditional gender roles in both the domestic and public division of labor, meant that women in Kella, like women throughout eastern Europe, bore a "double" or "triple" burden. As several feminist scholars have pointed out, the rights and privileges accorded to women under state socialism as well as its ideology of worker-mothers also served to reinforce as "natural" women's traditional role in the home, thereby underscoring as well women's roles as biological regenerators of the socialist nation and as socializers of its citizens (Einhorn 1993; Funk 1993a; Nickel 1993).[10]

The effort to negotiate such paradoxical policies and dogma affected women's daily lives on a very personal level. Echoing aspects of the socialist state's arguments that stressed the emancipation of women in the GDR relative to the FRG, one woman in her late twenties explained, "I think women here [in the GDR] were freer. In terms of work, in terms of everything. One always heard that women were somewhat oppressed in the West because they stayed home and were housewives. Women had a say here, in politics and in work." She paused and smiled, then continued. "Women here had to do as much as men and more. They worked eight hours and then came home and kept working. But I couldn't do it all. I couldn't work eight hours, keep up my household and THEN, on top of that, say 'I raised my children to be good socialists.' I just wasn't able to do that. I'd like to see the woman who did."

A woman in her early sixties, Emma Hauser, recalled a "typical day":

In the mornings after the alarm clock rings, who gets up first? The
woman. Who makes coffee? The woman. Who makes breakfast? The
woman. Even though I also had to go to work. That's the way it was in
most cases. The woman took care of everything, and when everyone else
was out the door, I didn't take any time to drink my coffee. I just made
a quick sandwich for myself, gulped it down, and left. That's what life
was like here. One day like the next.

For many women in Kella, the day often began before dawn and
ended after midnight. It included at least six hours of work outside the
home, several hours of cooking and cleaning at home, child care, and, for
many families with land in the LPG, regular work at the collective farm.
A gendered division of labor existed within the sphere of the second
economy as well: responsibility for securing food provisions, a time-
consuming effort involving hours in queues as well as bartering and negotiating, fell primarily to women (Pine 1993). Furthermore, village
women were the ones who usually heated the family home, a task that
entailed building and regularly attending to a fire in the coal-burning
stove; in the summer they canned fruits and vegetables from the garden
for winter consumption.

In Kella, this responsibility for the domestic sphere was reinforced by
the strong presence of the Catholic church. As in many areas of Europe,
religion in Kella is a gendered domain in which women are held more
strictly to rules of church attendance, confession, and mourning (compare Cowan 1990; Dubisch 1995). Church and state gender ideologies
were thus often in conflict: while the state encouraged, indeed demanded, that women work outside the home and promoted the workplace as the central locale for social interaction, religious teachings
stressed the importance of women as mothers and nurturers in the private sphere of the family. Reciting biblical teachings, the "religious virtuoso" Emma Hauser explained, "The Lord first made Adam, that was
the first. The man, that's the stronger sex. And then he said, 'It's not good
that he's alone,' so he made him a helper. That's what it says in the Bible,
a helper. So one should know that the woman is only a helper for the

man. One hundred percent equal rights, that won't ever happen." Although the relationship between church teachings, popular conceptions of womanhood, and gender roles is itself complex and fluid, many devout women looked to the Virgin Mary as an ideal of a self-sacrificing nurturer in their daily lives (Dubisch 1996; Loizos 1988).[11]

Women negotiated this tension between church and state gender ideologies in different ways. A woman in her early forties, Barbara Becker, for example, fulfilled all the duties of a socialist worker-mother: she worked six hours in the clips factory, put in her required hours at the LPG, and served as a village council member. At home, however, she strove to emulate not socialist prescriptions for motherhood but, she explained, religious ideals of motherhood derived from the model of the Virgin Mary. She attended church daily, took full responsibility for domestic chores, cared lovingly for her husband and children, and silently endured verbal and occasional mild physical abuse from her senile mother. Barbara is a popular and beloved community member; her high status and resulting symbolic capital were, I believe, the product of her capacity to negotiate and demonstrate socialist and religious ideologies of womanhood.

Emma Hauser similarly attempted to negotiate this tension. Her biblical reference, for example, emerged during the same conversation in which she acknowledged and lamented a "triple burden" in the division of domestic labor. For her, the biblical reference was an explanation and justification of the gender inequalities she experienced and perceived in her daily life. When I asked if she truly believed that women were created for the purpose of assisting men, Emma laughed and replied, "No. Ach, I'm not as narrow-minded as that. On the contrary. Sometimes I tell my husband what to do. My sister-in-law, she serves her husband. Lays out everything for him to wear—including his hankie and socks. I don't do that. I just put everything in the closet. He knows where it is."

Emma's acknowledgment of the inequity of a triple burden, claims to progressive attitudes regarding women's roles, and affirmation of traditional religious ideologies of womanhood do not represent a contradiction on her part; rather, it is indicative of the diversity of representations and self-representations that are part of the construction and expression of gender identities. The tension between traditional religious and state socialist ideologies of gender—as well as contradictions within them—and these women's negotiation of those tensions demonstrate how gender is produced heterogeneously (Ginsburg and Tsing 1990: 5). In this sense, gender may be viewed as the product of a dynamic interplay between the internalization, negotiation, and contestation of diverse and competing gender ideologies. This dynamic has become especially evident since the fall of the Wall.

FROM WORKER TO HOMEMAKER?

Eighteen months after the Berlin Wall fell, the clips factory in Kella closed. Women were also the first to be let go from the toy factory in a neighboring village, where most of the other women from Kella had worked. With few prospects for future employment, especially for workers over the age of forty, the majority of women were relegated to the domestic sphere and became full-time homemakers for the first time in their lives. Having viewed work as a duty rather than a right, some women welcomed this change. Most women, however, did not. The loss of access to and control of relevant information about personalities and events in the community was only one factor in these women's sudden isolation. "It was stupid work," one woman recalled, "but at least we saw each other and talked to each other. Now people just run past each other. It wasn't just the work, but the companionship."

Apart from close friends and relatives, women largely stopped seeing each other except for occasional encounters at Sunday mass or the village Konsum. Feelings of superfluousness and financial insecurity, as well as the loss of a worker identity inculcated through forty years of state ideology and physical labor, contributed to many women's confusion and depression. "My friend Sylvia," one woman told me, "she just sits at home and cries." Another woman in her midforties, who often shared with me her feelings of depression and isolation, explained sadly: "This idea that a woman should stay at home and only do her housework came all at once. It happened overnight, too quickly." And in a different context, a younger woman made a similar remark: "Many women don't know what to do with themselves any more. What am I supposed to do standing over the soup pot all day?"

As in other postsocialist societies, women's participation in the political sphere has also declined dramatically due to the abolition of socialist gender quotas. We may recall from chapter 2 that Kella's mayor of ten years, Ursula Meyer, was ousted by the village council in May 1990 despite an overwhelming majority of the village popular vote; furthermore, there were no female candidates in the 1994 village council election. The dissolution of other organizations in which women had been active and of several women's groups immediately following the Wende have also contributed to a decrease in women's involvement in the public sphere.

These changes have been accompanied by the incorporation of the former GDR into a new nation-state whose social policies and legal systems direct women toward the family, motherhood, and part-time work (De Soto 1994; Rosenberg 1991). In contrast to the men who have found work following the closing of East German factories, village women who have work are employed only part-time. Although this is largely due to the West German job market for women, it is also the result of West German ideologies and images of womanhood channeled through the large and the small: from the media, to the regional Employment Bureau, to discussions and interactions with West German friends and relatives.

In the realm of everyday life, these various transformations have led to a reevaluation and reorganization of family relations, women's time and work, and gender roles. As throughout eastern Europe, the disappearance of an active second economy, informal networks, and alternative groups since the collapse of state socialism has resulted in a "newly valorized public" that, as Susan Gal has pointed out, is often conceptually defined as male while the private is defined as naturally female (Gal 1996). Furthermore, whereas under socialism many women had earned as much as or slightly less than their husbands, the decline in women's income through unemployment or part-time work has increased their economic dependence on men. Because many couples have continued to maintain separate bank accounts and share household expenses, a practice that made sense for dual income families, many women are now struggling to manage on limited budgets while their husbands are able to afford relative luxuries. In many cases, the reduction of women's work hours has also increased their responsibilities for domestic work. "My husband used to help occasionally with the dishes or with the children," one woman told me, "but now that I'm at home while he works full-time he says I should do it."

With the closing of nurseries, day-care centers, and after-school programs, many women have also suffered from "a latent bad conscience about their children" (Nickel 1993: 147). Echoing western German suspicions of external child care as a threat to the family, women frequently expressed to me how they "now realize" that the former system of day care had been bad for children.[12] One unemployed young woman explained, "Now I want to take some time for the children. They used to know me only as someone who ran around frantically. . . . In retrospect I think it was actually quite bad for the kids—I didn't have any time for them, and they were in day care all day. I didn't see it at the time, only after I experienced the difference." In a similar remark, an unemployed middle-aged woman told me, "That women should work, that came from above [the state]. In many ways it was good to work, this togetherness [in the factory], but whether it was good for the family is another question." Even though this woman criticized the socialist policy of women's paid employment, she acknowledged that such rebukes have only really become common since the Wende: "Nobody said these things before."

Women's time and space have also been transformed by these changes. Many women have gone from the factory floor or village council not only to the kitchen but also to the department stores and shopping centers. During the socialist period, shopping had meant hours spent in long lines, bartering, and dealing with the numerous tensions among shoppers competing for scarce consumer goods. Shopping as recreation is thus something entirely new to women here, and many of them enjoy it. "I feel freer now," one woman told me, citing the liberating effects of frozen dinners, central oil heating, and the availability of a range of consumer goods. "I can do what I want. I go shopping, not necessarily to buy things but to look." After re-unification, women in Kella began to attend Tupperware parties in each other's homes. One woman from the village became an Avon cosmetics representative; another began to sell Amway products.[13] The arrival of new catalogs from *Otto* or *Quelle* provided occasions to get together and comparison shop.

The realm of consumption, and, as noted in the previous chapter, the effort to acquire a cultural fluency in it, has not merely provided a new source of activity or entertainment. Consumption has also been a gendered initiation rite for women into the new society, a realm in which the implications of the "transition" for women have been reflected and, to a large extent, constituted. Anthropologists have widely recognized that commodities can carry with them particular cultural doctrines (Comaroff and Comaroff 1990; McCracken 1988; Miller 1995; Sahlins 1988; Wilk 1994). Frequently, I would add, these doctrines can be highly gendered.

To illustrate, I turn to a Tupperware party held in Kella more than a year after the Wende. Following in its decades-old tradition of home marketing, the company apparently saw a market niche in the former GDR. The enthusiastic salesperson at the gathering I attended in Kella, Sabine Schneider, was a native villager. Her training in sales tactics at a seminar for Tupperware representatives, combined with her own creative asides, provided Sabine with a story for nearly every plastic container she presented: "This one is perfect for keeping dinners warm while the men are away at *Frühschoppen,*" or "I always send this one to school with the kids."[14] Her audience of seven women marveled at the range of offerings and possibilities: "An onion would fit in here," "This would be good for leftover ground pork," and "This is just right for milk," Sabine informed them.

Not only was consumption presented as a social and gendered activity, but the products themselves were laden with explicit and implicit gender ideologies. Above all, the plastic containers conveyed a certain cult of domesticity. A woman's domain, as the marketing's setting itself indicated (we were seated around the kitchen table), was naturally in the private sphere of the family home, caring for her husband while he partook of traditionally male activities, or for her children as they entered the outside world. The large offering and diversity of plastic Tupperware containers seemed to represent the triumph of capitalist abundance and the new possibilities it offered for women to be better nurturers and homemakers. By the end of the evening, Sabine's audience had apparently been converted: she sold more than 500 marks' worth of Tupperware products.

The transformation from a communist to a consumption-oriented regime was perhaps best exemplified by the seminar offerings of the regional Women's Equality Office. Introduced after re-unification to address the unique needs and interests of women in the "New Federal States," these state- and local-level offices provided financial support to women's groups and funded educational programs throughout the former GDR.[15] Although publicized in Kella, these meetings were held thirty kilometers away in Heiligenstadt and were thus rarely attended by village women. Nevertheless, the lecture and seminar topics conveyed a message about what women had to learn in the new system. Often cosponsored by the prominent West German Sparkasse Bank, seminar topics included "Wishing, Planning, Buying," "Fashioning One's Life and Consumption Behavior," "Shopping to Your Advantage," and "Mother Doesn't Work! (What Value Does Housework Have?)."

All of this would seem to support a thesis that the unemployment of women and the upgrading of motherhood and femininity since re-unification have returned women to the private sphere and transformed socialist worker-mothers into homemakers or feminine consumers (for example, Dölling 1993; Einhorn 1993; Nickel 1993). While there are certain truths to this argument in Kella, the situation in this borderland region—and, I would suggest, in other postsocialist societies as well—is more complex than that. The contrasting and competing ideologies of womanhood have produced a tension; like other tensions in social life, this one is contested both individually and collectively, often in very subtle ways.

NEGOTIATING GENDER IN THE BORDERLAND

One way to analyze the tension produced by contrasting ideologies of womanhood is to explore a more concrete and literal one: the tension between East and West, between Ossis and Wessis. As we saw in the previous chapter, these distinctions are a part of everyday life in the German borderland. They are also often structured in gendered terms.

Gendered distinctions and identities are constructed and expressed, for example, as village women point to the losses they have suffered as women under the new system. After nearly a year of silence following the Wende in which any mention of the advantages of the socialist system was met with accusations of being "red" or "one of them," it was women in the village who first initiated discussions about the positive aspects of life under socialism. Some began to point to the advantages and opportunities for political participation enjoyed by women in the GDR: "Women were supposed to be included [in politics]. Women had a role that was totally different from the role they have today: for example, in the village council. That really wasn't so bad, that system. Women's roles were different because they had more possibilities. Whoever wanted to could participate. And the results are better when women are part of the decision making because they have a different understanding of many things." Many women lamented the loss of state-sponsored child care and generous maternity benefits. The loss of these services, many argued, was evidence of the new state's "hostility to children" and was cited as one of the primary reasons for the drastically declining birthrate in Kella as well as throughout the former GDR.[16]

Both the new state and its western citizens were accused of being hostile to children. Paralleling many of the Catholic church's arguments, several women pointed to the influx of western materialist values as being responsible for the sinking birthrate. "People in the West don't want to have more than one child because it would cut into their money for house and car," one woman in her late twenties told a group of friends. Another woman agreed: "They're really hostile to children over there. It's easier to find an apartment if you have four dogs than if you have one child."

Motherhood itself thus became a contested and appropriated category.[17] Women in Kella mocked their western neighbors for delaying childbearing, pointing to the advantages of having children at a young age.[18] "They [western German women] wait until they're thirty to have their first child! And then it's too overwhelming for them." Village women working in the West reported establishing solidarity with their eastern German colleagues by referring to their average age of child-bearing ("*We* had our children early, didn't we?"). Having children at a younger age was perceived not only as a result and reflection of the socialist state's commitment to children but also as a reflection of their own values and priorities.

Demonstrating how historical memory can be a complex interactional and gendered phenomenon, village women have similarly reappropriated a socialist identity as worker-mothers as a means of distinguishing themselves from West German women. During one of many discussions about women "over there," a women in her late twenties explained, "All women could work here. What do I mean by could? All women *had* to work. What woman in Kella didn't work? In the West they don't have to. Their husbands earn enough. I know of one woman who goes swimming on Mondays, takes dance lessons on Tuesdays, goes to sauna on Wednesdays. They don't know what to do with their time." The notion that women should work outside the home remains so strong here, in fact, that several women have sought paid employment mainly to avoid village gossip. "My husband actually earns enough now, and I would rather stay at home with the children," one woman confessed to me, "but I got a job because I didn't want people to talk about me."

Many women's longing for a return to paid employment and social interaction through work was temporarily fulfilled through the institution of the "ABM School" in Kella.[19] This government-subsidized job and retraining program, designed not only to create jobs but also to make a dent in regional and national unemployment statistics, employed twenty-four women from Kella, most of them in their midforties; all but one were former clips-factory workers. Women in this make-work program spent three days a week working for the village: landscaping, painting public buildings or fences, or assisting in various other community improvement projects (Figure 20). There was a noticeable difference in the village's appearance after just several weeks of this work.

The other two weekdays were spent in class, where women were supposedly to be retrained as florists or gardeners. However, women were not only instructed in plant biology or other related subjects; they were also provided training in the West German political and economic sys-

Figure 20.   "ABM women" doing landscape work for the village, 1992.
(Photograph by the author)

tem with subjects like business administration and politics. In this civic
education, with striking parallels to the educational function of the socialist work brigade, women learned about the structure of the West German government, the definition and functionings of a joint stock company, and the organization of the European Union. Many women used
the opportunity to inquire about employee rights, unemployment laws,
or maternity benefits.

A heightened social consciousness, similar to that exhibited during
the silk-painting sessions, was present among women here and was recognized by other members of the community. One young woman whose
mother was part of the project commented: "It's really nice. I saw the
women this week walking up the hill together. They were nicely dressed
and laughing, happy to be together again." Even when they began to realize how little they were actually being paid and that the planned year
of training would not be enough to complete any kind of certification as
florists or gardeners, most women pointed to the social function of work
as its most meaningful aspect.[20] As one woman explained, "In a way

we're being stupid because we're being taken advantage of. But it's worth it to the women to be together." Another woman, in her use of socialist terminology, similarly reflected a sense that this temporary "school" was a reenactment of the socialist clips factory: "It's fun to be in the brigade, and good to be with the women again."

The (re)creation of this gendered space, modeled in the women's minds after their experience together in the clips factory, provided frequent occasions for village women to contrast their experience with that of women in West Germany. Discussions often consciously stressed the social function of work as well as their identity as workers. "We're used to this," many women told me, "*we're* used to working." The daily contact not only renewed an exchange of gossip and shared information that had occurred in the factory but also provided an opportunity for women to assert an identity as eastern Germans in contrast to images and stereotypes of Wessis, particularly western German women.

The image against which such identities as eastern German women have been constructed and reaffirmed, as I argued in the previous chapter, is frequently a constructed and imagined Other. In this case, it was an image that often resembled the West German homemaker of the 1960s and early 1970s. As one young woman explained, "They don't have to work drüben because they're too busy with their *housework!* We have often made fun of that, of women in the West who list 'housewife' as their profession." In a similar vein, another woman told me, "We used to envy women drüben who don't have to work. But now we don't." While this image of West German women has changed as contact between East and West increases and as villagers have learned that many West German women do work outside the home, women in Kella are often quick to point out that this is part-time work: "*We* are used to working full-time," many say.

These gendered distinctions between East and West are part of the dynamic of boundary maintenance and invention described in the previous chapter. In the construction of Otherness that entails the reading of bodies, for example, it has been women's bodies that are especially read. As one woman from Kella explained, "Women are most easily recognized [as Ossis]. You see the differences immediately. Especially with older and [middle-aged] women. Women from drüben still wear makeup. Their hair is stylish. But here, women aren't confident enough of themselves to even speak over there. They have these unstylish, frizzy perms and no makeup."

In the first years after the fall of the Wall, when the most visible signs of difference were markers of Ossis, women from the East could be identified by their clothing, makeup, hairdos, accessories, body hair, dental work, or skin complexion. Several women employed in the West were made fun of for not shaving their legs; others became obsessed with their skin complexion after advertisements and tanned West German women told them of the benefits of tanning salons. "The difference [between them and us] is noticeable," one woman commented to her group of friends. "They can afford to take care of themselves and look good. Think of how much cosmetics cost. You can just tell."

In an effort to "catch up" and blend in, many women discarded their East German clothes, changed their hairstyles, and spent their severance pay on a new kitchen (including Tupperware products) or an expensive set of pots and pans. The female corollary to the male automobile, these western products represented not merely the women's domestic sphere in contrast to male mobility; they also reflect an effort to be more like western women with the convenience of time-saving western appliances. The marketing slogan for a particular set of pots and pans sold through company-sponsored in-home demonstration parties (similar to the Tupperware presentation) appealed to this perceived image of the western woman who was liberated by technology: "Less time in the kitchen, more time for yourself." Nearly half of the village women attending these demonstrations purchased the set, despite the exceedingly high price tag of 2,000 marks (approximately U.S.$1,200).

Women's attempts to emulate the West have also been influenced by a different set of competing gender ideologies: between traditional gender roles (mediated in part by the strong presence of the Catholic church, certain policies of the former socialist state, and an upgrading of domesticity since re-unification) and western feminist ideas (mediated by the media, contact with other West Germans, and the presence of westerners in the village—including my husband and myself). This too has influenced

religious practice and other aspects of daily life. Some women have contested and renegotiated gendered divisions of domestic labor. Others
have challenged strict, gendered mourning practices by refusing to wear
black for a year. In a comment that typically equated "being modern"
with "being western," one woman explained: "[Mourning dress] is just
not modern any more. [Such traditions] will eventually cease to exist."
Thus while the laws and policies of the FRG may direct women toward
the family and motherhood, other currents that contest this view have
influenced women's lives and the negotiation of gender as well.

Thus the women of Kella may strive to behave and look like western
German women, but they also resist the pressure to do so. As I argued in
the previous chapter, this paradox reflects the complex and contradictory aspects of identity in the borderland. A conversation in 1991 with
two women in their late twenties, Ingrid and Anna, about their smocks
(Kittel) first brought this to my attention. The common attire of female
factory workers under socialism, the Kittel was a key symbol of working
women in the GDR, especially after the Wende. At a church gathering
where middle-aged women were wearing their smocks while serving
tables, Ingrid remarked, "You know, I never wear my smock any more.
I used to run around the house all day in one, but not anymore since
the Wende. It's because of those [women] drüben. Nobody there wears a
smock anymore. It's not modern." During the course of her comment I
noticed Ingrid becoming more interested in this topic, which she then
pursued with a mutual friend, Anna, when she joined our conversation,
not having heard Ingrid's first remark:

INGRID: Anna, do you still wear a smock?
ANNA: No.
INGRID: Since when?
ANNA: Since the Wende.

Several weeks later, I ran into both women independently wearing their
smocks again. Because I saw both women almost daily, I knew this was a
practice they had only recently renewed. When I commented on this to
Ingrid, she grinned and said, "I guess after we talked about it I realized I

could wear it again." When I asked Anna, she explained, "[The wearing of smocks] subsided in the first years after the Wende, but somewhere it's a part of us."

The smock incident was similar to other assertions of eastern German identities described in the previous chapter. As in many of those instances, it took place in the realm of consumption—itself a highly gendered and gendering phenomenon—where distinctions between East and West, as well as those within the village, have been expressed, experienced, negotiated, and contested, both before and since the fall of the Wall.

INGRID'S COLLAR

One final story will illustrate the contradictory, complex, and playful nature of borderland identities as well as illuminate the gendered aspect of boundaries and national identity. This story involves another conversation with Ingrid, who asked me one day how women in America wear their shirt collars. I told her I didn't really know. Somewhat taken aback and almost irritated by my ignorance, she said: "Well, now it's modern to wear your collar up. That's how women do it in the West. Here [in the former GDR] women wear their collars down." Ingrid seemed to be struggling to figure out not only current fashion etiquette for shirt collars but also where she, as an Ossi who both mimicked and resisted what she perceived to be Wessi standards, fit in. For weeks after our conversation, I couldn't help noticing that on some days she was wearing her collar up, on other days down. Then, one night at a dinner party, I looked across the table and saw that her collar was askew—a rare occurrence for someone as concerned with her appearance as Ingrid: one side of her collar was up, the other one was down.

To me, this probably fortuitous position of Ingrid's collar was loaded with meaning, symbolizing the interstitiality of the borderland, the way in which its residents are somehow betwixt and between East and West, as well as the constructed and gendered nature of these distinctions. Of course the uneven collar was most likely the result of Ingrid's indecision over how to dress for the dinner party; she probably had switched the collar back and forth until she had to leave, when she apparently was unable to check it one last time. As in the preceding weeks, her tampering with the collar entailed a gendered negotiation of and play with identity—a metaphor for identity in the borderland; indeed, for identity itself.

The tensions between East and West, as well as the tension produced by each system's contrasting ideologies of gender and womanhood, continue to be assimilated and negotiated in multiple and diverse ways. The fact that women's experiences and negotiations of these changes are highly differentiated points to the need to avoid homogenizing generalizations about women in eastern Europe (Funk 1993a). Instead, we must remain alert to these tensions and the interstices they produce (Hauser, Heyns, and Mansbridge 1993), for it is in these border zones—both real and imagined—that gender and national distinctions are constructed, negotiated, contested, and experienced in everyday life.

7 | The Dis-membered Border

Werner Schmidt, one of the few "really reds" in Kella, once told me, "If you want to conquer a [political] system, and conquer it quickly, then you have to portray this system in the ugliest colors possible. That's how it is. And that can be dirty work." Werner was commenting on the West German media's frequent comparisons of the GDR with the Third Reich, a portrayal that was part of a general and rapid devaluation of the East German past by dominant West German discourses. As we saw in chapter 2, Werner himself felt victimized by these attempts to "overcome the past." Not only did they unjustly connect him, as a devout former party member, to crimes committed by the Stasi and Communist Party leaders, he felt, but the characterization of the East German past as an obstacle—an implicit assumption in the notion of "overcoming the past"—also undermined some of the very foundations of his identity and personhood.

206

I begin with Werner's perceptive insight because it suggests several related themes I explore in this chapter: the way in which memory is an interactive, malleable, and highly contested phenomenon, the asymmetrical nature of remembering in united Germany, and the role of the past in the present.

My focus here is on the construction, production, and negotiation of memory since the fall of the Wall. I concentrate on several arenas in which this production and negotiation take place, including performative ceremonies, national and local discourses of memory, and struggles over the commemoration of the past. More specifically, I analyze two events in the community's recent past that reflect a dialectic of remembering and forgetting that is still occurring throughout united Germany: a parade in honor of German re-unification in October 1990 and the unsuccessful attempt by village leaders to preserve, as a memorial, sections of the three-meter fence that had surrounded and enclosed Kella between 1952 and 1989. My aim here is to examine an interplay between local and extralocal processes of remembering; I argue that memory and its representations both structure and are structured by representations of the past at a broader, often national, level.[1] I am interested here in commemorations as well as silences, in the role of the past in negotiating, contesting, and rebuilding the present.

SELF-RE-PRESENTATIONS

Like many of the re-unification festivities held throughout Germany on October 3, 1990, the community's unity celebration was in many ways a carefully orchestrated media event.[2] It was broadcast on a regional television network that had reported on Kella during the summer of 1990 and subsequently opted to base its coverage of re-unification events in the former Schutzstreifengemeinde. Under the glare of media lights, television cameras, and film crews, villagers performed, improvised, and invented a variety of rituals in honor of the historic occasion. The church-related observances, including a candlelight procession to the chapel on the eve of re-unification and a traditional mass the next morning, had been planned far in advance. But when the television network notified Kella's mayor, Karl Hartmann, two weeks before October 3 of its intention to cover the village's celebration that day, the community was galvanized. "If television is coming," Karl told me, "I thought we'd better really celebrate!"

The resulting parade, organized by an informal committee headed by the village mayor, was an elaborate commemoration and display of the village's past, present, and anticipated future, a "definitional ceremony" in which individuals as well as a collectivity told stories about themselves and itself to themselves as well as to others.[3] Throughout the parade these stories were linked to national histories—a way of connecting personal and community biographies to a nationally shared past and also, it seemed, a way to put Kella back on the map.

The procession, which began at the border crossing and circled through the village, contained numerous depictions of events and institutions in the community's history. All contributions to the parade by village residents were conceived, funded, and constructed by the participants themselves. Several women who had worked in the local factory dressed in smocks and carried trays of cigars to depict an earlier phase of the factory's history; a few carried signs bearing socialist slogans that had once hung on the walls of their workplace ("My Hand for My Product") (Figure 21). Another group of women, also dressed in smocks, carried baskets and farming tools to represent "LPG Women." Others wore the Eichsfeld traditional dress of cape and hat to portray women from a much earlier period. Men carrying farming tools and a sign "LPG Silberklippe" depicted the collective farm that had been located in Kella for several years before being merged with other LPGs in the region. An old wagon loaded with furniture bore the sign "In 1952 We Had to Leave," representing those who were deported during the forced evacuations in the spring of that year (Figure 22); and on top of a Trabant was a sign that read "Ordered 1964. Received 1990," referring to the long wait involved in obtaining an automobile in the GDR.

The most popular and loudest exhibit of the village's past during the parade was a float containing a reconstruction of the border itself (Figure 23). Across the back of a large, open truck bed, parade participants replicated the Grenze by mounting several feet of the former border

Figure 21. Women in Kella's unity parade recall the old cigar factory ("My Hand for My Product"), 1990. (Photograph in the collection of the author)

fence, complete with authentic warning signs and barbed wire. On one side of the fence were three young men dressed as border guards; on the other stood several young villagers shouting angrily "We want out! We want out!" while pounding the ground with sticks, pitchforks, and signs reading "We want our freedom." A photograph of the communist party leader Erich Honecker that had once adorned the walls of all public buildings hung on the side of the truck with a caption containing his well-known pledge, "Everything for the good of the people." An adjacent caption contained several villagers' interpretation of the meaning of this slogan after widespread revelations of party leaders' excesses: "I was the people." On the truck's other side hung a banner recalling the Wende: "When freedom draws near, not even barbed wire inspires fear!"

In the context of the parade, such representations of the past were affirmations of the present. Following the float of the reconstructed border, for example, was a group of participants from East and West sym-

Figure 22. The 1990 unity parade included a portrayal of deportations from Kella ("In 1952 We Had to Leave"). (Photograph in the collection of the author)

bolically linked by carrying garland arches adorned with red, gold, and black ribbons. Another group of villagers followed displaying a sign that read "Hurrah! The people from Hesse can come again!" Similarly, the wagon of those expelled in 1952 was followed by an automobile bearing the sign: "Now we can come back again"; behind the East German Trabi was a West German Ford. These juxtapositions served to illustrate not only positive changes since the Wende but also the hardships these changes had overcome.

Other representations of the present, referred to as "the new period," included a small basket of East German products next to a large and nearly overflowing shopping cart filled with western goods; children from the village kindergarten with signs bearing the crossed-out abbreviations FRG and GDR were followed by children carrying a large placard with the word "Germany" in bold letters. One woman from Kella

Figure 23. A float made of reconstructed border materials enlivened the re-unification celebrations, 1990. (Photograph in the collection of the author)

had constructed a large doll wearing a *Tarnkappe* (pointed cone hat), which, according to legend, makes those who wear it invisible. "For the people who must disappear in the new period," she explained, referring to former Stasi informants and powerful party members. Her husband's contribution to the parade made a similar critical reference. He carried several spades and a sign that read, "For sale: spades to dig up western relatives," referring to former party members who had denied having western relatives (often because they were prohibited from contact with the West) but who had sought them out after the fall of the Wall.[4] Members of the Eschwege volunteer fire department and a group representing a women's club in the nearby village of Grebendorf were among the western German participants.

Accompanied by a marching band and a trumpet choir from Eschwege, the parade, along with hundreds of spectators, made its way to the village soccer field, where the GDR flag was lowered for the last time and

Figure 24. Lowering the GDR flag for the last time on October 3, 1990. (Photograph in the collection of the author)

replaced with the West German one (Figure 24). After brief remarks from the mayors of Kella and adjacent western communities, villagers attempted (largely in vain) to sing along with the West German national anthem. Together with local politicians from the West, Kella's mayor planted a "Tree of Unity" as a symbol of renewal and a growing together of the two Germanies.

In the tongue-in-cheek ceremony that followed, the GDR flag was placed over a small black casket built especially for the occasion (Figure 25). It was then carried by four pallbearers in mourning dress to its

Figure 25. Carrying the GDR to its grave (in the unity parade, 1990).
(Photograph in the collection of the author)

final resting place near the soccer field, where the flag and casket were
ceremoniously burned. "They carried the GDR to its grave," one woman
later explained, smiling.

The party that followed lasted for days, in part because it coincided
with Kirmes. The time is fondly remembered as a high point in the community's recent past. "The weather was so beautiful—like high summer—and everything was so joyful," one woman recalled, "and so many
people! We hadn't had that many people here in forty years. It was the
best day of my life!" She smiled sheepishly: "Even better than my wedding day!"

In addition to demonstrating how quickly the past may be remade
into and reshaped by memory, the festivities and many of its perfor-

mances also reflected an emerging discourse of victimization in relation to the community's, and nation's, socialist past. The reconstructed border, for example, imposed a meaning and memory on the village's experience as a Schutzstreifengemeinde by depicting its residents as prisoners fighting for their freedom, using language that would have been unthinkable under socialism, rather than as the relatively complacent citizens that most villagers had actually been. The priest's sermon during that morning's mass reflected a similar use of language: "For forty years we lived in bondage. Let us pray that we don't fall into bondage again." Locals interviewed by the omnipresent television reporters seemed to be telling them what they wanted to hear: "This wasn't a democratic but rather a dictatorial regime," one villager said, "and I never want to hear of it again!" Another elderly women, visibly nervous in front of a microphone and television camera, lamented: "They [the Communists] took forty years of our lives!"

Like other representations of the past, however, such discourses of victimization have been questioned and contested. While watching a videotape of the television report from Kella, for example, one woman became outraged at her fellow villager's comments. "He never experienced so much hate here! How can he say that? In fact, he earned most of his money from the reds! I simply can't stand to hear such things." Her friend agreed: "How can they say they took forty years of our lives? We had our life here, our Heimat, and we did a lot in those forty years."

A conversation between a mother and son reflected similar contestations over interpretations of the past. The forty-year-old son, Thomas Spiegel, cautioned against accepting people's judgment of the past from today's perspective. "People have a different judgment today than they used to," he explained:

> For example, the case of Martin Schneider [the young man who was sentenced to prison after his aborted escape in 1983]. When that happened and he went to prison, people thought it was bad, but the rules were known. The horror and agitation that people display today is new.
>
> We used to sit and work in our garden in Kella, but we never really took note of the fence. It is wrong to say that the population felt oppressed.

His mother vehemently objected: "I always felt unfree, and always had misgivings about the fence. We were always afraid!" But her son reiterated: "It's only after the fact that people feel oppressed. Almost everyone participated passively. Eighty to ninety percent of the population kept the GDR going. The further we come away [from the socialist past], the more we scrub ourselves clean."

FROM VICTIMIZATION TO NOSTALGIA

Such discussions at the local, even familial, level take place in the context of national debates and discourses about the East German past. Referred to broadly as *Vergangenheitsbewältigung,* a term originally used in West Germany in relation to the Nazi period, these debates have been largely dominated by the West German press, politicians, and intellectuals. They have focused on a range of issues, including calls for a reevaluation of Germany's Nazi past;[5] debates over what to do with and about East Germany's Stasi heritage, which have often compared the GDR to the Third Reich; criminal trials of former border guards and other representatives of the GDR state, which for many eastern Germans represented a kind of victor's justice; and the controversy surrounding the famous East German author Christa Wolf,[6] the "second historians' debate," which called into question the value of GDR culture as well as the nature and apportioning of guilt (Huyssen 1995: 51). As one of Wolf's critics wrote, echoing an argument made by Michael Stürmer during the 1986 Historians' Debate, "This is no academic question. He who determines what was also determines what will be" (Ulrich Greiner, cited in Huyssen 1995: 51).

At issue were not only questions of history and memory but also a reopening and reevaluation of the German national question itself. The need to move beyond a burdened past and create a common history, a central assumption of Vergangenheitsbewältigung, was perceived in these debates as being critical to a new understanding of German nationhood and national identity. Implicit in this notion is the assumption that the past is something that must and can be overcome in order to "construct an alternative agenda for the future" (Huyssen 1995: 52),

rather than viewing historical memory as an ongoing process of understanding, negotiation, and contestation.

My aim here, however, is not to analyze the complex and extensive
postunification debates surrounding history and memory, the German
nation, or Vergangenheitsbewältigung.[7] Instead, I seek to illuminate and
contextualize an interplay between local and extralocal processes of remembering. The national debates surrounding Stasi revelations, guilt
and responsibility, and Vergangenheitsbewältigung, for example, produced a "rhetoric of accusation and self-righteousness" in which former
GDR citizens were either victims or perpetrators, with few gray areas in
between (Huyssen 1995: 37). Furthermore, as Claudia Koonz has pointed
out, the emergence of new forms of memory and historical representation at concentration-camps like Buchenwald or Sachsenhausen recast
eastern Germans as victims of Soviet occupation forces; this new form of
"GDR memory" not only expanded the categories of victimhood "beyond the anti-Fascists memorialized in the East and the victims of the
Holocaust mourned in the West" but reflected a more general discourse
of victimization in relation to the GDR past (1994: 275). These various
discourses of victimization provided the context for representations and
expressions like the Tarnkappe, spades, and border reconstruction during Kella's re-unification festivities.

These discourses have also produced many images of suffering that
emerged after the Wende. The exchange between Thomas Spiegel and his
mother, as well as the reconstructed boundary and other references to
the border during Kella's unity parade, for example, illustrate how the
fence, or the Grenze as a whole, quickly came to be a powerful image
of suffering after the Wende, a metonym for the GDR itself.[8] This was
evident not only in the widespread media representations of the fall of
the Wall but also in the local merging of the fence's image with the religious symbolism of the cross, as with the Seventh Station and other
crosses made of fencing and barbed wire described in chapter 3. As powerful images of suffering, these "new memory symbols" (Jones 1994: 161)
stand for all that is now regarded as having been wrong with the socialist regime.

Such images and discourses have carried with them the potential to be
internalized, reproduced, and expressed in the form of personal memo-

ries, often with multiple intentions. I was occasionally told, for example, of the mines and trip-wire shooting devices that surrounded Kella, even though such fortifications were never actually installed in the area. "We lived here as if we were in jail," said one woman, whose son, I later learned, had been an active Grenzhelfer and suspected Stasi informant. Her comment seemed to lend credence to Thomas Spiegel's warning about judging the past from the perspective of the present, about the simultaneous solidification of boundaries and blurring of distinctions between victims and perpetrators.

As we saw in chapter 2, this boundary between victim and perpetrator is constantly shifting as it is negotiated, constructed, and contested in everyday practices and discourses. According to some villagers, "everyone somehow participated." Others measure complicity according to definitive categories such as party member, Grenzhelfer, or village-council representative. For some residents, these categories carry equal weight; for others, party members or Stasi informants were the only true perpetrators. Several villagers have self-righteously accused those who sent their children to the Jugendweihe ceremony of being guilty of complicity. Others use church attendance as an important measure of resistance.

Indeed, the Catholic church has played an important role in mediating and constituting such discourses of guilt and victimization. While preaching the Christian doctrine of forgiveness, it has also been quick to claim its own institutional as well as its members' victim status. In March 1990, for example, several thousand residents of the Catholic Eichsfeld gathered on the symbolic ground of the Hülfensberg pilgrimage site to dedicate a plaque in honor of the "victims of the past," as the presiding priest explained. The inscription on the plaque, at the base of the Konrad Martin Cross, reads:

Pilgrims from East and West
Pray for the victims
Of fascist and
Stalinist dictatorships!

Lord, let their suffering
Be a blessing to our land!

In the language of this commemoration, the entire GDR past was labeled as "Stalinism," ignoring the fact that Stalinist rule—characterized by deportations, mass arrests, and internment camps—had largely ended in East Germany by the mid-1950s; its crimes were equated with those of the Nazi regime that had preceded it. The experience of Eichsfeld Catholics under socialism was similarly compared with that of the Kulturkampf victim, Konrad Martin. "Bishop Konrad Martin was made to suffer because of his beliefs," said the priest conducting the ceremony, "and through his memory the Catholic population of the GDR was brought to action. . . . I don't know of any other group that maintained its protest against the regime more than the Catholic church. We mustn't forget this resistance. Especially those who suffered in the Sperrgebiet. . . . We mustn't forget the victims of the past, of Stalinism and National Socialism."

Similar messages were conveyed by other church officials, including the local priest in Kella. Voices like those of Thomas Spiegel, who warned against the church's self-glorifying post-Wende claims to resistance and leadership during the 1989 demonstrations, were rare. "The church was guilty of the same kind of opportunism as were most of the people," he argued. For many villagers, however, loyal church membership and participation were sufficient evidence of victim status: the practice of religion under socialism as an expression of and reason for resistance was thus reappropriated in defining gradations of complicity, as well as in constructing a memory of the socialist past.

Thus as the old official histories are discredited—in the toppling of socialist monuments, renaming of streets and rewriting of history books— new histories are constructed, produced, and contested in a variety of ways (Watson 1994). The devaluing of the socialist past has been challenged, for example, by a retreat to the forms of nostalgia described in chapter 5. In an ongoing dialectic of remembering and forgetting, discourses of victimization have given way to, and continue to oscillate between, discourses of nostalgia and mourning—demonstrating the shifting, multiple, and infinitely malleable nature of memory. At times one discourse may be compelling, at other times not.

The reason for this, it seems to me, lies in the way in which historical memory is interactively constructed. In the previous chapter I described how village women have reappropriated a socialist identity as worker-mothers as a means of distinguishing themselves from West German women. Similarly, many villagers have pointed to the lost advantages of the socialist system. At first voiced in a cautious statement that "Socialism wasn't all that bad," early defenses of the former GDR focused on the economic and social security of the socialist system. Gradually, however, these defenses frequently came to be expressed as nostalgia and mourning for an East Germany that had never existed. In this discourse of nostalgia, metaphors of community and kinship have become increasingly prevalent. "We used to live like one big family here," I was often told, "now no one has time for any one else."

Rather than focusing on guilt or victimization, these nostalgic discourses of the past may also entail a novel form of willful forgetting, or silence: the choice *not* to know.[9] In the midst of Stasi revelations and "witch-hunts" waged largely in the West German press, villagers' initial enthusiasm for obtaining access to the mysteries of the Stasi files quickly dissipated. With very few exceptions, residents of Kella have decided not to file for access to their own Stasi files, at least for the moment. Although guided by an awareness of the potential risks involved in gaining access to one's personal file (including the possibility that a Stasi informant could be a friend or family member, a revelation that could be particularly disruptive in such a small community), the decision not to know is not merely a pragmatic one. It is also a reaction, I believe, to the discrediting of the GDR past, a critical resistance to partaking in the construction of new histories and memories. These pockets of subversive silences are an important element of an ongoing and interactive negotiation and contestation of historical memory.

Not only can every act of remembering be an act of forgetting; it can also work the other way around.

"THIS FENCE SHALL REMAIN STANDING"

In contrast to many postsocialist societies, in which new histories are being created out of formerly unsanctioned memories of the past (Watson 1994: 4), the discrediting of old official histories in the former GDR has been almost instantaneously replaced with the imposition of new ones. The production of historical memory is deeply imbedded in the dynamics of East and West German power relations; like other sites of cultural confrontation, remembering in the new Germany has been largely asymmetrical.

Nowhere has this been more evident than in local and national contestations over representations and commemorations of the socialist past. As socially constructed and negotiated events involving struggles over the control and appropriation of historical knowledge (Cohen 1994: 246), commemorations may be quite revelatory. In united Germany, they have often entailed the construction, reconfiguration, or dismantling of the institutions, symbols, memorials, monuments, and other public-memory sites of the former GDR. The removal of the Lenin statue in East Berlin, the renaming of streets and public buildings formerly dedicated to prominent communist figures throughout eastern Germany, and the nearly complete dismantling of the Berlin Wall are but a few examples of such inverted commemorations. Occasionally these inverted commemorations have been accompanied by a public ceremony; usually, they are not. The rush to avoid the kind of collective forgetting that characterized post-Nazi Germany by uncovering, confronting, and hence "overcoming" East Germany's burdened past has paradoxically been accompanied by a kind of "organized forgetting" (Connerton 1989: 14), an erasure of certain memory symbols and the creation and contestation of new ones.

A struggle in Kella between locals and the German federal government over the preservation of the former border fence highlights several of these issues; it also demonstrates the tremendous importance of the materiality of memory. Even before plans to dismantle the entire inter-German border were announced, village political leaders had submitted applications to Kreis officials hoping to maintain the border fencing near Kella as a memorial and potential tourist attraction. Two years after the fall of the Wall, when the responsibility for the former border structure was assigned to the newly founded Association for the Dismantling and Use of Old [former border] Installations, Ltd., it became clear that community leaders' plans were threatened. The corporation was contracted

Figure 26.   Removal of the border fence near Kella, 1992. (Photograph by the author)

by the Federal Defense Ministry to dismantle the fencing, guard towers, service roads, and all other structures that had been part of the former border. As with the Berlin Wall, whose concrete slabs were crushed into gravel for eastern German roads, many of the materials (especially metal fencing and concrete slabs) were resold to individuals and local businesses—further testimony for many locals that "the new regime only cares about money."

As the encroaching removal of the fence became visible from Kella, the village's mayor, Karl Hartmann, attempted to mobilize the community to combat the dismantling of this intensely symbolic structure (Figure 26). At a large gathering of the local Heimatverein, Karl announced that "the federal government has issued orders to remove the fence and service road. It is supposed to be returned to its original state." When the audience expressed its outrage at this development, he continued: "In the case of arable land [removing the fence] is certainly the right thing to do. But not like here, especially when the service road makes such a good walking path. A part of the border structure should remain as a memorial. In the last few years, many things have been determined too quickly [for us]. And now we want to be the ones to decide about this." At Karl's suggestion, the group passed a resolution to preserve the service road and sections of the border fence near Kella.

The majority sentiment, although not unanimous, entailed more than a concern for memory, for the "symbolic importance" of the border, as one man stressed, or for "preserving the border structure for future generations because even the young children won't remember it years from now," as another woman explained. The desire to keep the fence was also an expedient one, based on the (misguided) anticipation of a burgeoning local tourist industry. The border as tourist attraction was especially stressed by community members working to promote tourism in the region.[10] "That is what really distinguishes our village," one of these men argued. "The border is the first thing visitors want to see when they come to Kella."[11]

Although a small minority, some residents did not share these sentiments. One man angrily claimed he felt like he was "living in Buchenwald" and demanded the immediate removal of the fence. Others simply explained, "We don't need to be reminded of that. We had to live with it for forty years, and now we don't want to see it anymore." For these opponents of the memorial effort, a museum was the proper place to memorialize the border.

Over a period of nearly two years, Kella's mayor appealed to county, state, and federal officials to preserve sections of the fence and service road. Together with other supporters of the memorial, he hung hand-painted signs on sections of the fence to mark them for preservation: "This fence shall remain standing." Karl supported his requests to state authorities with arguments about the importance of the former border structure as a memorial and tourist attraction as well as with references to resolutions passed by both the Heimatverein and village council. An early written communication, for example, argued: "As a village in the 500-meter Sperrgebiet, our experience of the harshness of the old regime was more than skin deep. The border installations represent a part of our community's history. . . . Our residents and our village council therefore demand that these installations be maintained as monuments and memorials for posterity, as well as for a potential tourist attraction in the future."[12] Later, sensing the ineffectiveness of these arguments, Karl appealed on environmentalist grounds, pointing out the threat posed by the dismantling of the fence and service road to the unique vegetation and animal life that had developed along the border region. "The village administration in Kella will not tolerate a dismantling of these installations," he wrote, "for this would mean a massive destruction of flora and fauna."

Stressing orders to dismantle "completely" the former border installations as well as the "not insignificant dangers" the structures allegedly posed to local residents, authorities denied the community's requests.[13] In a move eerily reminiscent of the fenced enclosure of the village pilgrimage chapel in the 1950s—a symbolic and literal demonstration of the socialist state's authority—the border fence was removed from Kella in the summer of 1993.[14]

Local voices were thus ultimately and conclusively silenced in this clash between local and official memories. As David Cohen has noted, struggles over the production of history often entail a "pathology of ownership" (1994: 246). What was being contested here was not only ownership of the actual border fence (a real issue, for the land on which it stood had been returned to private ownership), but also ownership of the form, content, and manner of commemoration. It was, in a sense, a contest over the ownership, appropriation, and meaning of this *lieu de mémoire* (Nora 1989), which for locals had been invested with additional meaning after the Wall as an image of suffering.

WHAT REMAINS

The physical remains of the past in Kella consist of icons of faith and images of suffering—the wooden cross adorned with barbed wire, the renovated chapel, the crucifixes that mark community boundaries—set against a backdrop of the recent destruction of the landscape and memory through the removal of the former border fence. The gashes

Figure 27.   The border museum near the town of Bad Sooden-Allendorf
includes a characteristic patrol road, border fencing, and watch tower.
(Photograph by the author)

in the earth where the fence and service road were once located will heal,
just as vegetation soon covered and nearly concealed the metal fencing
once the political border became obsolete in 1989. As the landscape heals,
however, evidence of the past will be increasingly effaced, relegated to
museums, the officially sanctioned mode of memory and amnesia.

In the numerous border museums that are now scattered along the former border,[15] the past has been neatly arranged, displayed, and distilled
(Figure 27). Containing decontextualized objects of the border, including
towers, fencing, border-police jeeps, observation stands, signs, and deac-
tivated trip-wire installations, the museums serve not merely to inform
but to legitimate the new German nation-state by providing testimony to
the necessity of overcoming Germany's division. Indeed, most border
museums contain, or are themselves memorials to, "the victims of the division of Germany." One museum, for example, states its mission on a
plaque near the entryway: "To overcome the scars of Germany's division

and to do justice to the countless victims of the border." A brochure describing this museum begins:

> Although the metal grating, barbed wire, barricades, and trip wires have been dismantled, the land mines removed, [and] the watch towers blown up, . . . everyone who had to live with and suffer under this despicable border that divided Germany for forty years will not forget it. But what about future generations who, thank God, will not know the most perfect and gruesome fortification system in history? Who never saw it or were allowed to see it? This museum is to be maintained . . . as a memorial to a piece of German history.

Many border museums, including the one near Kella, are outgrowths of West German voluntary associations founded long before the fall of the Wall for the purpose of educating visitors about the "peculiarities" of the inter-German border.[16] Intended not only as memorials but also as efforts to fight a kind of "forgetting" that results from what another (eastern German) museum brochure describes as the "disappearance of the border from the landscape," the border museums are visited by Germans from both East and West,[17] including many school classes.

The re-membering of the border in this context—the product of its dis-membering in another—exemplifies certain uses of the past in affirming the present. Or, as Paul Connerton has written in an observation uncannily similar to Werner Schmidt's insight quoted at the beginning of this chapter: "To pass judgment on the practices of the old regime is the constitutive act of the new order" (1989: 7).

The various means and forms of remembering, however—including everyday negotiations of guilt and complicity, alternative memory symbols, and subversive silences—illustrate the inherently interactive, malleable, and contestable nature of memory. What remains of the past in Kella, therefore (as elsewhere in the former GDR), is this ongoing process of production and negotiation of memory, a dynamic that continues to shape and transform people's relationship to their past as it shapes the boundaries, and interstices, of remembering and forgetting.

Epilogue: The Tree of Unity

During re-unification celebrations on October 3, 1990, residents of Kella, visitors, and local politicians from West Germany planted an oak sapling near the village soccer field. The Tree of Unity was intended to symbolize renewal and the growing together of the two Germanies after forty years of division. A year later, the tree was dead, symbolizing for many villagers the lost hopes and expectations of re-unification itself (Figure 28). "Of course it died," one woman told me, flipping her wrist forward and shaking her head to emphasize what many perceived to be the obvious symbolic connection between the tree's death and disappointing developments since re-unification. A new tree was planted by village workers without ceremony several months later, this time surrounded by a piece of the former border fence to protect it, people said, from animals and other elements. The tree is thriving (Figure 29).

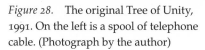

Figure 28.   The original Tree of Unity, 1991. On the left is a spool of telephone cable. (Photograph by the author)

Figure 29.   The replacement Tree of Unity, surrounded by a piece of the former border fence, 1996. (Photograph by the author)

Like the wooden cross at the Seventh Station, the border fencing around the Tree of Unity only later acquired symbolic value. Originally intended as a functional solution to the problem of protecting the sapling, the iron fencing was like other materials from the border that were readily available and being used throughout the village to practical ends. The tree became symbolic as it began to thrive in its new, enclosed location. Many villagers, pointing to the merely functional purpose of the fencing, failed to see an irony in this development. Others, in an "argument of images" (Fernandez 1986), related it to their experience and interpretation of recent events: "Put the fence back up and [the tree] grows," one young man chuckled. Although stated with humor, his comment invoked a series of cultural references in local and national discourses on both sides of the former border—ranging from T-shirts to jokes to heated confrontations between East and West—that called for putting back up the Wall.

The Tree of Unity reflected not only the serendipitous and multifarious nature of symbols but also the creativity, and often humor, with which people have manipulated, negotiated, and even sustained a liminal condition during a period of turbulent change. Like many of the incidents, anecdotes, and stories I have described in this book, the Tree of Unity might be dismissed by some as trivial or inconsequential; accusations of "mereness" are often leveled at anthropology (Herzfeld 1997). What such allegations overlook, however, is that processes of social change are most intimately experienced and thus often most discernible in the minutiae of everyday life. Further, as Bourdieu and Foucault (among others) have argued, the very triviality of everyday practices is a key element of their power; it is in the routines and intimacies of daily life that cultural forms acquire their taken-for-granted (or, in Bourdieu's terminology, "doxic") quality.

As I have attempted to show in a variety of contexts throughout this book, the nation-state may frequently become most effectively anchored in the trivialities of daily life, for it is in everyday practices that the experience of national belonging and state power is both activated and contested. Under socialist rule, and especially in borderlands like Kella, the state permeated most realms of daily life, ranging from the penetrating presence of the border and its culture of surveillance to village social life, which was structured by factory work brigades, state mass organizations, and lengthy shopping queues. Since re-unification, the pervasive presence of the new (West) German nation-state, frequently defined and promoted in terms of a consumer market economy and economic prosperity,[1] has been, and continues to be, manifested and experienced in equally quotidian domains: in daily negotiations of new consumption practices; in the decline of face-to-face interaction that has resulted, in part, from the closing of state-owned factories and cooperatives; in transformations in religious practices attributed to the influx of a consumer society; in the Tupperware parties and silk-painting sessions that coincided with the loss of maternity, child-care, and employment benefits for women; and, perhaps most noticeably for residents of Kella, in the nearly complete dismantling of the former border structure.

Yet it is also in the trivialities of daily life that such anchorings are contested—subtly, often silently, and sometimes not even fully consciously:

> It is the realm of partial recognition, of inchoate awareness, of ambiguous perception, and, sometimes, of creative tension: that liminal space of human experience in which people discern acts and facts but cannot or do not order them into narrative descriptions or even into articulate conceptions of the world. . . . It is from this realm, we suggest, that silent signifiers and unmarked practices may rise to the level of explicit consciousness, of ideological assertion, and become the subject of overt political and social contestation—or from which they may recede into the hegemonic, to languish there unremarked for the time being. (Comaroff and Comaroff 1991: 29)

Under socialism, this spectrum of contestations included GDR flags wedged between windows on state holidays, greetings disguised as housecleaning to relatives standing on the western side of the border, a blue Aral gasoline bumper sticker pasted on the inside of a kitchen cupboard, a playful yet critical performance at carnival, or regular attendance at mass. In the first years after the fall of the Wall, critiques of the new order were similarly expressed in gestures of tacit dissent as well as conscious opposition: in carnival songs and monologues, decisions to leave lucrative employment in the West for lower-paying work with other Ossis in the former GDR, the resuscitation of women's Kittel, choosing the Trabi over a western car, and investing with symbolic meaning an iron fence around a tree.

If measured by their success in arresting the absorption of the East by the West, such practices may not be considered truly resistive. Ultimately, of course, West German political, economic, and sociocultural forms and institutions will continue to prevail. However, moments and processes of transition are not to be measured solely by their political outcomes. In the process of this transition between two German states, people have invented, and to some extent ritualized, cultural practices that both reflect and constitute profound identity negotiations and transformations. In Kella, these negotiations have frequently entailed the emergence of certain rites of passage that mark a transition: a trip to the Braunrode hill overlooking Kella, borderlining walks along the old boundary, even a first visit to McDonald's. Like many aspects of every-

Figure 30.   The village center, 1991.
(Photograph by the author)

day life under socialist rule in Kella, these ritualistic practices have often been informed by the contextual specificity and dense materiality of the now vanished territorial border.

When I returned to Kella in 1996, the village looked, felt, smelled, and sounded more "western." Most brown coal ovens had been replaced by oil heating, largely eliminating the distinctive odor of "GDR air." Many Trabis were also gone, not because they were no longer desirable but because they could not pass the rigorous vehicle inspections of West Germany. Because of the widespread availability and relative inexpensiveness of formerly coveted food products like meat and eggs, gone too was the raising of livestock and poultry for domestic consumption—and

Figure 31. The village center, 1996. (Photograph by the author)

along with it, the rural sounds of pigs, chickens, and sheep as well as corresponding local rituals associated with animal slaughtering. The roads were newly paved, and the village center had been "renewed" with a small parking area, a decorative fountain, a renovated and privatized local pub, and a freshly laid cobblestone street (Figures 30 and 31). The old clips factory was being remodeled as a duplex apartment, and more houses, including four new homes, glistened with clean white (and one yellow) stucco. Kella's face-lift was so remarkable, in fact, that in 1996 the community was awarded first prize in a statewide competition for Thuringia's most beautiful village.

Although many of the material signs of eastern German distinctiveness are gone, fault lines remain. Etched into memory and legible in the scarred landscape that is saturated with meanings, the border lives on. It is reproduced, reinvented, and transgressed in the intimacies of daily contact: during encounters while shopping, working, driving, hiking. Indeed, during my visit in 1996, practices of constructing Otherness on both sides of the former border were still part of daily life. During shopping trips to Eschwege, or when encountering hikers in the hills surrounding Kella, bodies were still being read and classified as "East" or "West." "We *are* Ossis," one villager proudly told me, "and we want to remain Ossis!"

Crossing the border thus remains an act of declaration—one which, for most residents of Kella, now belongs to the routines of daily life. When people return home from their workplaces, shopping excursions, or visits in the West, they leave the hegemonic space of a foregone conclusion, an unrealized yet inevitable trajectory of re-unification, and reenter a Heimat of an increasingly vanishing past, where the institutions, structures, and appearances of a once familiar life are rapidly receding to the realm of memory, and amnesia. This movement back and forth may prevent the solidification of identities at either end, as many border theorists would suggest, but it can also produce an acute consciousness of in-betweenness. Like the inscription of the literal border onto space and bodies during socialist rule, so too has a state of transition been incorporated into daily life. People may no longer be taking their foot off the gas pedal when approaching the site of a former border checkpoint, but they are constantly confronted with symbolically loaded choices of identification, affirmation, or contestation created by the collapse of this significant frame of reference. Many of the negotiations and ritualizations of these choices embody the liminal realm from which they have emerged: walking the former borderline, playing with a collar, constructing a cross out of barbed wire, noticing a thriving tree.

One of the many paradoxes of the borderland, then, is that ambiguity creates clarity. Indeed, perhaps this is the ultimate symbolism of the Tree of Unity: Not only does the flourishing tree ironically signify an alternative vision of "Germanness"—of eastern German particularism, consciousness, and Eigen-Sinn—that defiantly contests official master narratives of a united Germany, it also represents a kind of lucidity created out of the chaos and failures of transition, symbolized for many in the demise of the first little tree. In the literal and figurative borderlands of human experience, cultural forms are not always taken for granted.

In this study of one community after the fall of the Berlin Wall, I have attempted to unpack the different meanings of a borderland by examining the creation, maintenance, transformation, and invention of different kinds of boundaries and border zones in daily life. Borders, I have argued, are zones of ambiguity and liminality as well as places of intense and articulated lucidity; in fact, these qualities are often mutually constitutive. I have aimed not only to provide here an account of the confluence of the local and the extralocal in this unique historical moment but also to portray certain processes and particulars of *negotiation*, a term that itself denotes a process of defining spaces between things as well as of drawing distinctions and commonalities—a process of creating both clarity and confusion, indicative of experience in the borderland; indeed, of much experience itself.

Glossary of Terms

Abhauen	escape over the border
Ackersmann	plowman; in Kella, the term denotes patron farmers who plowed villagers' fields
Arbeiter	worker
Bauer, Bauern	farmer; in Kella, the term denotes landholders
Begrüßungsgeld	"welcome money," 100 marks that were given to each East German citizen during his or her first visit to West Germany
Beziehungen	connections
Braunrode	hill on the western side of the border overlooking Kella, close to the hilltop "window to Kella"
Bückwaren	scarce goods for which the store clerk had to "bend" down
DFD	Demokratischer Frauenbund Deutschlands (Democratic Women's Federation)

Dorfchronik	village chronicle
drüben	"over there"—the other side of the border in both East and West
Eichsfeld	Catholic enclave in Protestant central Germany
Eingaben	legally sanctioned complaints under socialism
Einwohnerversammlungen	town meetings
Elternhaus	parent house
Fasching	annual pre-Lent carnival
FDJ	Freie Deutsche Jugend (Free German Youth), the youth organization of the East German SED (Communist) party
Gemeinde	community, municipality
Gemeindehaus	community (village) administration building
Geschichtsverein	voluntary association for the study and preservation of history
Glauben	religious faith
Grenze	border, most frequently used in referring to the border between East and West Germany
Grenzer	border guard
Grenzhelfer	border-guard helper
Grenzordnung	order of the border
Großbauer	large farmer / property holder; in Kella, the term alludes to families who farmed ten to twenty hectares
Hamsterkauf	"hamster," or hoarding purchase
Heimat	literally, *home* or *homeland;* a discourse of belonging, place, and identity
Heimatverein	voluntary association dedicated to the cultivation of Heimat
Hülfensberg	the Eichsfeld's most sacred pilgrimage site, ten kilometers from Kella and within the highly restricted Schutzstreifen
Jugendweihe	socialist state initiation ceremony intended as a secular equivalent to the Catholic first communion and Protestant confirmation
Kampfgruppe	People's Militia

Kirmes	annual village festival commemorating the anniversary of the church's dedication in October 1854
Kittel	smock, a potent symbol of working women in the GDR
Konsum	state-owned retail chain that operated as Kella's only store
Kreis	administrative district, similar in function to a county in the United States
LPG	Landwirtschaftliche Produktionsgenossenschaft, state-owned collective farm
Männerballett	men's ballet, a performance involving cross-dressing at the annual Fasching festivities
Mittelbauer	property holder / farmer who owned five to ten hectares
Nachholungsbedarf	"need to catch up," alluding to the perceived need of eastern Germans to "catch up" materially, politically, socially, culturally, and economically to the western Germans
Neues Forum	New Forum, one of the 1989 civic movements
NVA	Nationale Volksarmee, the GDR army
Ordnung und Sicherheit der Grenze	order and security of the border
Ortschronik	local chronicle written during the GDR period
Ossi	colloquial name for eastern Germans
Republikflucht	unlawful border crossing from the GDR to the FRG
Schutzstreifen	500-meter-wide security zone edging the border on the GDR side; only people with special passes were permitted to enter the zone
Schutzstreifengemeinde	village in the high-security zone
Schwesternhaus	church-owned facility in Kella that housed a Catholic kindergarten and a small nursing home staffed by three resident nuns
SED	Sozialistische Einheitspartei, the East German Communist Party

Sperrgebiet	five-kilometer-deep restricted zone along the East-West boundary; like the Schutzstreifen, only people with special passes were permitted to enter
Stasi	East German state security police
streifenlaufen	patrol of the sand strip along the alarm fence
Trabi	nickname for a Trabant, an East German automobile
Treuhand	federal organization in charge of privatizing former East German industry
VEB	Volkseigener Betrieb, publicly (state-) owned factory in the GDR
Vergangenheitsbewältigung	"overcoming the past," originally used in West Germany in relation to the Nazi period but now also used in referring to East Germany's socialist past
Volksfest	festival
Volksfrömmigkeit	popular faith
Volkskirche	people's church
Volkspolizei	People's Police, the East German police
Volkspolizeihelfer	People's Police helper
Wende	"turning point," the fall of the Berlin Wall and the collapse of socialist rule
Werbefahrt	corporate-sponsored commercial trip
Wessi	colloquial name for western Germans
Westpakete	western packages
Wossi	Ossi who takes on exaggerated characteristics of Wessis
Zivilverteidigung	civil defense
Zoni	somewhat derogatory, colloquial term for eastern German, stemming from the Soviet zone of occupation during the early postwar period
Zufluchtsort	place of refuge
Zwischenraum	space between

Notes

INTRODUCTION

1.   I have chosen the hyphenated terms *re-unification* and *re-unified* to refer to the union of the FRG and the GDR on October 3, 1990. Although I am aware of the arguments that point to the teleological and ideological implications of the term *reunification*, as well as the fact that the territories united in 1990 do not represent Germany in an earlier state, I am also concerned that the omission of any term reflecting a previous union of this region as one country silences critical elements of Germany's past: the fact, for example, that Germany was divided in 1945 for a reason. Further, the area that I discuss in this book has experienced a resumption of earlier economic and social ties across regional, religious, and former national borders. My use of the hyphen is thus a compromise, an effort to avoid the naturalizing connotations of *reunification* while reflecting a sensitivity to certain histories of divisions and recent restorations. At times I do use the word *unity*, however, as a literal translation of the official German term *Einheit*.

2.   In this sense, a study of boundaries relates to a long-term interest of anthropology in social classification and structure as reflected in the spatial organization of social groups (Durkheim and Mauss 1963; Evans-Pritchard 1940; Lévi-Strauss 1963).

3.   For notable exceptions, see Cole and Wolf 1974; Donnan and Wilson 1994b; Flynn 1997; Frankenberg 1957; Kelleher 1994. Wilson and Donnan 1998, published as my book was in press, provides a rich collection of anthropological case studies of international borders as well as a lucid overview of an anthropology of borders in the context of nation and state formation.

4.   A limited sample of this recent literature, some of which is discussed below, includes: Behar 1993, Gupta and Ferguson 1992, and Rosaldo 1989 in anthropology; a special issue of the German journal *Sowi* on boundaries (March 1991) in history; and Bhabha 1994, Calderón and Salvídar 1991, Castillo 1995, Hicks 1991, Michaelsen and Johnson 1997 in cultural and literary studies. Paralleling views of Chicana and Chicano poets and fiction writers like Gloria Anzaldúa (1987) or Federico Campbell (1995). Many of these studies on boundaries and borderlands are also closely linked to, and draw their insights from, other attempts to theorize interstitiality and hybridity: for example, in studies of postcolonialism (Bhabha 1994; Hannerz 1987) or of transnational diasporas (Rouse 1991). As part of this recent trend, the theme of the 1995 meetings of the American Ethnological Society was "Border Anthropologies."

5.   Such writings include the classic *With His Pistol in His Hand,* by Américo Paredes (1958), as well as Alvarez 1995; Anzaldúa 1987; Bauman and Abrahams 1981; Campbell 1995; Kearney 1991; Limón 1992, 1994; Martinez 1994; Paredes 1993; Vélez-Ibáñez 1996.

6.   For example, Bhabha 1994; Hicks 1991; Johnson and Michaelsen 1997. One could argue that a metaphorical or figurative borderland is foregrounded in the pioneering works of both Renato Rosaldo and Gloria Anzaldúa, as well.

7.   My thanks to the participants in the panel on "Border Incidents" (annual meetings of the American Anthropological Association, November 1996; Mary Steedly and Lindsay French, organizers) for illuminating and clarifying my thinking on these issues.

8.   See also Michaelsen and Johnson 1997, particularly the essay by Alejandro Lugo.

9.   Compare Borneman 1991, 1992.

10.   See, for example, Hann 1980, 1985; Humphrey 1983; Kideckel 1993; Kligman 1988; Nagengast 1991; Verdery 1991, 1996. The work of John Borneman (1991, 1992, 1997) has provided an extremely valuable precedent for anthropological studies of socialism in the East German context.

11.   On the "capitalist triumphalism" surrounding the collapse of socialism, see

Borneman 1991; Hann 1993; Verdery 1996. For discussions of different trajectories of postsocialism, see, for example, Berdahl, Bunzl, and Lampland, 1999; De Soto and Anderson 1993; Kideckel 1995; Verdery 1996.

12.   The exceptions include Kearney 1991 on the U.S.-Mexican border and Wilson 1994 on the Irish border.

13.   Of course, any focus on the particular resonates with a long-standing emphasis in anthropology on case studies and genealogical methods.

14.   See, for example, the village monographs by Anderson and Anderson 1966; Friedl 1962; Friedl 1974; Netting 1981; and Laurence Wylie's classic study, *Village in the Vaucluse* (1957). For some of the first village monographs in the German context, see Golde 1975 and Spindler 1973; see also De Soto 1989 for a more recent theoretical and ethnographic perspective. The wealth of scholarship in German, some of which more or less successfully transcends the "village study paradigm," includes Frahm and Hoops 1987; Ilien and Jeggle 1978; Kaschuba and Lipp 1982, as well as the innovative work of social historians on both sides of the Atlantic like Becker 1990; Medick 1997; Sabean 1984, 1990, 1998.

15.   See, for example, Chirot 1976; Cole and Wolf 1974; Schneider and Schneider 1976.

16.   The term stems from Behar 1990.

17.   For particularly sophisticated justifications of the trivial and overviews of importance of "the everyday," see Comaroff and Comaroff 1997, esp. pp. 29-35; Lüdtke 1995.

18.   The question of experience has been the subject of much theoretical and political scrutiny both within and outside anthropology. For an especially illuminating and nuanced discussion of this issue, see Steedly 1993. See also Bruner 1986; Jackson 1989; Scott 1991.

19.   The relatively recent and rich literature on everyday life in the GDR includes Kaelble, Kocka, and Zwahr 1994; Kocka and Sabrow 1994; Lüdtke and Becker 1997; Niethammer, von Plato, and Wierling 1991.

20.   My positioning as an American, outsider, and non-Catholic undoubtedly affected certain aspects and trajectories of my research in Kella. A West German, for example, might have come away with very different materials and interpretations due to the nature of East-West tensions that dominated much of village experience and discourse at the time. Any attempt to assess the implications of my particular positioning would be difficult from my vantage point and would remain speculative without having available study of the village or similar village situations by investigators who were differently situated. However, I believe the point warrants brief mention in order to provide some perspective on my choice and weighting of informants and interpretations. I discuss in greater depth the issues surrounding my positioning in relation to dilemmas of fieldwork in postsocialist societies in Berdahl n.d.

CHAPTER 1

1.   The Eschweger Klosterbräu is a local brewery. The restaurant closed a few years before the fall of the Wall.

2.   Led by the reformer Thomas Müntzer in 1525, the Eichsfeld was briefly converted to Protestantism following the Reformation. Under the direction of the archbishop of Mainz, however, members of the newly founded Jesuit order succeeded in converting the region's population back to Catholicism during a sweeping Counter-Reformation.

3.   The Eichsfeld dialect is an important aspect of local identity. Like other regional dialects in Germany, however, it is spoken primarily by people born before 1945. Local historical journals (*Eichsfelder Heimathefte* and, until it dissolved after the Wende, *Eichsfelder Heimatstimmen*) publish regular columns that include regional idiomatic expressions, jokes, vocabulary, and discussions of writing local dialect. Although younger people may understand the local dialect, they do not speak it together or with their elders. The cultivation of a threatened local dialect is thus perceived to be a primary function of the regional Heimatvereine. In Kella, for example, the newly founded Heimatverein Kella sponsors regular "dialect evenings," in which poems and stories are performed in the local dialect. On a methodological note, the local dialect presented few language problems for me during fieldwork because high German was spoken in most contexts.

4.   This account, along with several other children's narratives of the Americans' arrival in Kella, is included in a church chronicle written in 1946 by I. Degenhardt, a priest who served in Kella during the war years. This chronicle is in the Kella church archives and is one of four "chronicles" referred to throughout this book. The others are: a village history published in honor of Kella's 825th anniversary (*Festschrift*, hereafter cited as Müller and others 1966); a local chronicle (*Ortschronik*) written during the GDR period, as required by the state; a village chronicle (*Dorfchronik*) started in the 1990s, which incorporates much of the information in the previous three chronicles. The latter Dorfchronik, carefully handwritten in a large, leather-bound volume, contrasts sharply with the loose, typed forms of the Ortschronik. All three chronicles are housed in the village archive.

5.   On "GDR language," see, for example, Lüdtke 1997a.

6.   In the Christian tradition, the fourteen Stations of the Cross depict the events leading up to and including Christ's crucifixion.

7.   Twenty-eight villagers out of a working-age population of 163 are listed in the Festschrift as being involved in home textile production in 1765 (Müller and others 1966: 10).

8.   For a more extensive overview and description of Eichsfeld migrant work-

ers, see Schnier and Schulz-Greve 1990. For a more thorough history of economic development in the Eichsfeld, see Riese 1980.

9.　Village employment/occupations in 1985 (the last date before the Wende for which such figures were compiled) were:

EMPLOYMENT/OCCUPATION	NUMBER
VEB Spielwaren Pfaffs. (toy factory)	108
BT Solidor (Kella suspender-clips factory)	82
Construction workers in Heiligenstadt	28
Road-construction workers	10
Schoolteachers	7
Day-care workers	6
Village administration	5
Forestry (in Heiligenstadt)	5
Stockyard (in Heiligenstadt)	2
Catholic kindergarten	3
Konsum	3
Beauticians	2
Post-office workers	2
Pub	2
Nursery	4
Truck drivers	3
Independent craftsperson: carpenter	2 (total employees)
Independent craftsperson: smith	2 (total employees)
Independent craftsperson: mason	1
Independent craftsperson: folk artist	1
Other	12

Source: Kella village archives.

10.　On the senses in fieldwork and anthropological practice, see Stoller 1989.

11.　After the currency union on July 1, 1990, East German stores carried mostly western products. Some causes and consequences of this changeover are discussed in chapter 5. Although the local store came under private ownership in 1991, it was still called *Konsum* by village residents.

12.　Between 1952 and 1989, Kella's population declined from approximately 800 to 600 inhabitants. Age groups, however, remained fairly evenly dispersed, as reflected in village demographics compiled in 1985:

AGE GROUP	NUMBER OF RESIDENTS
1–3 years	41
3–6	28
6–16	69

16–25	105
24–40	98
40–55	145
55–65	58
over 65	75

Source: 1987 Report on Population Structure of Kreis Heiligenstadt, Kella village archives.

13.   The church-sponsored kindergarten (described in chapters 2 and 3) was still in operation.

CHAPTER 2

1.   For insightful ethnographic analyses of the mutually constitutive relationship between the state and its citizens in the context of the "modern" (western) nation-state, see Herzfeld 1992, 1997.

2.   Michel de Certeau also employs the term *Zwischenraum*—"a middle place, composed of interactions and inter-views"—in his discussion of spatial practices and frontiers. His usage is thus similar to the borderland metaphor I employ throughout this book; it does not denote the interstitial spaces of state power in the way that I am using it here (de Certeau: 1984: 127).

3.   For an overview of state organizations and popular participation in an urban context, see Rueschemeyer 1991.

4.   For a sophisticated model of the political economy of socialism in relation to the organization and allocation of production and consumption, see Konrad and Szelenyi 1979; Kornai 1992; Verdery 1996.

5.   For an interesting study in the Hungarian context of factory production rituals and the ways in which they counter-productively generated resentment and opposition to socialism, see Burawoy and Lukács 1992.

6.   Although the presence of and infiltration by Stasi spies was common knowledge among GDR citizens, the extent of Stasi thoroughness was discovered only after the fall of the Wall. According to most estimates, the agency had more than 90,000 full-time employees, supplemented by another 500,000 official or occasional informants (Rosenberg 1995: 290). More than half of the adult population of the GDR reportedly had personal Stasi files. Following numerous debates surrounding the future of the Stasi files in 1990, they were placed in the independent hands of what is referred to as the "Gauck Authority" after Joachim Gauck, an East German dissident pastor from Rostock. One of the unique aspects of the German "lustration" law is that victims may have access to their own files. After the Stasi files were opened in January 1992, the Gauck Authority was flooded with requests; by November 1993 it had received more than 2 million re-

quests—more than 12 percent of the population of the former GDR. For an accessible discussion of the Stasi legacy see Rosenberg 1995. See also Gauck's own assessment (Gauck 1991). For an account of one of the most famous stories of this legacy, a case of a dissident married couple, see Wollenberger 1992.

The identity of Stasi informants in Kella will most likely not be revealed until residents obtain access to their individual Stasi files, which could take years. Rumor has it that there were between twelve and fifteen Stasi informants within the village, although no one was able to explain to me where that number came from.

7.   According to GDR law, a member of the defendant's community must serve as a "social plaintiff" in such cases. Werner was asked by the village council to serve in this capacity and viewed his role as both plaintiff and defender.

8.   At the time of the municipal elections in May 1990, communities in this region adopted West German municipal government rules. Members of the village council were elected first; the council then elected one of its members mayor.

9.   On Eingaben in the GDR, see also Merkel 1997 and Mühlberg 1996.

10.   "Black" refers to the Christian Democratic Union, part of the "multi-party facade" (Childs 1988: 127) in the GDR and a refuge for Christians.

11.   Localities were required by the state to maintain a local chronicle (Ortschronik), which was regularly subject to state inspection.

12.   As many scholars have pointed out (for example, Bakhtin 1984; Burke 1978; De Soto n.d.; Fernandez 1986; Gilmore 1987; Scott 1990), carnival has a long history in Europe as a means of and forum for mocking political authority. James Scott, for example, argues that carnival may be viewed as "an institutionalized form of political disguise" (1990: 173).

13.   "Zone," a reference to the zone of Soviet occupation, is a nickname for East Germany that derives from the immediate postwar period.

14.   As with other rhymed songs and chants quoted throughout the book, I have taken some leeway in my translation here in order to capture the creativity of the original German rhyme. Original German:

> Ich bin ein Mädchen aus der Zone, ich wohne in Kella—am Ende dieser Welt.
> Ich hab' ein schönes Häuschen mit Garten, ein Auto und auch 'ne Menge Geld.
> Trotz einem schönen Kneipchen, der Kirmes, dem Fasching fühl ich mich so allein.
> Ich träume von den schönen Städten, von Dallas, von Denver, dort möchte ich
>   gern sein!!!

> Ein Prinz muß kommen und meinen Traum erfüllen
> und meine Sehnsucht stillen nach dieser großen Welt.
> Holt er mich mit 'nem tollen Wagen, wird er mich leise fragen . . .
> . . . Doch aber—ohne Schein—kommt er ja gar nicht rein!!!

15.   German:

> Da sah ich den Zaun, er war wie aus Watte
> und es gab keinen, der gegen die Grenzer was hatte

Kein Mensch hatte das Braunrode im Sinn
denn jeder der wollte, kam über Eisenach nach Eschwege hin.

16.   German: "Es gab keinen der einen anderen verpetzte; und damit das ganze Dorf in Bewegung versetzte."

17.   After 1971 East Germans were permitted to enter West Germany (contingent on state approval) for "urgent family events," such as weddings, deaths, anniversaries, or birthdays. Before that, only retired persons had been permitted to visit West Germany once a year. Prior to 1964, however, travel had been restricted to prominent individuals who were deemed trustworthy by the state.

18.   It is likely that the Stasi kept files on close to 100 percent of the adult population of Kella, owing to the village's location in the Schutzstreifen and the fact that most residents were in contact with western relatives. Emma, like many villagers, initially was intrigued by the possibility of applying for access to her Stasi file. Like most other villagers, she has since decided against it. The politics of decisions surrounding whether to file for access to these files is discussed in chapter 7.

19.   For an informed and more detailed discussion of this resolution and Moscow's possible involvement in it, see Potratz 1993.

20.   From Order No. 38/52 of the "Head of the Central Administration of the German People's Police" (Potratz 1993: 61; translation mine).

21.   According to Potratz (1993: 61), local mayors were notified of the planned deportations shortly before they took place, so this scenario is entirely plausible. In Thuringia (of which Kella is a part) alone, 1,807 people slated for evacuation fled to West Germany before they could be deported (Potratz 1993: 64). For more on the evacuations of 1952 and 1961, see Bennewitz and Potratz 1994.

22.   Access to these families' Stasi files might illuminate the state's rationale for these events, but for the purposes of my argument here that does not matter. What is important is the uncertainty and fear generated by the deportations. None of the family members has gained access to its file, however, and as far as I know, none has even applied for it.

23.   As Verdery has pointed out, the categories of this "us" versus "them" chasm, which existed in every eastern European socialist country, could be quite elastic (1996: 94).

24.   Based on my own reading of these documents, now in the village archives, the reports were primarily concerned with the general mood of the population: how people were responding to current events; their complaints about consumer goods; whether production goals were being met; the activities of the mass organizations and village council; and the progress of the village's own norms in the planned economy, including recycling and local agricultural production. In the reports of the 1960s and 1970s, individuals were mentioned by name, but only in

relation to events that were common knowledge (arrests for drunkenness, career changes, and the like). During the 1980s, few individual names appeared in these monthly reports. The contents of these reports are thus similar to the reported banality of the majority of the Stasi files, which were similarly imagined to contain important, damaging, and accurate information. On the contents and function of information reports generally, as well as in the context of 1950s factory life more specifically, see Lüdtke 1997b.

25.   See also the important work of the proponents of Alltagsgeschichte ("the history of everyday life"), who have argued for reducing "the gaping distance between rulers and ruled" in the Nazi period through an examination of the ways in which authority is established and reproduced in the routinized and habitual practices of daily life (Lüdtke 1995).

CHAPTER 3

1.   Traditionally, however, Catholics work until the afternoon church service on Good Friday.

2.   According to Konrad Jarausch, thirty-five of these groups promoted peace, thirty-nine focused on ecology, twenty-three dealt with both, twenty-nine addressed Third World issues, ten promoted human rights, and a few dealt with draft resistance and feminism (1994: 38).

3.   This was pointed out by Charles Maier during a GDR History Graduate Student Workshop, Harvard University, April 1993.

4.   The exhibit was sponsored by the Institut für Europäische und Deutsche Politik.

5.   According to local legend, the Hülfensberg is where the missionary St. Boniface converted the region to Christianity. Its name derives from the Hülfenskreuz, a famous crucifix from the Middle Ages that is in its chapel. It has been a pilgrimage site since the fourteenth century (Linge and Schmidt 1967).

6.   Plans to complete the "chapel at the Eichsfeld cross" were put on hold immediately after the fall of the Wall in favor of what were felt to be more pressing expenditures like renovations to the Hülfensberg itself. Construction was resumed in 1993.

7.   Bohlman (1996) has similarly pointed out how pilgrimages perform and thereby ascribe meaning and legibility to the landscape. The literature on pilgrimage within and outside anthropology is voluminous: on Christian pilgrimage, for example, see Crain 1992; Dubisch 1995; Eade and Sallnow 1991; Nolan and Nolan 1989; and, of course, the seminal work of Victor Turner (1974, 1978, 1979).

8.   This literature includes Bausinger and Köstlin 1980; Greverus 1979; Weigelt

1984. Regarding the idea of Heimat in film, see Kaes 1989; Kaschuba 1989. Edgar Reitz's nine-hour television series entitled *Heimat,* which appeared on German television in 1984, is one of the more recent and widely discussed treatments of Heimat in film. For discussions of critical reaction to this film, see the special issue of *New German Critique* 36 (1985). On the relation between the idea of Heimat, German nationalist discourses, and racist categories of exclusion, see Peck 1996. See also Linke 1995, 1997 for provocative discussions of race, violence, and nation in German political culture.

9.   Many of the Heimatvereine were subsumed by the GDR Cultural Ministry and were thus subject to state control.

10.   Poster in Heiligenstadt, GDR, July 1990.

11.   During my fieldwork, I attempted to remain alert to the possible embellishment of "resistance" stories as memory of the events was remade in the telling. Despite new claims to victim status (see chapter 7), I believe that the practices of both popular and institutionalized religion provided a means of contesting state power. This argument is supported by Kubik 1994 and Nagengast 1991, among others.

12.   Emma was denied a travel permit to attend a brother's birthday in the West, and the Hausers' oldest son was prohibited from attending high school in Heiligenstadt despite the fact that he was at the top of his elementary-school class.

13.   According to the mayor and her assistants, one Stasi officer visited the mayor's office at least once a month. If they saw him coming, they told me, they would try to sneak out the back door. The mayor always tried to have one of her assistants present during the questioning, she explained, but occasionally the official would seek out one of the women at their homes for furthering questioning.

14.   Many of the details, including much of the prose, from this 1946 church chronicle are reproduced both in the 1966 Festschrift (Müller and others 1966) and the recent Dorfchronik.

15.   These 1933 voting statistics are cited in the recent Dorfchronik. The 1946 church chronicle mentions the arrest in October 1945 of village Nazi party members by the Soviets. All were released. A few days later, Kella's mayor, who reportedly had initially withheld information about his work as assistant regional superintendent for the Nazi party in order to retain his position as mayor, was rearrested. According to reports passed on by a fellow prisoner several years later, he was imprisoned and died at Buchenwald. Descriptions of these arrests appear in older villagers' accounts of the immediate postwar period as well. Unlike the aura of mystery and uncertainty surrounding the 1952 deportations, however, the arrest of Nazi party members (with the obvious exception of the village mayor's imprisonment and death at Buchenwald) is generally perceived as justifiable action.

16.   My understanding of the terms *symbol* and *image* recognizes the important dynamic and evolutionary relationship of the two within both cultural processes and individual experience (Fernandez 1965). Specifically, I use the *symbol* to denote those items "possessed of fully conceptualized and often articulated meanings" and the *image* to describe those "tokens of communication" that are "pregnant with felt but unconceptualized meanings" (Fernandez 1986: 31). As James Fernandez has argued, over time, images (like the Seventh Station) may become important symbols in cultural interaction; they may also be important elements of the "argument of images" in human interaction, in which "quite different domains are brought together in unexpected and creative ways" (Fernandez 1986: viii).

17.   This is true of both the Catholic church and, especially, the Protestant church in the GDR. Protestant churches whose sanctuaries were packed at the time of the Wende now report dwindling attendance.

18.   One of the principal reasons for confessing to other clergy, I was told, was that Father Münster had an unfortunate tendency to ignore the confessional oath of secrecy (a common sentiment behind anticlericalism [e.g., Herzfeld 1985; Mintz 1982]): items discussed in confession would occasionally be included in sermons. Although the identities of the persons involved were never revealed, in a small community like Kella, they did not have to be.

19.   These include, above all, the end of Kella's geographical isolation. Under socialism, villagers were able to keep track of one another's comings and goings as well as the occasional visitors from outside Kella. Now, with the freedom to travel and receive visitors, keeping track of such details is impossible. This process was accelerated with the closing of local factories, where information was exchanged and shared.

20.   Examples of this manipulation included Father Münster's testing the loyalty of his most dedicated followers (primarily women) by scheduling Bible-study groups on the evening of Kirmes. He also frequently attempted to be the center of social events involving visitors to Kella, often by scheduling them at his home. My husband and I were frequently challenged by this strategy. His actions toward us indicated that as a foreign and potentially disruptive presence in the village, we, too, needed to be monitored. For a more self-reflexive discussion of the personal dynamics surrounding the priest and his relationship to parishioners both during his tenure and surrounding his departure, see Berdahl n.d.

21.   The Focolare movement, started in southern Italy in 1943 and officially sanctioned by Pope John Paul II, now exists in more than 180 countries. It has several million "adherents" and more than 80,000 core members (Urquhart 1995: 6).

22.   Much to the chagrin of many villagers, for example, Father Münster never learned the lyrics to the "Eichsfeldlied." Furthermore, he often confessed to his devoted Focolare followers that he viewed many of the required duties of a

priest—presiding over mass and pilgrimages, for example—as distractions from his main goal of furthering the ideals of the ecumenical movement.

CHAPTER 4

1.   Compare Barrett 1978, Brandes 1975, Gilmore 1982, and Pitt-Rivers 1977 on gossip, nicknames, and the politics of reputation in Spain.

2.   On cross-cultural readings of *Dallas*, see Liebes and Katz 1990.

3.   This statistic is drawn from oral histories of older villagers as well as property records kept in the GDR, now housed in the village archive. The Bauern of Kella were among the 41.5 percent of farmers in eastern Germany who owned between five and fifty hectares and were thus considered independent and economically viable. The majority of small farmers (56 percent) owned between one-half and five hectares, while a small minority of large landowners (2.5 percent) owned farms of more than fifty hectares, which accounted for nearly 40 percent of the agriculturally useful land in East Germany (Dornberg 1968: 183). The term *Großbauer* usually refers to the small minority of landholders with fifty hectares or more, but in Kella it is a relative term and is used interchangeably with *Bauer*.

4.   One of these Großbauer was also the local pub owner, another category with a high rate of deportees in 1952. Because he owned more than seven hectares of land and, especially, because he served as an Ackersmann for several villagers, I have included him in the category of village Großbauer.

5.   That is, questioned, harassed, counseled.

6.   Of the thirteen individuals listed as currently or formerly employed by the LPG in a 1987 village census, for example, only four were members or descendants of one of the five remaining Großbauern families.

7.   As part of a planned economy, each independent craftsman, as well as the village itself, was allotted a certain amount of materials every year under the state's centralized economic plan. These allotments corresponded to the appropriation of materials and/or building permits to community members, whose requests were integrated into the community's economic plan and often took years to grant.

8.   See, for example, Carole Nagengast's (1991) study of Polish peasant-workers and Martha Lampland's (1995) historical ethnography of a Hungarian agricultural collective for more nuanced analyses of class and social differentiation under socialism. For a different context, see Katherine Verdery's (1991) analysis of the role of intellectual elites in national cultural production in Romania.

9.   Katherine Verdery (1991), for example, rightly cautions against using Bourdieu's terms, like *investments* or *profits*, because of their inappropriateness for socialist societies. I would disagree with her avoidance of the term *capital*, however,

for reasons that my analysis of social differentiation in this chapter should reveal. Furthermore, the use of certain terms like *capital* may also highlight continuities between socialist and postsocialist societies. See also Carole Nagengast's (1991) analysis of class stratification in a Polish rural community, which draws on Bourdieu's forms of capital, although in a manner that is fairly different from my discussion here.

10.   For a more thorough descriptions and analyses of the political economy of socialism, see, for example, Burawoy and Lukács 1992; Konrad and Szelenyi 1979; Kornai 1992; Stark and Nee 1989; Verdery 1996.

11.   A small sample of the diverse writings on the "informal" or "second" economy in socialist societies includes Åslund 1985; Cole 1985; Grossman 1987; Hankiss 1990; Hann 1990; Pine 1993; Sampson 1986; Wedel 1986.

12.   For a similar phenomenon in a different context, see writings on Quanxi in China (for example, Yan 1996).

13.   This interconnection was perhaps most evident in Hungary's "mixed economy." See Hann 1990; Szelenyi 1989.

14.   Gaus lived in the GDR from 1974 to 1981 as the FRG's first representative in East Germany.

15.   Compare the literature on patronage and influence peddling in the Mediterranean (for example, Boissevain 1974; Campbell 1964; Gellner and Waterbury 1977).

16.   For an excellent analysis of barter in a variety of contexts, see Humphrey and Hugh-Jones 1992. Barter may coexist with other forms of exchange, they argue, and may also create social relations. I would concur that there is no one definition of barter; instead, it is best understood in its social context.

17.   At the time of the Wende in 1989, five independent master craftsmen were living in Kella: a smith, a mason, a carpenter, and two painters. Because so many local men were trained as craftsmen, however, exchanges of services were not limited to these craftsmen. The independent operations did have access to centrally allotted materials that were not available to workers employed in factories.

18.   "GDR consumer culture" has become the subject of a rich and rapidly expanding body of literature. See, for example, Diesener and Gries 1992; Merkel 1995; Neue Gesellschaft für Bildende Kunst 1996; Pence 1997; Veenis 1997.

19.   A similar argument is made by Steven Sampson, who, in pointing out the prestige of social connections, argues that "procuring scarce resources is itself a means of demonstrating 'social wealth', and East Europeans themselves have understood that it is social wealth rather than possession of cash that is important in these societies" (Sampson 1986: 60).

20.   Most prices in Exquisit shops were prohibitively expensive in East German terms: one young woman from Kella, for example, recalled spending a month's salary on a western blouse.

21.   The social prestige of western goods in socialist societies is by now a well-known fact. See, for example, Cole 1985; Sampson 1986. In the GDR context, see Diesener and Gries 1992; Merkel 1995; Veenis 1997.

22.   My observations of such displays in Kella are confirmed as more widespread practices in the GDR by Merkel 1995 and Veenis 1997.

23.   In contrast to the current FRG legal system, moonlighting work brigades were encouraged by the GDR as a way of fulfilling state plans and overcoming inadequate state resources in housing and construction. In Kella, such work brigades could provide substantial supplemental income, particularly for the crew leader.

24.   Of the five remaining Großbauer families, only two, "J. R." and one other family, were able to perpetuate their status as village elites. The other three went to work alongside other villagers in local factories or the LPG and never accumulated unusual amounts of other forms of wealth and capital under socialism.

25.   Kella's status as a Schutzstreifengemeinde that could be viewed from the West meant that its residents with house facades visible from the other side of the border had privileged access to building materials from the state.

26.   In describing symbolic capital, Pierre Bourdieu notes that symbolic investments may take the form of ritual, aid to the needy, and so forth, and suggests that symbolic capital is a form of credit (Smart 1993: 391; Bourdieu 1977: 18).

27.   Approximately two-thirds of working-age villagers were employed during my fieldwork, although the figure fluctuated constantly. One-quarter of the working-age population had found employment in the West. The vast majority of those working in the West were under the age of thirty-five, thus making the income differences a generational issue as well.

28.   For a sensitive and incisive account of the history and complexities of production ideologies in relation to actual labor practices the GDR, see Lüdtke 1994.

29.   Most former property owners are now leasing their land once held by the LPG to a recently formed agricultural cooperative. Only two small farmers, including "J. R.," have reclaimed their land and are attempting to farm it on the side.

CHAPTER 5

1.   On the symbolic dimensions of the Berlin Wall and its aftermath, see Borneman 1998.

2.   "Green Border" alludes to the relative permeability of the border during these years. The term *green* evokes the rural landscape of which the border was a part and contrasts its earlier porousness with the later impenetrability of the gray concrete and the metal fencing.

3.   See also *Die Grenze im Eichsfeld* (Stadt Duderstadt 1991).

4.   Archival sources and older villagers indicate that the population of Kella declined from approximately 800 to 600 residents during these years.

5.   Cited in "Wir machen alles gründlich" 1991. According this estimate, 123 of the 201 border fatalities occurred on the inter-German border and 78 died at the Berlin Wall.

6.   Until it became legal to watch western television in 1971, East German schoolchildren were frequently subjected to the "Sandman test." Both East and West German television aired a brief children's show, *The Sandman,* before the evening news. Following the show, a clock would appear on the screen until the beginning of the news. The West German clock had small lines in place of numbers; the East German, clock small dots. Teachers would ask children if the clock after their *Sandman* had lines or dots, thus revealing whether parents were watching western or eastern television.

7.   The extent of state control depended on a variety of factors, especially on local behavior. After an attempted or successful escape, for example, the state would tighten its control considerably, setting early curfews and increasing its border surveillance. Such regulations were also the results of party directives, themselves products of inter-German cold war relations. With the change in travel restrictions in the mid-1970s, for instance, areas in the Sperrgebiet and Schutzstreifen also experienced a slight relaxation in control. By the late 1980s, there were fewer controls at the barriers.

8.   For a rich anthology of border stories (primarily from the West German side) and an analysis of their structure, see Hartmann and Künsting 1990, 1993.

9.   For ethnographic accounts of the construction of localities and the mutually constitutive relationship between stories and places, see also Basso 1984; Feld and Basso 1996; Hirsch and O'Hanlon 1995; Stewart 1996.

10.   Peter Sahlins (1989) makes a similar argument about the French-Spanish border in the Pyrenees. See also Celia Applegate (1990) on identity in the German Pfalz region.

11.   There is already a very large scholarly and popular literature on the collapse of socialist rule in the GDR. See, for example, Fulbrook 1995; Jarausch 1994; Maier 1997. For oral history accounts, see Philipsen 1992.

12.   Similar to the concept of Heimat, the Elternhaus symbolizes one's childhood roots, family, and belonging.

13.   Thorsten was particularly close to his western cousin, now in her midforties, for she had lived with his family until she left the GDR illegally as a young adult. They kept in close contact after her departure through letters and annual visits. The family would meet her in Heiligenstadt because she was not permitted into the Sperrgebiet.

14.   Katje, Thorsten's girlfriend at the time, was also in her midtwenties.

15.   Christoph, Thorsten's brother, left via Hungary during the summer of 1989.

16.   McDonald's was often one of the first stops for first-time border crossers from the GDR. For discussions and comparative analyses of McDonald's as symbol and practice, see Ritzer 1993; Watson 1997.

17.   See also Borneman 1992: "In the days and weeks after the opening, East Germans gorged themselves on the symbolic goods of West German nationness. . . . They flocked to the shopping centers and stores in a consumptive orgy that kept West German businesses open long after the state-mandated (and sacred) closing hours, and they sought those items that most define the West German self: cars, indexing power and prosperity, pornography, symbolizing pleasure and free time, travel out of their country, jeans of the sort identifying one as *westlich* [western]" (p. 321).

18.   Except for a few members of the younger generation who participated in the Monday demonstrations in Heiligenstadt, most villagers had been relatively quiet prior to the fall of the Wall. The Catholic Eichsfeld joined the wave of protests sweeping the GDR several months after the first demonstrations began in Leipzig. Hans-Gerd Adler (1990) gives a detailed account of the Wende in the Eichsfeld.

19.   Werner Henning, whose parents still live in Kella, was elected head of the District Council on December 12, 1989. He was the first democratically elected district president in the GDR. He was reelected in 1994.

20.   The phrase "the Wall in our heads" stems from Peter Schneider's novel *The Wall Jumper* (1983, first published in 1982 as *Der Mauerspringer*) and has entered popular discourse since the Wende. In the novel, published seven years before the fall of the Wall, Schneider accurately predicted that "it will take us longer to tear down the Wall in our heads than any wrecking company will need for the Wall we can see" (p. 119). For more general reports on East-West tensions throughout Germany, see Distanz, Entäuschung, Haß 1992: 30–37; Der neue Kalte Krieg 1993. Numerous national surveys support the increasing East-West division as well. See, for example, Erst vereint, nun entzweit 1993; Das Ost-Gefühl: Heimweh nach der alten Ordnung 1995.

21.   For a more detailed discussion of the Treuhand, see Maier 1997: 290–303; Christ and Neubauer 1991.

22.   The restructuring of East German universities entailed the dissolution of departments and institutes, the dismissal of East German faculty members (20 percent of the professors and 60 percent of the midrank faculty [Maier 1997: 305]), the recruitment of West German academics, and the concomitant influx of West German research agendas.

23.   More than half of the men and many of the younger women from Kella found employment in the West within two years of the Wende. Border crossings thus became largely one-sided as villagers began to shop and work in the west-

ern town of Eschwege. Only seven kilometers from Kella, Eschwege was much closer than Heiligenstadt, the nearest eastern town.

24. A typical joke stressed the ignorance and stupidity of eastern Germans: "What does DDR stand for?" "Der Doofe Rest" (the stupid rest—referring to eastern Germans who remained in the GDR after the exodus in 1989). For more on jokes during this period of transition, see Brednich 1990; Stein 1993.

25. Trabis contrast sharply with the West German Mercedes, BMWs, and Porsches and quickly became a symbol of socialist inefficiency, backwardness, and inferiority after the Wende. Although Trabi jokes were told in the GDR as well, they took on new meaning when reappropriated in the tellings of West Germans. The following jokes reflect a transformation in East-West relations:

> "Why aren't Trabis painted yellow?" "So people don't confuse them with mailboxes."
> "How do you double the value of a Trabi?" "Fill it up with gasoline."
> "Why does the Trabi have two slits in the roof?" "So the idiots who drive them can stick their donkey ears out the top."
> "The only reason to junk a Trabi is if the driver is still inside."

26. The colonial metaphor has frequently been employed to describe the asymmetrical power relations between eastern and western Germany after reunification (see, for example, Dümcke and Vilmar 1996). However, I would concur here with John Borneman (1992) that, while there certainly have been elements of internal colonization following the Wende, the situation differs from most colonial contexts due to a long history of shared language, kinship ties, and cultural traditions.

27. One of the most pressing issues following re-unification involved questions of property ownership in the former GDR. Expropriations occurred not only during the Nazi regime but under socialism as well. Just before re-unification, the Bonn government ruled to return all properties lost on the grounds of "race, politics, religion or philosophical outlook" between 1933 and 1945. The Unification Treaty of 1990 adopted the policy of "return before compensation," giving the return of property to former owners priority over monetary compensation for it. As many opponents of the policy had predicted, it has both stalled investment in the former GDR and produced and aggravated mounting tensions between East and West. By the end of 1992, more than 2 million property claims had been filed in the former GDR. The majority of these, including those in Kella, remain unresolved.

28. This property dispute has since been resolved. Emma's half-brother, who had no legal claims to the garden because it had been bequeathed to Emma and her full siblings by their mother, accepted money in payment for the family house (inherited from their father's side). The other two siblings obtained their respective strips of the garden. Only three meters wide, even together the strips were

too narrow to build on, as her siblings reportedly intended. When I visited Kella in 1996, I learned that just before Emma's brother died, a few months earlier, he had bequeathed his portion of the garden to her. "'I finally want to be able to sleep peacefully,'" he had told her. Realizing that she would not be able to do anything with her narrow strip, Emma's sister offered to sell it to the Hausers for 5,000 marks. Emma eventually obtained the remaining portion of the garden for a compromise sum of 3,000 marks.

29.   I owe this term to William Kelleher (n.d.), whose work on the border in Northern Ireland has similarly pointed out how boundary maintenance may be sustained through the reading of bodies.

30.   For a sympathetic and even-handed discussion of East-West German stereotypes in the context of different work enterprises, see Müller 1993; for an analysis of German-German relations as reflected in expressive culture, see Stein 1993; and for discussion of the public mood surrounding East-West relations following re-unification, see McFalls 1995.

31.   This consumption metaphor was also used to describe the "sell out" of the East to the West. As one villager remarked, "They [the West Germans] conquered us through advertisements and products, but we wanted to be conquered that way."

32.   I thank Janelle Taylor for the phrase "fluency in consumption."

33.   Werbefahrten are not unique to the former GDR, but this marketing strategy proved to be particularly successful here because it provided unsuspecting easterners with an opportunity for inexpensive travel.

34.   In *Entdecken, Erleben, Handeln* 1991. Even the title of the textbook conveys a subtle message of what eastern Germans had to learn in the new system. Although the first two words are fairly straightforward—*Entdecken* (discover) and *Erleben* (experience)—the third word, *Handeln*, means both "to proceed" and "to do business."

35.   On legends and legend analysis specifically, see, for example, Bausinger 1980; Dégh and Vázsonyi 1978; Fine 1992. Brednich (1991: 15–28) addresses West German legends about the GDR after the fall of the Wall.

36.   The depth and diversity of narrative scholarship in anthropology, folklore, history, literary studies, and performance theory (among other disciplines) obviously cannot be addressed in a single footnote. A few recent exemplary works in anthropology include Abu-Lughod 1993 on storytelling and "writing against culture"; Bauman 1986 on the analysis of storytelling and performance; Narayan 1989 on narrative in religious teachings; Steedly 1993 on narrative experience; and Stewart 1996 on cultural poetics and narrative space.

37.   I thank Stefan Wolff for this anecdote from Leipzig. The Berlin examples stem from "Wir lieben die Heimat" 1995. Another particularly interesting manifestation of "Ostalgia" and eastern German identity in many areas of the former GDR is the revival of the Jugendweihe ceremony. See Wolbert 1995, n.d.

38.   See, for example, Abu-Lughod 1990; Comaroff and Comaroff 1990; Hebdige 1988.

39.   German:

> Das Pokerspiel der Treuhand regt uns kleine Lichter auf
> Die Wessis kommen, sahnen ab, und wir gehn dabei drauf
> Das Beste wär, wir teilen das Eigentum des Volkes auf
> an uns, denn nur alleine wir haben Recht darauf
>
> Das ganze Leben ist ein Quiz
> Und wir sind nur die Kandidaten
> Das ganze Leben ist ein Quiz
> ja, und wir raten, raten, raten
> Und wiedermal, wir können's nicht fassen,
> haben wir uns total verarschen lassen?

40.   German:

> Nun sehen wir es ein, wir passen nicht rein
> in euere zivilisierte Welt
> Bei uns regiert noch Kraft und Mut, wir sind noch
> ehrlich, stark und gut,
> bei euch regiert hingegen nur das Geld.

41.   German: "Der Fuchs ist schlau und stellt sich dumm, beim Wessi ist es
andersrum."

42.   Here I differ with some of the conclusions drawn by Borneman (1992: 313–
34; 1993). Although he is extremely effective in outlining the unidirectional nature of power involved in the politics of German re-unification, Borneman overlooks the complexities and subtleties with which western hegemony has been negotiated and contested in everyday life. I believe it is premature to argue, as he
does, that "unification has served to confirm the values of West Germanness,"
that eastern Germans "began a process of self-dissolution" (1992: 322), and that
"East Germans have remained speechless and have thus internalized these projections" of them as "inferior in space and behind in time" (1993: 5).

43.   *Eigen-Sinn* is a multifaceted term that denotes self-will, self-affirmation,
reappropriation, and playful autonomy. It is a central concept in Alf Lüdtke's
analyses of workers' everyday life and shop-floor dynamics (Lüdtke 1993a;
1993b) but has far broader and very useful implications for theorizing the dynamics of power, alienated social relations, and the politics of everyday life more
generally.

44.   I am indebted to discussions with Andrew Bergerson, who has described
notions of liminality through "walking the walls" in pre–World War II Alt-
Hildesheim (Bergerson 1998). See also Flynn 1997 for an excellent discussion of
the strategic manipulation of ambiguity in the context of transborder exchange
along the Bénin-Nigeria border.

CHAPTER 6

1.   In choosing gender as a category of analysis, as a border zone of social life around which certain lines may become salient, my focus on women here is admittedly one-sided. This is in part a product of the realities of fieldwork: I had more access to and interaction with women than with men. It is mostly the product, however, of the realities of life for women since re-unification: women have been disproportionately affected by rising unemployment, reductions in generous maternity and child-care benefits, the loss of access to free and legal first-trimester abortion, and the introduction of the West German legal system that directs women toward motherhood and part-time work (see De Soto 1994).

2.   Several recent collections of interviews with women in the former GDR provide illuminating illustrations of this point. See Dodds and Allen-Thompson 1994; Fischer and Lux 1990.

3.   I am primarily talking about the 1970s and 1980s here. Although these decades share similarities with the years that preceded them, it would be misleading to generalize about the entire forty years of socialist rule. Furthermore, the period I discuss is one that represents the experiences and memories of most of the women in Kella.

4.   According to a 1987 village census, 78 out of the 146 working-age women in Kella (53 percent) were employed in the clips factory. Only two women were not employed outside the home: one worked as a bookkeeper for her self-employed husband; the other was a folk artist who sold her crafts to the state.

5.   Built in 1911 by the local innkeeper and leased to a regional cigar-manufacturing company, for several decades the factory employed local women to roll cigars until production ceased during World War II. It was reopened in 1953 under the direction of a state-owned factory.

6.   Doina Harsanyi has noted a similar function of a Romanian factory, which women she interviewed viewed as "as much a place to socialize as a means to make money" (1993: 45).

7.   As in many socialist states, gender-equity laws in the GDR were the product of a demand for labor power as well as ideology (see Verdery 1996: 64).

8.   Although there were never any women in the politburo and few in the upper echelons of the GDR political organization, the number of women involved in local politics was relatively high. In the early 1980s, for example, approximately one-quarter of city mayors were women (Dodds and Allen-Thompson 1994: 10).

9.   "This personality follows the precepts of socialist morality, such as community spirit, feelings of duty and responsibility toward state and society, and an optimistic outlook on life and the aims of socialism" (Lemke 1989: 60).

10.   For insightful discussions of the intersections of gender and nation in relation to socialist "parent" or "father" states, see Dölling 1991; Verdery 1996.

11.   For an excellent brief overview of the history of the Cult of Mary and insightful critique of anthropological studies of Marian devotion, particularly in terms of challenging conventional interpretations of the relationship between the Cult of Mary and gender and family roles, see Dubisch 1995.

12.   As Ute Gerhard points out, these suspicions that child care "undermines the family" are reflected in national statistics: in West Germany, only 5 percent of children under the age of three are in day-care facilities outside the home (1991–1992: 19). Following the Wende and especially after violence against foreigners perpetrated by eastern German youths, the GDR day-care system was used by conservatives in arguments against increased support for child care in general.

13.   Most of these small enterprises petered out after their novelty wore off and budgets were tightened. The entrepreneurs' failure to cultivate clientele outside the small circle of the village also contributed to the brief life of their businesses.

14.   *Frühschoppen* are the Sunday morning festivities during Kirmes, when the male participants traditionally consume many alcoholic beverages.

15.   For a brief history of the Women's Equality Office (Gleichstellungsstelle), with its origins in 1980s West Germany, and an analysis of differences and conceptualizations of the office after re-unification as reflective of differences among feminist concerns in the old and new federal states, see Ferree 1991–1992.

16.   Paralleling national statistics in the former GDR, the birthrate in Kella dropped by 70 percent in the first three years following the Wende, from an average of 10.6 births per year between 1969 and 1989 to an average of 3 between 1990 and 1992. Between 1992 and 1995, the birthrate rose again slightly in Kella, to 5.6 births per year (statistics compiled from village church records).

17.   Motherhood also became a point of contention in East and West German feminist dialogues. See, for example, Streit 1991–1992.

18.   On average, women in the GDR had their first child by the age of twenty-three, several years younger than their West German counterparts (Kolinksy 1993: 261).

19.   *ABM,* or *Arbeitsbeschaffungsmassnahmen,* are government grants to create temporary jobs or retraining programs.

20.   This ABM project, started in the spring of 1992, was intended to provide employment for one year. It came to an abrupt halt several months later but was resumed in 1994.

CHAPTER 7

1.   I have hyphenated *re-presentations* to stress a dynamic of agency and performance involved in practices of historical representation. Re-presentations entail the act of presenting something *again* and are thus important elements in the construction of memories and identities. Or, as Edward Bruner has written, not

only does experience "structure expressions," but "expressions structure experience" (1986: 6).

2.   My account of Kella's re-unification celebration is based on the recollections and photographs of numerous participants as well as on a videotape of the events filmed by the television network Thüringer Fernsehen. I watched the videotape several times with different groups of villagers, which enabled me to ask for clarifications and interpretations in a variety of contexts.

3.   The phrase "definitional ceremony" stems from Barbara Myerhoff, whose insightful definition is worth quoting here for its relevance to the context in Kella: "Definitional ceremonies deal with problems of invisibility and marginality; they are strategies that provide opportunities for being seen and in one's own terms, gathering witness to one's worth, vitality, and being" (1986: 267).

4.   To many villagers whose contact with western relatives had made them subject to certain harassments and scrutiny under socialism (being prohibited from using certain western goods in school or being questioned or placed under increased scrutiny due to western contacts, for example), this represented the ultimate hypocrisy.

5.   Calls for a re-evaluation of the Nazi past stemmed largely from the contrasting constructions of memory in East and West Germany. On the one hand, West Germany went through a politicized process of "confronting" this past, particularly in the late 1970s and 1980s, which culminated in the Historians' Debate of 1986, a heated controversy over the uniqueness of Nazi crimes. Initiated by historians on the political right and contested by critics on the left (led by Jürgen Habermas), the central issue in this dispute focused on whether Nazi genocide was comparable with other national atrocities. Underlying these debates were questions of German nationhood and the burdens of the past. See Historikerstreit 1988; Maier 1988. East Germany, on the other hand, implemented an official memory of National Socialist fascism as the outcome of capitalist and imperialist agendas. Nazi victims were labeled "antifascists," thereby largely erasing from memory Jews and other victims of the Holocaust. The term *antifascism* figured prominently in socialist language and ideology throughout GDR history: The border was "protection" from the "fascists" in the West, for example, and good "antifascist" socialist citizens would continue the fight against fascism. The use of this term thus rhetorically linked GDR citizens to Nazi victims, an identification that was further inculcated through Jugendweihe and FDJ induction rituals at former concentration-camp sites. For a discussion of differences in memory construction in East and West Germany, see Herf 1997.

6.   The Christa Wolf debate emerged after the publication of her story, *Was Bleibt* (What Remains) in June 1990. Written in 1979 and kept in a drawer until after the Wende, *Was Bleibt* describes a day in the life of the author under Stasi surveillance. Wolf was attacked on a variety of fronts, especially for the timing of the

book's publication and for attempting to claim victim status when she had enjoyed numerous privileges as an intellectual and alleged GDR state laureate. She was also accused of failing to criticize the SED regime forcefully before its demise. The criticisms of Wolf not only raised questions of the role and responsibility of intellectuals under socialism, the apportioning of guilt, and the value of GDR culture but also forced leftist intellectuals in the West to consider their own responsibility for elevating Wolf and other East German writers with a "dissident bonus" while ignoring certain realities of the SED regime. For a thoughtful discussion and analysis of the Wolf debate, see Huyssen 1995: 49–66.

7.   On memory and identity in the former GDR, see Ten Dyke n.d.; One Nation, Which Past? 1997, esp. Wierling 1997.

8.   See also Borneman 1998 for a discussion of how the "GDR is often reduced, both colloquially and in formal legal discourse, to its *Grenzregime,* border regime—to the entire system of rules and regulations intended to demarcate East Germany from its West German counterpart, to enclose, bound and reconstitute its 'people'" (p. 164).

9.   I am indebted to David Cohen's (1994) discussion of silences and commemorations, which has influenced my analysis of the Stasi issue here.

10.   Several men from the village, including Mayor Karl Hartmann, were involved in an effort to promote regional tourism in the southern Eichsfeld. Driven by a pride in their Heimat as well as a belief in the potential economic benefits of tourism, these men were briefly involved in a regional Eichsfeld tourist organization and initiated community improvement projects to make the locale attractive to tourists. Such projects, often funded by the state and made possible by ABM labor, included the construction of hiking trails, lookout points, and picnic areas; the creation or renovation of public spaces like a village center and fountain; and the erection of signs and benches throughout the area. Many renovations followed models and/or suggestions of western specialists. As one western German planner who presented his ideas in a public lecture explained, "The most important thing is to bring out the authentic village character." Among other things, the lack of a village infrastructure to support even a small tourist industry (guest accommodations, for example) has hindered the realization of these goals. Although most improvements were welcomed by the community, many did not go uncontested. As one young villager wrote me after the recent (1994) installation of a small fountain in the village center, "Maybe this will get us out of our identity crisis. But does preserving the 'village character' always mean it has to be old?"

11.   After uttering his remark, this villager looked to me to substantiate his view: all American and West German visitors we received during our time in Kella were most interested in viewing the former border structure. Indeed, as mentioned in the book's Introduction, despite my efforts to claim otherwise,

many villagers expressed a hope that publication of my study would help promote tourism in their community.

12.   Letter from Gemeindevertretung Kella to Kreisverwaltung Amt für Umwelt und Natur, February 24, 1992.

13.   Letter from the Federal Defense Ministry to Gemeindevertretung Kella, July 23, 1992. Karl's last-ditch efforts to use ecological arguments were similarly denied when authorities determined that there would be no damage to the environment (correspondence between the Federal Defense Ministry and Gemeindevertretung Kella, June 29, 1993).

14.   The service road surrounding Kella was left standing pending further action, although the rest of this road has been removed along with the fencing. Much to many residents' chagrin, a small section of the fence was left standing near a neighboring village.

15.   The border museum closest to Kella, Schifflersgrund, is near the town of Bad Sooden-Allendorf, approximately twenty kilometers away.

16.   Statement by Arbeitskreis Grenzinformation e.V. at the entrance to the Schifflersgrund border museum.

17.   In the first years after its opening in 1991, the Schifflersgrund border museum received significantly more visitors from western Germany than from eastern Germany.

EPILOGUE

1.   See especially Borneman 1992; Habermas 1991. For a discussion of the gendered dimensions of a national identity founded on the principal of economic prosperity, see Carter 1997.

Works Cited

Abu-Lughod, Lila. 1990. The Romance of Resistance: Tracing Transformations of Power through Bedouin Women. *American Ethnologist* 17 (1): 41–55.

———. 1991. Writing against Culture. In *Recapturing Anthropology: Working in the Present,* ed. Richard G. Fox, 137–62. Santa Fe, N.Mex.: School of American Research Press.

———. 1993. *Writing Women's Worlds: Bedouin Stories.* Berkeley: University of California Press.

Adler, Hans-Gerd. 1990. *Wir Sprengen unsere Ketten: Die friedliche Revolution im Eichsfeld.* Leipzig: Thomas Verlag.

Altman, Yochanan. 1989. Second Economy Activities in the USSR: Insights from the Southern Republic. In *Corruption, Development and Inequality: Soft Touch or Hard Graft?* ed. Peter M. Ward, 58–187. New York: Routledge.

Alvarez, Robert R., Jr. 1995. The Mexican-U.S. Border: The Making of an Anthropology of Borderlands. *Annual Review of Anthropology* 24: 447–70.

Anderson, Robert T., and Barbara Gallatin Anderson. 1966. *Bus Stop for Paris: The Transformation of a French Village.* New York: Anchor Books.

Anzaldúa, Gloria. 1987. *Borderlands / La Frontera: The New Mestiza.* San Francisco: Spinsters / Aunt Lute Books.

Appadurai, Arjun. 1986. Introduction: Commodities and the Politics of Value. In *The Social Life of Things: Commodities in Cultural Perspective*, ed. Arjun Appadurai, 3–63. Cambridge, England: Cambridge University Press.

———. 1993. Consumption, Duration, and History. *Stanford Literature Review* 10 (1–2): 11–33.

———. 1996. *Modernity at Large: Cultural Dimensions of Globalization*. Minneapolis: University of Minnesota Press.

Applegate, Celia. 1990. *A Nation of Provincials: The German Idea of Heimat*. Berkeley: University of California Press.

Åslund, Anders. 1985. *Private Enterprise in Eastern Europe: The Non-Agricultural Private Sector in Poland and the GDR, 1945–1983*. London: Macmillan.

Badone, Ellen. 1990. Introduction. In *Religious Orthodoxy and Popular Faith in European Society*, ed. Ellen Badone, 3–23. Princeton, N.J.: Princeton University Press.

Bakhtin, Mikhail. 1984. *Rabelais and His World*, trans. Helene Iswolsky. Bloomington: Indiana University Press.

Barrett, Richard A. 1978. Village Modernization and Changing Nicknaming Practices in Northern Spain. *Journal of Anthropological Research* 34 (1): 92–108.

Barth, Fredrik, ed. 1969. *Ethnic Groups and Boundaries: The Social Organization of Culture Difference*. Boston: Little, Brown.

Basso, Keith H. 1984. "Stalking with Stories": Names, Places, and Moral Narratives among the Western Apache. In *Text, Play, and Story: The Construction and Reconstruction of Self and Society*, ed. Edward M. Bruner, 19–55. Washington, D.C.: 1983 Proceedings of the American Ethnological Society.

Bauman, Richard. 1986. *Story, Performance, and Event: Contextual Studies of Oral Narrative*. Cambridge, England: Cambridge University Press.

Bauman, Richard, and Roger D. Abrahams, eds. 1981. *"And Other Neighborly Names": Social Process and Cultural Image in Texas Folklore*. Austin: University of Texas Press.

Bausinger, Hermann. 1980 [1968]. *Formen der Volkspoesie*. Berlin: E. Schmidt.

Bausinger, Hermann, and Konrad Köstlin, eds. 1980. *Heimat und Identität: Probleme regionaler Kultur*. Neumünster: Karl Wachholtz Verlag.

Baylis, Thomas A. 1974. *The Technical Intelligentsia and the East German Elite: Legitimacy and Social Change in Mature Communism*. Berkeley: University of California Press.

Becker, Peter. 1990. *Leben und Lieben im einem kalten Land: Sexualität im Spannungsfeld von Ökonomie und Demographie. Das Beispiel St. Lambrecht 1600–1850*. Frankfurt am Main: Campus Verlag.

Behar, Ruth. 1990. The Struggle for the Church: Popular Anticlericalism and Religiosity in Post-Franco Spain. In *Religious Orthodoxy and Popular Faith in European Society*, ed. Ellen Badone, 76–112. Princeton, N.J.: Princeton University Press.

————. 1993. *Translated Woman: Crossing the Border with Esperanza's Story.* Boston: Beacon Press.

Beidelman, T. O. 1989. Agonistic Exchange: Homeric Reciprocity and the Heritage of Simmel and Mauss. *Cultural Anthropology* 4 (3): 227–59.

Bennewitz, Inge, and Rainer Potratz. 1994. *Zwangsaussiedlungen an der innerdeutschen Grenze: Analysen und Dokumente.* Berlin: Christoph Links Verlag.

Berdahl, Daphne. n.d. Mixed Devotions: Religion, Friendship, and Fieldwork in Post-Socialist East Germany. In *Fieldwork Dilemmas: Anthropologists in Postsocialist States,* ed. Hermine De Soto and Nora Dudwick. Madison: University of Wisconsin Press. In press.

Berdahl, Daphne, Matti Bunzl, and Martha Lampland, eds. 1999. *Altering States: Ethnographies of Transition in Eastern Europe and the Former Soviet Union.* Ann Arbor: University of Michigan Press. In press.

Bergerson, Andrew S. 1998. A History of Neighborliness in Alt-Hildesheim, 1900–1950: Custom, Transformation, Memory. Ph.D. diss., University of Chicago.

Bhabha, Homi K. 1994. *The Location of Culture.* London: Routledge.

Bohlman, Philip. 1996. The Final Borderpost. *Journal of Musicology* 14 (4): 427–52.

Boissevain, Jeremy. 1974. *Friends of Friends: Networks, Manipulators, and Coalitions.* Oxford: Blackwell.

Borneman, John. 1991. *After the Wall: East Meets West in the New Berlin.* Boston: Basic Books.

————. 1992. *Belonging in the Two Berlins: Kin, State, Nation.* Cambridge, England: Cambridge University Press.

————. 1993. Time-Space Compression and the Continental Divide in German Subjectivity. *Oral History Review* 21 (2): 41–57.

————. 1997. *Settling Accounts: Violence, Justice, and Accountability in Postsocialist Europe.* Princeton, N.J.: Princeton University Press.

————. 1998. *Grenzregime* (Border Regime): The Wall and Its Aftermath. In *Border Identities: Nation and State at International Frontiers,* ed. Thomas M. Wilson and Hastings Donnan, 162–90. Cambridge, England: Cambridge University Press.

Bourdieu, Pierre. 1977. *Outline of a Theory of Practice,* trans. Richard Nice. Cambridge, England: Cambridge University Press.

————. 1984. *Distinction: A Social Critique of the Judgement of Taste,* trans. Richard Nice. Cambridge, Mass.: Harvard University Press.

————. 1985. The Social Space and the Genesis of Groups. *Theory and Society* 14 (6): 723–44.

————. 1986. The Forms of Capital. In *Handbook of Theory and Research for the Sociology of Education,* ed. John G. Richardson, 241–58. Westport, Conn.: Greenwood Press.

————. 1987. What Makes a Social Class? On the Theoretical and Practical Existence of Groups. *Berkeley Journal of Sociology: A Critical Review* 32: 1–17.

Bourdieu, Pierre, and Loïc J. D. Wacquant. 1992. *An Invitation to Reflexive Sociology.* Chicago: University of Chicago Press.

Brandes, Stanley H. 1975. The Structural and Demographic Implications of Nicknames in Navanogal, Spain. *American Ethnologist* 2 (1): 139–48.

Brednich, Rolf Wilhelm. 1990. Trabi-Witze. Ein populäres deutsches Erzählgenre der Gegenwart. *Volkskunde in Niedersachsen* 7 (1): 18–35.

————. 1991. *Die Maus im Jumbo-Jet: Neue sagenhafte Geschichten von Heute.* Munich: C. H. Beck Verlag.

Brettell, Caroline B. 1990. The Priest and His People: The Contractual Basis for Religious Practice in Rural Portugal. In *Religious Orthodoxy and Popular Faith in European Society,* ed. Ellen Badone, 55–75. Princeton, N.J.: Princeton University Press.

Bringa, Tone. 1995. *Being Muslim the Bosnian Way: Identity and Community in a Central Bosnian Village.* Princeton, N.J.: Princeton University Press.

Bruner, Edward M. 1984. Introduction: The Opening up of Anthropology. In *Text, Play, and Story: The Construction and Reconstruction of Self and Society,* ed. Edward M. Bruner, 1–16. Washington, D.C.: American Ethnological Society.

————. 1986. Experience and Its Expressions. In *The Anthropology of Experience,* ed. Victor W. Turner and Edward M. Bruner, 3–32. Urbana: University of Illinois Press.

Burawoy, Michael, and János Lukács. 1992. *The Radiant Past: Ideology and Reality in Hungary's Road to Capitalism.* Chicago: University of Chicago Press.

Burke, Peter. 1978. *Popular Culture in Early Modern Europe.* New York: New York University Press.

Calderón, Héctor, and José D. Salvídar, eds. 1991. *Criticism in the Borderlands: Studies in Chicano Literature, Culture, and Ideology.* Durham, N.C.: Duke University Press.

Campbell, Federico. 1995. *Tijuana: Stories on the Border,* trans. Debra A. Castillo. Berkeley: University of California Press.

Campbell, John K. 1964. *Honour, Family, and Patronage: A Study of Institutions and Moral Values in a Greek Mountain Community.* Oxford: Clarendon Press.

Carrier, James. 1994. *Gifts and Commodities: Exchange and Western Capitalism since 1700.* London: Routledge.

Carter, Erica. 1997. *How German Is She? Postwar West German Reconstruction and the Consuming Woman.* Ann Arbor: University of Michigan Press.

Castillo, Debra. 1995. Borderlining: An Introduction. In *Tijuana: Stories on the Border,* by Federico Campbell, trans. Debra A. Castillo, 1–26. Berkeley: University of California Press.

Childs, David. 1988. *The GDR: Moscow's German Ally.* London: Unwin Hyman.

Chirot, Daniel. 1976. *Social Change in a Peripheral Society: The Creation of a Balkan Colony.* New York: Academic Press.

Christ, Peter, and Ralf Neubauer. 1991. *Kolonie im eigenen Land: Die Treuhand, Bonn und die Wirtschaftskatastrophe der fünf neuen Länder.* Berlin: Rowohlt.

Christian, William A., Jr. 1989. *Person and God in a Spanish Valley.* Rev. ed. Princeton, N.J.: Princeton University Press.

———. 1996. *Visionaries: The Spanish Republic and the Reign of Christ.* Berkeley: University of California Press.

Clifford, James, and George E. Marcus, eds. 1986. *Writing Culture: The Poetics and Politics of Ethnography.* Berkeley: University of California Press.

Cohen, Anthony P. 1987. *Whalsay: Symbol, Segment, and Boundary in a Shetland Island Community.* Manchester: Manchester University Press.

———, ed. 1982. *Belonging: Identity and Social Organisation in British Rural Cultures.* Manchester: Manchester University Press.

———. 1986. *Symbolising Boundaries: Identity and Diversity in British Cultures.* Manchester: Manchester University Press.

Cohen, David William. 1994. *The Combing of History.* Chicago: University of Chicago Press.

Cole, John W. 1977. Anthropology Comes Part-Way Home: Community Studies in Europe. *Annual Review of Anthropology* 6: 349–78.

———. 1985. Problems of Socialism in Eastern Europe. *Dialectical Anthropology* 9 (1–4): 233–56.

Cole, John, and Eric Wolf. 1974. *The Hidden Frontier: Ecology and Ethnicity in an Alpine Valley.* London: Academic Press.

Comaroff, Jean, and John L. Comaroff. 1990. Goodly Beasts and Beastly Goods: Cattle and Commodities in a South African Context. *American Ethnologist* 17 (2): 195–216.

———. 1991. *Of Revelation and Revolution: Christianity, Colonialism, and Consciousness in South Africa,* vol 1. Chicago: University of Chicago Press.

Comaroff, John L., and Jean Comaroff. 1997. *Of Revelation and Revolution: The Dialectics of Modernity on a South African Frontier,* vol 2. Chicago: University of Chicago Press.

Connerton, Paul. 1989. *How Societies Remember.* Cambridge, England: Cambridge University Press.

Connor, Walter D. 1979. *Socialism, Politics, and Equality: Hierarchy and Change in Eastern Europe and the USSR.* New York: Columbia University Press.

Cowan, Jane K. 1990. *Dance and the Body Politic in Northern Greece.* Princeton, N.J.: Princeton University Press.

Crain, Mary. 1992. Pilgrims, "Yuppies," and Media Men: The Transformation of an Andalusian Pilgrimage. In *Revitalizing European Rituals,* ed. Jeremy Boissevain, 95–112. New York: Routledge.

Creed, Gerald W. 1995. An Old Song in a New Voice: Decollectivization in Bulgaria. In *East European Communities: The Struggle for Balance in Turbulent Times,* ed. David A. Kideckel, 25–46. Boulder, Colo.: Westview Press.

Darnton, Robert. 1991. *Berlin Journal 1989–1990.* New York: W. W. Norton.

de Certeau, Michel. 1984. *The Practice of Everyday Life,* trans. Steven Rendall. Berkeley: University of California Press.

Dégh, Linda, and Andrew Vázsonyi. 1978. The Crack in the Red Goblet or Truth and Modern Legend. In *Folklore in the Modern World,* ed. Richard M. Dorson, 253–72. The Hague: Mouton.

Denich, Bette. 1994. Dismembering Yugoslavia: Nationalist Ideologies and the Symbolic Revival of Genocide. *American Ethnologist* 21 (2): 367–90.

De Soto, Hermine G. 1989. The Delayed Transformation: Experiences of Everyday Life in a Village in the Black Forest. Ph.D. diss., University of Wisconsin–Madison.

———. 1994. "In the Name of the Folk": Women and Nation in the New Germany. *Women's Law Journal, University of California, Los Angeles* 5 (1): 83–102.

———. In press. Reading the Fools' Mirror: Reconstituting Identity against National and Transnational Political Practices. *American Ethnologist.*

———. n.d. Contesting Female Personhood: Comparison of East and West German Legal Cultures in the Process of Unification. In *Gendered Histories, East German Women after Socialism.* Unpublished manuscript.

De Soto, Hermine G., and David G. Anderson, eds. 1993. *The Curtain Rises: Rethinking Culture, Ideology, and the State in Eastern Europe.* Atlantic Highlands, N.J.: Humanities Press.

De Soto, Hermine G., and Christel Panzig. 1995. From Decollectivization to Poverty and beyond: Women in Rural East Germany before and after Unification. In *East-Central European Communities: The Struggle for Balance in Turbulent Times,* ed. David A. Kideckel, 179–96. Boulder, Colo.: Westview Press.

Diesener, Gerald, and Rainer Gries. 1992. "Chic zum Geburtstag unserer Republik": Zwei Projekte zur Produkt- und Politikpropaganda im Deutsch-Deutschen Vergleich. *Geschichtswerkstatt* 25: 56–69.

Distanz, Entäuschung, Haß: Die deutsch-deutsche Mauer im Kopf. 1992. *Der Spiegel,* August 17.

Djilas, Milovan. 1957. *The New Class: An Analysis of the Communist System.* New York: Frederick A. Praeger.

Dodds, Dinah, and Pam Allen-Thompson. 1994. *The Wall in My Backyard: East German Women in Transition.* Amherst: University of Massachusetts Press.

Dölling, Irene. 1991. Between Hope and Helplessness: Women in the GDR after the "Turning Point." *Feminist Review* 39 (Winter): 3–15.

———. 1993. "But the Pictures Stay the Same . . .": The Image of Women in the

Journal *für Dich* before and after the "Turning Point." In *Gender Politics and Post-Communism: Reflections from Eastern Europe and the Former Soviet Union,* ed. Nanette Funk and Magda Mueller, 168–79. New York: Routledge.

Donnan, Hastings, and Thomas M. Wilson. 1994a. An Anthropology of Frontiers. In *Border Approaches: Anthropological Perspectives on Frontiers,* ed. Hastings Donnan and Thomas M. Wilson, 1–14. Lanham, Md.: University Press of America.

———, eds. 1994b. *Border Approaches: Anthropological Perspectives on Frontiers.* Lanham, Md.: University Press of America.

Dornberg, John. 1968. *The Other Germany.* New York: Doubleday.

Drakulic, Slavenka. 1991. *How We Survived Communism and Even Laughed.* New York: W. W. Norton.

Dubisch, Jill. 1990. Pilgrimage and Popular Religion at a Greek Holy Shrine. In *Religious Orthodoxy and Popular Faith in European Society,* ed. Ellen Badone, 113–39. Princeton, N.J.: Princeton University Press.

———. 1995. *In a Different Place: Pilgrimage, Gender, and Politics at a Greek Island Shrine.* Princeton, N.J.: Princeton University Press.

Dümcke, Wolfgang, and Fritz Vilmar, eds. 1996. *Kolonialisierung der DDR: Kritische Analysen und alternativen des Einigungsprozesses.* Münster: Agenda Verlag.

Durkheim, Emile, and Marcel Mauss. 1963 [1903]. *Primitive Classification,* trans. Rodney Needham. Chicago: University of Chicago Press.

Eade, John, and Michael J. Sallnow, eds. 1991. *Contesting the Sacred: The Anthropology of Christian Pilgrimage.* New York: Routledge.

Einhorn, Barbara. 1993. *Cinderella Goes to Market: Citizenship, Gender and Women's Movements in East Central Europe.* London: Verso Press.

Entdecken, Erleben, Handeln. 1991. Berlin: Volk und Wissen Verlag GmbH.

Erst vereint, nun entzweit. 1993. *Der Spiegel,* January 18.

Evans-Pritchard, E. E. 1940. *The Nuer.* New York: Oxford University Press.

Fabian, Johannes. 1983. *Time and the Other: How Anthropology Makes Its Object.* New York: Columbia University Press.

Feld, Steven, and Keith H. Basso, eds. 1996. *Senses of Place.* Sante Fe, N.Mex.: School of American Research Press.

Fernandez, James W. 1965. Symbolic Consensus in a Fang Reformative Cult. *American Anthropologist* 67 (4): 902–29.

———. 1986. *Persuasions and Performances: The Play of Tropes in Culture.* Bloomington: Indiana University Press.

———. 1990. Enclosures: Boundary Maintenance and Its Representations over Time in Asturian Mountain Villages (Spain). In *Culture through Time: Anthropological Approaches,* ed. Emiko Ohnuki-Tierney, 94–127. Stanford, Calif.: Stanford University Press.

Ferree, Myra Marx. 1991–1992. Institutionalizing Gender Equality: Feminist Politics and Equality Offices. *German Politics and Society* 24–25 (Winter): 53–66.

Fine, Gary Alan. 1992. *Manufacturing Tales: Sex and Money in Contemporary Legends.* Knoxville: University of Tennessee Press.

Firliet, Elzbieta, and Jerzy Chlopecki. 1992. When Theft Is Not Theft. In *The Unplanned Society: Poland during and after Communism,* ed. Janine R. Wedel, 95–109. New York: Columbia University Press.

Fischer, Erica, and Petra Lux. 1990. *Ohne uns ist kein Staat zu machen: DDR-Frauen nach der Wende.* Cologne: Kiepenheuer and Witsch.

Fischer, Hans Friedrich. 1991. The Catholic Church in the GDR: A Look back in Anger. *Religion in Communist Lands* 19 (3–4): 211–19.

Flynn, Donna K. 1997. "We Are the Border": Identity, Exchange, and the State along the Bénin-Nigeria Border. *American Ethnologist* 24 (2): 311–30.

Foucault, Michel. 1979. *Discipline and Punish: The Birth of the Prison.* New York: Vintage Books.

Frahm, Eckart, and Wiklef Hoops, eds. 1987. *Dorfentwicklung: Aktuelle Probleme und Weiterbildungsbedarf.* Tübingen: Tübinger Vereinigung für Volkskunde.

Frankenberg, Ronald. 1957. *Village on the Border: A Social Study of Religion, Politics, and Football in a North Wales Community.* London: Cohen and West.

Friedl, Ernestine. 1962. *Vasilika: A Village in Modern Greece.* New York: Holt, Rinehart and Winston.

Friedl, John. 1974. *Kippel: A Changing Village in the Alps.* New York: Holt, Rinehart and Winston.

Fulbrook, Mary. 1995. *Anatomy of a Dictatorship: Inside the GDR, 1949–1989.* New York: Oxford University Press.

Funk, Nanette. 1993a. Abortion and German Unification. In *Gender Politics and Post-Communism: Reflections from Eastern Europe and the Former Soviet Union,* ed. Nanette Funk and Magda Mueller, 194–200. New York: Routledge.

———. 1993b. Introduction: Women and Post-Communism. In *Gender Politics and Post-Communism: Reflections from Eastern Europe and the Former Soviet Union,* ed. Nanette Funk and Magda Mueller, 1–14. New York: Routledge.

Fustel de Coulanges, N. D. 1980 [1864]. *The Ancient City: A Study on the Religion, Laws, and Institutions of Greece and Rome.* Baltimore, Md.: Johns Hopkins University Press.

Gal, Susan. 1994. Gender in the Post-Socialist Transition: The Abortion Debate in Hungary. *East European Politics and Societies* 8 (2): 256–86.

———. 1996. Feminism and Civil Society. *Replika:* 75–82.

Gauck, Joachim. 1991. *Die Stasi-Akten: Das unheimliche Erbe der DDR.* Reinbek bei Hamburg: Rowohlt.

Gaus, Günter. 1986. *Wo Deutschland Liegt: Eine Ortsbestimmung.* Munich: Deutscher Taschenbuch Verlag.

Gebhardt, Winfried, and Georg Kamphausen. 1994. *Zwei Dörfer in Deutschland: Mentalitätsunterschiede nach der Wiedervereinigung.* Opladen: Leske und Budrich.

Geertz, Clifford. 1973. *The Interpretation of Cultures.* New York: Basic Books.

———. 1983. *Local Knowledge: Further Essays in Interpretive Anthropology.* New York: Basic Books.

Gellner, Ernest, and John Waterbury, eds. 1977. *Patrons and Clients in Mediterranean Societies.* London: Duckworth.

Gerhard, Ute. 1991–1992. German Women and the Social Costs of Unification. *German Politics and Society* 24–25 (Winter): 16–33.

Gerlach, Vinzenz. 1985. *Das Eichsfeld.* Hanover: Niedersächsische Landeszentrale für politische Bildung.

Geyer, Michael. n.d. Introduction: Cultural Authority in Contemporary Germany. Unpublished manuscript.

Gilmore, David D. 1982. Some Notes on Community Nicknaming in Spain. *Man* 17 (4): 686–700.

———. 1987. *Aggression and Community: Paradoxes of Andalusian Culture.* New Haven, Conn.: Yale University Press.

Ginsburg, Faye, and Anna Lowenhaupt Tsing. 1990. Introduction. In *Uncertain Terms: Negotiating Gender in American Culture,* ed. Faye Ginsburg and Anna Lowenhaupt Tsing, 1–18. Boston: Beacon Press.

Golde, Günther. 1975. *Catholics and Protestants: Agricultural Modernization in Two German Villages.* New York: Academic Press.

Gordon, Arvan. 1990. The Church and Change in the GDR. *Religion in Communist Lands* 18 (2): 138–54.

Goven, Joanna. 1993. Gender Politics in Hungary: Autonomy and Antifeminism. In *Gender Politics and Post-Communism: Reflections from Eastern Europe and the Former Soviet Union,* ed. Nanette Funk and Magda Mueller, 224–40. New York: Routledge.

Greverus, Ina-Maria. 1979. *Auf der Suche nach Heimat.* Munich: C. H. Beck.

Grossman, Gregory, ed. 1987. *Studies in the Second Economy of Communist Countries.* Berkeley: University of California Press.

Gupta, Akhil, and James Ferguson. 1992. Beyond "Culture": Space, Identity, and the Politics of Difference. *Cultural Anthropology* 7 (1): 6–23.

Habermas, Jürgen. 1991. Yet again: German Identity—A Unified Nation of Angry DM-Burghers? *New German Critique* 52 (Winter): 84–101.

Hankiss, Elemér. 1990. *East European Alternatives.* Oxford: Clarendon Press.

Hann, C. M. 1980. *Tázlar: A Village in Hungary.* Cambridge, England: Cambridge University Press.

———. 1985. *A Village without Solidarity: Polish Peasants in Years of Crisis.* New Haven, Conn.: Yale University Press.

————. 1993. Introduction: Social Anthropology and Socialism. In *Socialism: Ideals, Ideologies, and Local Practices,* ed. C. M. Hann, 1–26. London: Routledge.

————, ed. 1990. *Market Economy and Civil Society in Hungary.* London: Frank Cass.

Hannerz, Ulf. 1987. The World in Creolisation. *Africa* 57 (4): 546–59.

Harsanyi, Doina Pasca. 1993. Women in Romania. In *Gender Politics and Post-Communism: Reflections from Eastern Europe and the Former Soviet Union,* ed. Nanette Funk and Magda Mueller, 39–52. New York: Routledge.

Hartmann, Andreas, and Sabine Künsting. 1990. *Grenzgeschichten: Berichte aus dem deutschen Niemandsland.* Cologne: S. Fischer Verlag.

————. 1993. Die erzählte Grenze. In *Grenzland: Beiträge zur Geschichte der deutsch-deutschen Grenze,* ed. Bernd Weisbrod, 15–27. Hanover: Verlag Hahnische Buchhandlung.

Hauser, Ewa, Barbara Heyns, and Jane Mansbridge. 1993. Feminism in the Interstices of Politics and Culture: Poland in Transition. In *Gender Politics and Post-Communism: Reflections from Eastern Europe and the Former Soviet Union,* ed. Nanette Funk and Magda Mueller, 257–73. New York: Routledge.

Hayden, Robert. 1994. Recounting the Dead: The Rediscovery and Redefinition of Wartime Massacres in Late and Post Communist Yugoslavia. In *Memory, History, and Opposition under State Socialism,* ed. Rubie S. Watson, 167–84. Santa Fe, N.Mex.: School of American Research Press.

————. 1996. Imagined Communities and Real Victims: Self-Determination and Ethnic Cleansing in Yugoslavia. *American Ethnologist* 23 (4): 783–801.

Hebdige, Dick. 1988. *Hiding in the Light: On Images and Things.* New York: Routledge.

Heiberg, Marianne. 1989. *The Making of the Basque Nation.* Cambridge, England: Cambridge University Press.

Herf, Jeffrey. 1997. *Divided Memory: The Nazi Past in the two Germanys.* Cambridge, Mass.: Harvard University Press.

Herzfeld, Michael. 1985. *The Poetics of Manhood: Contest and Identity in a Cretan Mountain Village.* Princeton, N.J.: Princeton University Press.

————. 1987. *Anthropology through the Looking-Glass: Critical Ethnography in the Margins of Europe.* Cambridge, England: Cambridge University Press.

————. 1991. *A Place in History: Social and Monumental Time in a Cretan Town.* Princeton, N.J.: Princeton University Press.

————. 1992. *The Social Production of Indifference: Exploring the Symbolic Roots of Western Bureaucracy.* Chicago: University of Chicago Press.

————. 1997. *Cultural Intimacy: Social Poetics in the Nation-State.* New York: Routledge.

Hicks, D. Emily. 1991. *Border Writing: The Multidimensional Text.* Minneapolis: University of Minnesota Press.

Hirsch, Eric, and Michael O'Hanlon, eds. 1995. *The Anthropology of Landscape: Perspectives on Place and Space.* Oxford: Clarendon Press.

Historikerstreit. 1988. *New German Critique* 44 (Spring-Summer). Special issue.

Hobsbawm, Eric, and Terence Ranger, eds. 1981. *The Invention of Tradition.* Cambridge, England: Cambridge University Press.

Holy, Ladislaw. 1996. *The Little Czech and the Great Czech Nation: National Identity and the Post-Communist Transformation of Society.* Cambridge, England: Cambridge University Press.

Humphrey, Caroline. 1983. *Karl Marx Collective: Economy, Society, and Religion in a Siberian Collective Farm.* Cambridge, England: Cambridge University Press.

———. 1995. Creating a Culture of Disillusionment: Consumption in Moscow, a Chronicle of Changing Times. In *Worlds Apart: Modernity through the Prism of the Local,* ed. Daniel Miller, 43–68. London: Routledge.

Humphrey, Caroline, and Stephen Hugh-Jones. 1992. *Barter, Exchange and Value: An Anthropological Approach.* Cambridge, England: Cambridge University Press.

Huyssen, Andreas. 1995. *Twilight Memories: Marking Time in a Culture of Amnesia.* New York: Routledge.

Ilien, Albert, and Utz Jeggle. 1978. *Leben auf dem Dorf: Zur Sozialgeschichte des Dorfes und zur Sozialpsychologie seiner Bewohner.* Opladen: Westdeutscher Verlag.

Ivy, Marilyn. 1995. *Discourses of the Vanishing: Modernity, Phantasm, Japan.* Chicago: University of Chicago Press.

Jackson, Michael. 1989. *Paths toward a Clearing: Radical Empiricism and Ethnographic Inquiry.* Bloomington: Indiana University Press.

Jarausch, Konrad H. 1994. *The Rush to German Unity.* New York: Oxford University Press.

Johnson, David E., and Scott Michaelsen. 1997. Border Secrets: An Introduction. In *Border Theory: The Limits of Cultural Politics,* ed. Scott Michaelsen and David E. Johnson, 1–39. Minneapolis: University of Minnesota Press.

Jones, Stephen F. 1994. Old Ghosts and New Chains: Ethnicity and Memory in the Georgian Republic. In *Memory, History, and Opposition under State Socialism,* ed. Rubie S. Watson, 149–66. Santa Fe, N.Mex.: School of American Research Press.

Kaelble, Hartmut, Jürgen Kocka, and Hartmut Zwahr, eds. 1994. *Sozialgeschichte der DDR.* Stuttgart: Klett-Cotta.

Kaes, Anton. 1989. *From Hitler to Heimat: The Return of History as Film.* Cambridge, Mass.: Harvard University Press.

Kaschuba, Wolfgang, ed. 1989. *Der Deutsche Heimatfilm: Bilder, Texte und Analysen zu 70 Jahren deutscher Filmgeschichte.* Tübingen: Tübinger Vereinigung für Volkskunde.

Kaschuba, Wolfgang, and Carola Lipp. 1982. *Dörfliches Überleben: Zur Geschichte materieller und sozialer Reproduktion ländlicher Gesellschaft im 19. Und frühen 20. Jahrhundert.* Tübingen: Tübinger Vereinigung für Volkskunde.

Kearney, Michael. 1991. Borders and Boundaries of State and Self at the End of Empire. *Journal of Historical Sociology* 4 (1): 52–74.

Kelleher, William. 1994. Ambivalence, Modernity, and the State of Terror in Northern Ireland. *PoLAR: Political and Legal Anthropology Review* 17 (1): 31–39.

———. n.d. Memory, the Past and Forgetting: 'Terror' and the Struggles over Representation in Contemporary Ireland. Unpublished manuscript.

Kennedy, Michael D., ed. 1994. *Envisioning Eastern Europe: Postcommunist Cultural Studies.* Ann Arbor: University of Michigan Press.

Kideckel, David A. 1993. *The Solitude of Collectivism: Romanian Villagers to the Revolution and Beyond.* Ithaca, N.Y.: Cornell University Press.

———, ed. 1995. *East European Communities: The Struggle for Balance in Turbulent Times.* Boulder, Colo.: Westview Press.

Kligman, Gail. 1988. *The Wedding of the Dead: Ritual, Poetics, and Popular Culture in Transylvania.* Berkeley: University of California Press.

———. 1990. Reclaiming the Public: A Reflection on Recreating Civil Society in Romania. *East European Politics and Societies* 4 (3): 393–438.

———. 1992. The Politics of Reproduction in Ceaucescu's Romania: A Case Study in Political Culture. *East European Politics and Societies* 6 (3): 364–418.

Kocka, Jürgen, and Martin Sabrow, eds. 1994. *Die DDR als Geschichte: Fragen—Hypothesen—Perspektiven.* Berlin: Akademie Verlag.

Kolinksy, Eva. 1993. *Women in Contemporary Germany: Life, Work, and Politics.* Oxford: Berg Publishers.

Kolosi, Tamas, and Edmund Wnuk-Lipinski, eds. 1983. *Equality and Inequality under Socialism: Poland and Hungary Compared.* Beverly Hills, Calif.: Sage Publications.

Konrad, George, and Ivan Szelenyi. 1979. *The Intellectuals on the Road to Class Power,* trans. Andrew Arato and Richard E. Allen. New York: Harcourt Brace Jovanovich.

Konstantinov, Yulian. 1996. Patterns of Reinterpretation: Trader-Tourism in the Balkans (Bulgaria) as a Picaresque Metaphorical Enactment of Post-Totalitarianism. *American Ethnologist* 23 (4): 762–82.

Koonz, Claudia. 1994. Between Memory and Oblivion: Concentration Camps in German Memory. In *Commemorations: The Politics of National Identity,* ed. John R. Gillis, 258–80. Princeton, N.J.: Princeton University Press.

Kornai, Janos. 1992. *The Socialist System: The Political Economy of Communism.* Princeton, N.J.: Princeton University Press.

Kubik, Jan. 1994. *The Power of Symbols against the Symbols of Power: The Rise of Solidarity and the Fall of State Socialism in Poland.* University Park: Pennsylvania State University Press.

Kürti, László, and Juliet Langman, eds. 1997. *Beyond Borders: Remaking Cultural Identities in the New East and Central Europe.* Boulder, Colo.: Westview Press.

Lampland, Martha. 1995. *The Object of Labor: Commodification in Socialist Hungary.* Chicago: University of Chicago Press.

Larsen, Sidel S. 1982. The Two Sides of the House: Identity and Social Organisation in Kilbroney, Northern Ireland. In *Belonging: Identity and Social Organisation in British Rural Cultures,* ed. Anthony P. Cohen, 131–64. Manchester: Manchester University Press.

Lass, Andrew. 1994. From Memory to History: The Events of November 17 Dis/membered. In *Memory, History, and Opposition under State Socialism,* ed. Rubie S. Watson, 87–104. Santa Fe, N.Mex.: School of American Research Press.

Lavie, Smadar, and Ted Swedenburg. 1996. Introduction: Displacement, Diaspora, and Geographies of Identity. In *Displacement, Diaspora, and Geographies of Identity,* ed. Smadar Lavie and Ted Swedenburg, 1–25. Durham, N.C.: Duke University Press.

Lemke, Christiane. 1989. Political Socialization and the 'Micromilieu': Toward a Political Sociology of GDR Society. In *The Quality of Life in the German Democratic Republic,* ed. Marilyn Rueschemeyer and Christiane Lemke, 59–76. Armonk, N.Y.: M. E. Sharpe.

Lévi-Strauss, Claude. 1963. *Structural Anthropology,* trans. Claire Jacobson and Brooke Grundfest. New York: Basic Books.

———. 1966. *The Savage Mind.* Chicago: University of Chicago Press.

Liebes, Tamar, and Elihu Katz. 1990. *The Export of Meaning: Cross Cultural Readings of Dallas.* New York: Oxford University Press.

Limón, José E. 1991. Representation, Ethnicity, and the Precursory Ethnography: Notes of a Native Anthropologist. In *Recapturing Anthropology: Working in the Present,* ed. Richard G. Fox, 115–36. Santa Fe, N.Mex.: School of American Research Press.

———. 1992. *Mexican Ballads, Chicano Poems: History and Influence in Mexican-American Social Poetry.* Berkeley: University of California Press.

———. 1994. *Dancing with the Devil: Society and Cultural Poetics in Mexican-American South Texas.* Madison: University of Wisconsin Press.

Linge, Rudolf, and Peter Schmidt. 1967. *Kirche und Glauben im Eichsfeld.* Leipzig: St. Bruno Verlag.

Linke, Uli. 1995. Murderous Fantasies: Violence, Memory, and Selfhood in Germany. *New German Critique* 64 (Winter): 37–59.

———. 1997. Gendered Difference, Violent Imagination: Blood, Race, Nation. *American Anthropologist* 99 (3): 559–73.

Loizos, Peter. 1988. The Virgin Mary and Marina Warner's Feminism. *London School of Economics Quarterly* 2 (2): 175–92.

Lüdtke, Alf. 1993a. *Eigen-Sinn. Fabrikalltag, Arbeitererfahrungen und Politik vom Kaiserreich bis in den Faschismus.* Hamburg: Ergebnisse Verlag.

———. 1993b. Polymorphous Synchrony: German Industrial Workers and the Politics of Everyday Life. *International Review of Social History* 38: 39–84.

———. 1994. "Helden der Arbeit"—Mühen beim Arbeiten. Zur mißmutigen Loyalität von Industriearbeitern in der DDR. In *Sozialgeschichte der DDR,* ed. Hartmut Kaelble, Jürgen Kocka, and Hartmut Zwahr, 188–213. Stuttgart: Klett-Cotta.

———. 1995. Introduction: What Is the History of Everyday Life and Who Are Its Practitioners? In *The History of Everyday Life: Reconstructing Historical Experiences and Ways of Life,* ed. Alf Lüdtke, trans. W. Templer, 3–40. Princeton, N.J.: Princeton University Press.

———. 1997a. Sprache und Herrschaft in der DDR. Einleitende Überlegungen. In *Akten. Eingaben. Schaufenster. Die DDR und ihre Texte: Erkundungen zu Herrschaft und Alltag,* ed. Alf Lüdtke and Peter Becker, 11–26. Berlin: Akademie Verlag.

———. 1997b. ". . . den Menschen vergessen" ?—oder: Das Maß der Sicherheit. Arbeiterverhalten der 1950er Jahre im Blick von MfS, SED, FDGB und staatlichen Leitungen. In *Akten. Eingaben. Schaufenster. Die DDR und ihre Texte: Erkundungen zu Herrschaft und Alltag,* ed. Alf Lüdtke and Peter Becker, 189–222. Berlin: Akademie Verlag.

Lüdtke, Alf, and Peter Becker, eds. 1997. *Akten. Eingaben. Schaufenster. Die DDR und ihre Texte: Erkundungen zu Herrschaft und Alltag.* Berlin: Akademie Verlag.

Ludz, Peter Christian. 1972. *The Changing Party Elite in East Germany.* Cambridge, Mass.: MIT Press.

Lugo, Alejandro. 1997. Reflections on Border Theory, Culture, and the Nation. In *Border Theory: The Limits of Cultural Politics,* ed. Scott Michaelsen and David E. Johnson, 43–67. Minneapolis: University of Minnesota Press.

Maier, Charles S. 1988. *The Unmasterable Past: History, Holocaust, and German National Identity.* Cambridge, Mass.: Harvard University Press.

———. 1997. *Dissolution: The Crisis of Communism and the End of East Germany.* Princeton, N.J.: Princeton University Press.

Martinez, Oscar J. 1994. *Border People: Life and Society in the U.S.-Mexico Borderlands.* Tucson: University of Arizona Press.

Mauss, Marcel. 1954. *The Gift: Forms and Functions of Exchange in Archaic Societies,* trans. Ian Cunnison. New York: W. W. Norton.

McCracken, Grant. 1988. *Culture and Consumption: New Approaches to the Symbolic Character of Consumer Goods and Activities.* Bloomington: Indiana University Press.

McFalls, Laurence H. 1995. *Communism's Collapse, Democracy's Demise? The Cultural Context and Consequences of the East German Revolution.* New York: New York University Press.

Medick, Hans. 1997. *Weben und Überleben in Laichingen 1650–1900: Lokalgeschichte als Allgemeine Geschichte.* Göttingen: Vandenhoeck und Ruprecht.

Meinhardt, Gunther. 1986. *Frohe Fest und alte Volksbräuche im Eichsfeld.* Gudenberg-Gleichen: Wartberg Verlag Peter Wieden.

Merkel, Ina. 1994. From a Socialist Society of Labor into a Consumer Society? The Transformation of East German Identities and Systems. In *Envisioning Eastern Europe: Postcommunist Cultural Studies,* ed. Michael D. Kennedy, 55–65. Ann Arbor: University of Michigan Press.

———. 1995. Consumer Culture in the GDR, or: How the Struggle for Anti-Modernity was Lost on the Battleground of Consumer Culture. Conference presentation at the German Historical Institute, Washington, D.C., October.

———. 1997. ". . . In Hoyerswerda leben jedefalls keine so kleinen viereckigen Menschen: Briefe an das Fernsehon der DDR.". In *Akten. Eingaben. Schaufenster. Die DDR und ihre Texte: Erkundungen zu Herrschaft und Alltag,* ed. Alf Lüdtke and Peter Becker, 279–310. Berlin: Akademie Verlag.

Mewett, Peter G. 1982. Exiles, Nicknames, Social Identities and the Production of Local Consciousness in a Lewis Crofting Community. In *Belonging: Identity and Social Organisation in British Rural Cultures,* ed. Anthony P. Cohen, 222–46. Manchester: Manchester University Press.

———. 1986. Boundaries and Discourse in a Lewis Crofting Community. In *Symbolising Boundaries: Identity and Diversity in British Cultures,* ed. Anthony P. Cohen, 71–87. Manchester: Manchester University Press.

Meyer, Hans Joachim. 1991. The Contribution of Catholic Christians to Social Renewal in East Germany. *Religion in Communist Lands* 19 (1–2): 89–94.

Michaelsen, Scott, and David E. Johnson, eds. 1997. *Border Theory: The Limits of Cultural Politics.* Minneapolis: University of Minnesota Press.

Milic, Andjelka. 1993. Women and Nationalism in the Former Yugoslavia. In *Gender Politics and Post-Communism: Reflections from Eastern Europe and the Former Soviet Union,* ed. Nanette Funk and Magda Mueller, 109–22. New York: Routledge.

Miller, Daniel, ed. 1995. *Worlds Apart: Modernity through the Prism of the Local.* London: Routledge.

Milosz, Czeslaw. 1991 [1953]. Ketman. In *From Stalinism to Pluralism: A Documentary History of Eastern Europe since 1945,* ed. Gale Stokes, 51–56. New York: Oxford University Press.

Mintz, Jerome R. 1982. *The Anarchists of Casas Viejas.* Chicago: University of Chicago Press.

Morley, David, and Kevin Robins. 1996. No Place like *Heimat:* Images of Home(land) in European Culture. In *Becoming National: A Reader,* ed. Geoff Eley and Ronald Grigor Suny, 456–78. New York: Oxford University Press.

Mühlberg, Felix. 1996. Wenn die Faust auf den Tisch schlägt. Eingaben als Strategie zur Bewältigung des Alltags. In *Wunderwirtschaft: DDR-Konsumkultur in den 6oer Jahren,* ed. Neue Gesellschaft für Bildende Kunst, 175–84. Cologne: Böhlau Verlag.

Müller, Birgit. 1993. Der Mythos vom faulen Ossi: Deutsch-deutsche Vorurteile und die Erfahrungen mit der Marktwirtschaft in drei Ostberliner Betrieben. *Prokla: Zeitschrift für kritische Sozialwissenschaft* 91 (23): 251–68.

Müller, Erhard, and others. 1966. *825 Jahre Kella (Eichsfeld): Festschrift.* Heiligenstadt: F. W. Cordier.

Munn, Nancy. 1973. Symbolism in a Ritual Context: Aspects of Symbolic Action. In *Handbook of Social and Cultural Anthropology,* ed. John J. Honigmann, 579–612. Chicago: Rand McNally.

———. 1983. Gawan Kula: Spatiotemporal Control and the Symbolism of Influence. In *The Kula: New Perspectives on Massim Exchange,* ed. Jerry W. Leach and Edmund Leach, 277–308. Cambridge, England: Cambridge University Press.

Myerhoff, Barbara. 1986. Life not Death in Venice. In *The Anthropology of Experience,* ed. Victor Turner and Edward M. Bruner, 261–88. Urbana: University of Illinois Press.

Nagengast, Carole. 1991. *Reluctant Socialists, Rural Entrepreneurs: Class, Culture, and the Polish State.* Boulder, Colo.: Westview Press.

Narayan, Kirin. 1989. *Storytellers, Saints, and Scoundrels: Folk Narrative in Hindu Religious Teaching.* Philadelphia: University of Pennsylvania Press.

Netting, Robert McC. 1981. *Balancing on an Alp: Ecological Change and Continuity in a Swiss Mountain Community.* Cambridge, England: Cambridge University Press.

Neue Gesellschaft für Bildende Kunst, ed. 1996. *Wunderwirtschaft: DDR-Konsumkultur in den 6oer Jahren.* Cologne: Böhlau Verlag.

Der Neue Kalte Krieg. 1993. *Der Spiegel,* May 17.

Nickel, Hildegard Maria. 1993. Women in the German Democratic Republic and in the New Federal States: Looking Backward and Forward (Five Theses). In *Gender Politics and Post-Communism: Reflections from Eastern Europe and the Former Soviet Union,* ed. Nanette Funk and Magda Mueller, 138–50. New York: Routledge.

Niethammer, Lutz, Alexander von Plato, and Dorothee Wierling. 1991. *Die volkseigene Erfahrung: Eine Archäologie des Lebens in der Industrieprovinz der DDR: 30 biografische Eröffnungen.* Berlin: Rowohlt.

Nolan, Mary Lee, and Sidney Nolan. 1989. *Christian Pilgrimage in Modern Western Europe.* Chapel Hill: University of North Carolina Press.

Nora, Pierre. 1989. Between Memory and History: Les Lieux de Mémoire. *Representations* 26 (Spring): 7–25.

One Nation, Which Past? 1997. *German Politics and Society* 15 (2). Special issue.

Osa, Maryjane. n.d. Religion, Politics and Social Change: Beyond Church-State Relations in Eastern Europe. Unpublished manuscript.

Das Ost-Gefühl: Heimweh nach der alten Ordnung. 1995. *Der Spiegel,* July 3. Special issue.

Paredes, Américo. 1958. *With His Pistol in His Hand: A Border Ballad and Its Hero.* Austin: University of Texas Press.

———. 1993. *Folklore and Culture on the Texas-Mexican Border,* ed. Richard Bauman. Austin: CMAS Books, Center for Mexican American Studies, University of Texas at Austin.

Peace, Adrian. 1986. "A Different Place Altogether": Diversity, Unity and Boundary in an Irish Village. In *Symbolising Boundaries: Identity and Diversity in British Cultures,* ed. Anthony P. Cohen, 107–22. Manchester: Manchester University Press.

Peck, Jeffrey M. 1996. Rac(e)ing the Nation: Is There a German "Home"? In *Becoming National: A Reader,* ed. Geoff Eley and Ronald Grigor Suny, 481–92. New York: Oxford University Press.

Pence, Katherine. 1997. Schaufenster des sozialistischen Konsums: Texte der ostdeutschen "consumer culture." In *Akten. Eingaben. Schaufenster. Die DDR und ihre Texte: Erkundungen zu Herrschaft und Alltag,* ed. Alf Lüdtke and Peter Becker, 91–118. Berlin: Akademie Verlag.

Philipsen, Dirk. 1992. *We Were the People: Voices from East Germany's Revolutionary Autumn of 1989.* Durham, N.C.: Duke University Press.

Pine, Frances. 1993. "The Cows and Pigs Are His, the Eggs Are Mine": Women's Domestic Economy and Entrepreneurial Activity in Rural Poland. In *Socialism: Ideals, Ideologies, and Local Practices,* ed. C. M. Hann, 227–42. New York: Routledge.

Pitt-Rivers, Julian. 1977. *The Fate of Shechem, or the Politics of Sex: Essays in the Anthropology of the Mediterranean.* Cambridge, England: Cambridge University Press.

Potratz, Rainer. 1993. Zwangsaussiedlung aus dem Grenzgebiet der DDR zur Bundesrepublik Deutschland im Mai/Juni 1952. In *Grenzland: Beiträge zur Geschichte der deutsch-deutschen Grenze,* ed. Bernd Weisbrod, 57–69. Hanover: Verlag Hahnsche Buchhandlung.

Rabinow, Paul. 1984. Introduction. In *The Foucault Reader,* ed. Paul Rabinow, 3–29. New York: Pantheon Books.

Ramet, Sabrina P. 1991. Protestants in East Germany, 1949–89: A Summing Up. *Religion in Communist Lands* 19 (3–4): 160–94.

Riegelhaupt, Joyce. 1984. Popular Anti-Clericalism and Religiosity in Pre-1974 Portugal. In *Religion, Power, and Protest in Local Communities: The Northern Shore of the Mediterranean,* ed. Eric R. Wolf, 83–114. Berlin: Mouton.

Riese, Werner. 1980. *Das Eichsfeld. Entwicklungsprobleme einer Landschaft.* Heidelberg: Meyn.

Ritzer, George. 1993. *The McDonaldization of Society: An Investigation into the Changing Character of Contemporary Social Life.* Thousand Oaks, Calif. Pine Forge Press.

Rogers, Susan Carol. 1991. *Shaping Modern Times in Rural France: The Transformation and Reproduction of an Aveyronnais Community.* Princeton, N.J.: Princeton University Press.

Rosaldo, Renato. 1989. *Culture and Truth. The Remaking of Social Analysis.* Boston: Beacon Press.

Rosenberg, Dorothy J. 1991. Shock Therapy: GDR Women in Transition from a Socialist Welfare State to a Social Market Economy. *Signs* 17 (1): 129–51.

Rosenberg, Tina. 1995. *The Haunted Land: Facing Europe's Ghosts after Communism.* New York: Vintage Books.

Rouse, Roger. 1991. Mexican Migration and the Social Space of Postmodernism. *Diaspora* 1 (1): 8–23.

Rueschemeyer, Marilyn. 1991. Participation and Control in a State Socialist Society: The German Democratic Republic. *East Central Europe / Europe du Centre-Est* 18 (1): 23–53.

Sabean, David Warren. 1984. *Power in the Blood: Popular Culture and Village Discourse in Early Modern Germany.* Cambridge, England: Cambridge University Press.

———. 1990. *Property, Production, and Family in Neckarhausen, 1700–1870.* New York: Cambridge University Press.

———. 1998. *Kinship in Neckarhausen, 1700–1870.* Cambridge, England: Cambridge University Press.

Sahlins, Marshall. 1988. Cosmologies of Capitalism: The Trans-Pacific Sector of the World System. *Proceedings of the British Academy* 74: 1–51.

Sahlins, Peter. 1989. *Boundaries: The Making of France and Spain in the Pyrenees.* Berkeley: University of California Press.

Sampson, Steven. 1986. The Informal Sector in Eastern Europe. *Telos* 66 (Winter): 44–66.

———. 1991. Is There an Anthropology of Socialism? *Anthropology Today* 7 (5): 16–19.

Schama, Simon. 1995. *Landscape and Memory.* New York: Alfred A. Knopf.

Schneider, Jane, and Peter Schneider. 1976. *Culture and Political Economy in Western Sicily.* New York: Academic Press.

Schneider, Peter. 1983. *The Wall Jumper,* trans. Leigh Hafrey. New York: Pantheon Books.

Schnier, Detlef, and Sabine Schulz-Greve, eds. 1990. *Wanderarbeiter aus dem Eichsfeld. Zur Wirtschafts- und Sozialgeschichte des Ober- und Untereichsfeldes seit Mitte des 19. Jahrhunderts.* Duderstadt: Mecke Druck und Verlag.

Scott, James C. 1990. *Domination and the Arts of Resistance: Hidden Transcripts.* New Haven, Conn.: Yale University Press.

Scott, Joan W. 1991. The Evidence of Experience. *Critical Inquiry* 17 (Summer): 773–97.

Simmel, Georg. 1908. *Soziologie. Untersuchungen über die Formen der Vergesellschaftung.* Leipzig: Verlag von Duncker and Humblot.

Slobin, Mark, ed. 1996. *Retuning Culture: Musical Changes in Central and Eastern Europe.* Durham, N.C.: Duke University Press.

Smart, Alan. 1993. Gifts, Bribes, and *Guanxi:* A Reconsideration of Bourdieu's Social Capital. *Cultural Anthropology* 8 (3): 388–408.

Smith, Roland. 1985. The Church in the German Democratic Republic. In *Honecker's Germany,* ed. David Childs, 66–82. London: Allen and Unwin.

Sowi (sozialwissenschaftliche Informationen). 1991. *Grenzen* 20 (3). Special issue.

Spindler, George. 1973. *Burgbach: Urbanization and Identity in a German Village.* New York: Holt, Rinehart and Winston.

SSRC Summer Seminar on Acculturation. 1953. Acculturation: An Exploratory Formulation. *American Anthropologist* 56 (6): 973–1002.

Stadt Duderstadt. 1991. *Die Grenze im Eichsfeld.* Göttingen: Verlag Göttinger Tageblatt.

Stark, David, and Victor Nee. 1989. Toward an Institutional Analysis of State Socialism. In *Remaking the Economic Institutions of Socialism: China and Eastern Europe,* ed. Victor Nee and David Stark, 1–31. Stanford, Calif.: Stanford University Press.

Steedly, Mary Margaret. 1993. *Hanging without a Rope: Narrative Experience in Colonial and Postcolonial Karoland.* Princeton, N.J.: Princeton University Press.

Stein, Mary Beth. 1993. The Present Is a Foreign Country: Germany after Unification. *Journal of Folklore Research* 30 (1): 29–43.

Stewart, Charles. 1991. *Demons and the Devil: Moral Imagination in Modern Greek Culture.* Princeton, N.J.: Princeton University Press.

Stewart, Kathleen. 1996. *A Space on the Side of the Road: Cultural Poetics in an "Other" America.* Princeton, N.J.: Princeton University Press.

Stewart, Susan. 1993. *On Longing: Narratives of the Miniature, the Gigantic, the Souvenir, the Collection.* Durham, N.C.: Duke University Press.

Stoller, Paul. 1989. *The Taste of Ethnographic Things: The Senses in Anthropology.* Philadelphia: University of Pennsylvania Press.

Strathern, Marilyn. 1982. The Village as an Idea: Constructs of Village-ness in Elmdon, Essex. In *Belonging: Identity and Social Organisation in British Rural Cultures,* ed. Anthony P. Cohen, 247–77. Manchester: Manchester University Press.

Streit, Petra. 1991–1992. Raising Consciousness. *German Politics and Society* 24–25 (Winter): 10–15.

Szelenyi, Ivan. 1988. *Socialist Entrepreneurs: Embourgeoisement in Rural Hungary.* Madison: University of Wisconsin Press.

———. 1989. Eastern Europe in an Epoch of Transition: Toward a Socialist Mixed Economy? In *Remaking the Economic Institutions of Socialism: China and Eastern Europe,* ed. Victor Nee and David Stark, 208–32. Stanford, Calif.: Stanford University Press.

Taylor, Lawrence. 1990. Stories of Power, Powerful Stories: The Drunken Priest in Donegal. In *Religious Orthodoxy and Popular Faith in European Society,* ed. Ellen Badone, 163–84. Princeton, N.J.: Princeton University Press.

Ten Dyke, Elizabeth. 1999. Memory, History and Remembrance Work in Dresden. In *Altering States: Ethnographies of Transition in Eastern Europe and the Former Soviet Union,* ed. Daphne Berdahl, Matti Bunzl, and Martha Lampland. Ann Arbor: University of Michigan Press.

Turner, Victor. 1967. *The Forest of Symbols: Aspects of Ndembu Ritual.* Ithaca, N.Y.: Cornell University Press.

———. 1969. *The Ritual Process: Structure and Anti-Structure.* Ithaca, N.Y.: Cornell University Press.

———. 1974. *Dramas, Fields, and Metaphors: Symbolic Action in Human Society.* Ithaca, N.Y.: Cornell University Press.

———. 1979. *Process, Performance, and Pilgrimage: A Study in Comparative Symbology.* New Delhi: Concept Publishing.

———. 1986. *The Anthropology of Performance.* New York: PAJ Publications.

Turner, Victor, and Edith Turner. 1978. *Image and Pilgrimage in Christian Culture: Anthropological Perspectives.* New York: Columbia University Press.

Urquhart, Gordon. 1995. *The Pope's Armada.* London: Bantam Books.

Van Gennep, Arnold. 1960. *The Rites of Passage,* trans. Monika B. Vizedom and Gabrielle L. Caffe. Chicago: University of Chicago Press.

Veenis, Milena. 1997. Fantastic Things. In *Experiencing Material Culture in the Western World,* ed. Susan M. Pearce, 154–74. London and Washington, D.C.: Leicester University Press.

Vélez-Ibáñez, Carlos G. 1996. *Border Visions: Mexican Cultures of the Southwest United States.* Tucson: University of Arizona Press.

Verdery, Katherine. 1991. *National Ideology under Socialism: Identity and Cultural Politics in Ceausescu's Romania.* Berkeley: University of California Press.

———. 1996. *What Was Socialism, and What Comes Next?* Princeton, N.J.: Princeton University Press.

Wacquant, Loïc J. D. 1987. Symbolic Violence and the Making of the French Agriculturalist: An Enquiry into Pierre Bourdieu's Sociology. *Australian and New Zealand Journal of Sociology* 23 (1): 65–88.

Watson, James, ed. 1997. *Golden Arches East: McDonald's in East Asia.* Stanford, Calif.: Stanford University Press.

Watson, Rubie S. 1994. Memory, History, and Opposition under State Socialism: An Introduction. In *Memory, History and Opposition under State Socialism*, ed. Rubie S. Watson, 1–20. Santa Fe, N.Mex.: School of American Research Press.

Wedel, Janine. 1986. *The Private Poland.* New York: Facts on File Publications.

———, ed. 1992. *The Unplanned Society: Poland during and after Communism.* New York: Columbia University Press.

"Wehre Dich Täglich." 1993. *Der Spiegel,* December 27.

Weigelt, Klaus, ed. 1984. *Heimat und Nation. Zur Geschichte und Identität der Deutschen.* Mainz: Hase and Koehler.

Wierling, Dorothee. 1997. The East as the Past: Problems with Memory and Identity. *German Politics and Society* 15 (2): 53–75.

Wilk, Richard. 1994. Consumer Goods as Dialogue about Development. In *Consumption and Identity,* ed. Jonathan Friedman, 97–118. London: Harwood Press.

Wilson, Thomas M. 1994. Symbolic Dimensions to the Irish Border. In *Border Approaches: Anthropological Perspectives on Frontiers,* ed. Hastings Donnan and Thomas M. Wilson, 101–18. Lanham, Md.: University Press of America.

Wilson, Thomas M., and Hastings Donnan. 1998. *Border Identities: Nation and State at International Frontiers.* Cambridge, England: Cambridge University Press.

"Wir lieben die Heimat." 1995. *Der Spiegel,* July 3.

"Wir machen alles gründlich": Die Todesgrenze der Deutschen (1): Schreibtischtäter aus Wandlitz. 1991. *Der Spiegel,* June 24.

Wolbert, Barbara. 1995. Jugendweihe: Zur Transformation einer rituellen Praxis. *Kuckuck: Notizen zu Alltagskultur und Volkskunde* 10 (2): 23–28.

———. n.d. Jugendweihe nach der Wende: Form und Transformation einer sozialistischen Initiationszeremonie. *Zeitschrift für Volkskunde.* In press.

Wolf, Christa. 1990. *Was Bleibt.* Berlin: Aufbau-Verlag.

Wolf, Eric. 1966. Kinship, Friendship, and Patron-Client Relations in Complex Societies. In *The Social Anthropology of Complex Societies,* ed. Michael P. Banton, 1–22. London: Tavistock Publications.

Wollenberger, Vera. 1992. *Virus der Heuchler: Innenansicht aus Stasi-Akten.* Berlin: Elefanten Press.

Wylie, Laurence. 1957. *Village in the Vaucluse.* Cambridge, Mass.: Harvard University Press.

Yan, Yunxiang. 1996. *The Flow of Gifts: Reciprocity and Social Networks in a Chinese Village.* Stanford, Calif.: Stanford University Press.

Index

Designer: BookMatters
Compositor: G&S Typesetters, Inc.
Text: 10/14 Palatino
Display: Bauer Bodoni
Printer and Binder: Thomson-Shore, Inc.